ISBN 0-8373-0904-2

C-904 CAREER EXAMINATION SERIES

This is your PASSBOOK® for...

Community Development Assistant

Test Preparation Study Guide

Questions & Answers

NLC

NATIONAL LEARNING CORPORATION

National Learning Corporation

212 Michael Drive, Syosset, New York 11791

(516) 921-8888
(800) 632-8888
(800) 645-6337
FAX: (516) 921-8743
www.passbooks.com
info @ passbooks.com

PRINTED IN THE UNITED STATES OF AMERICA

PASSBOOK®

NOTICE

NATIONAL LEARNING CORPORATION
212 Michael Drive
Syosset, New York 11791

Inquiries re licensing agreements should be addressed to:
The President
National Learning Corporation
212 Michael Drive
Syosset, New York 11791

PASSBOOK® SERIES

THE *PASSBOOK® SERIES* has been created to prepare applicants and candidates for the ultimate academic battlefield – the examination room.

At some time in our lives, each and every one of us may be required to take an examination – for validation, matriculation, admission, qualification, registration, certification, or licensure.

Based on the assumption that every applicant or candidate has met the basic formal educational standards, has taken the required number of courses, and read the necessary texts, the *PASSBOOK® SERIES* furnishes the one special preparation which may assure passing with confidence, instead of failing with insecurity. Examination questions – together with answers – are furnished as the basic vehicle for study so that the mysteries of the examination and its compounding difficulties may be eliminated or diminished by a sure method.

This book is meant to help you pass your examination provided that you qualify and are serious in your objective.

The entire field is reviewed through the huge store of content information which is succinctly presented through a provocative and challenging approach – the question-and-answer method.

A climate of success is established by furnishing the correct answers at the end of each test.

You soon learn to recognize types of questions, forms of questions, and patterns of questioning. You may even begin to anticipate expected outcomes.

You perceive that many questions are repeated or adapted so that you can gain acute insights, which may enable you to score many sure points.

You learn how to confront new questions, or types of questions, and to attack them confidently and work out the correct answers.

You note objectives and emphases, and recognize pitfalls and dangers, so that you may make positive educational adjustments.

Moreover, you are kept fully informed in relation to new concepts, methods, practices, and directions in the field.

You discover that you are actually taking the examination all the time: you are preparing for the examination by "taking" an examination, not by reading extraneous and/or supererogatory textbooks.

In short, this PASSBOOK®, used directedly, should be an important factor in helping you to pass your test.

COMMUNITY DEVELOPMENT ASSISTANT

DUTIES:

Assists in the preparation of contracts for rehabilitation projects for a community development agency. Assists in estimating construction necessary to complete renovations on clients' homes. Performs field visits to prepare cost estimates for work to be done. Assists in the awarding of contracts to licensed contractors after bids have been analyzed. Assists in conducting field inspections of building alterations and repairs to enforce adherence to building codes. Performs related work as required.

SUBJECT OF EXAMINATION

The written test is designed to cover knowledges, skills, and/or abilities in the following areas:

1. Understanding, interpreting, and applying housing and community development laws, rules, and regulations; and
2. Preparing written material.

HOW TO TAKE A TEST

I. YOU MUST PASS AN EXAMINATION

A. WHAT EVERY CANDIDATE SHOULD KNOW

Examination applicants often ask us for help in preparing for the written test. What can I study in advance? What kinds of questions will be asked? How will the test be given? How will the papers be graded?

As an applicant for a civil service examination, you may be wondering about some of these things. Our purpose here is to suggest effective methods of advance study and to describe civil service examinations.

Your chances for success on this examination can be increased if you know how to prepare. Those "pre-examination jitters" can be reduced if you know what to expect. You can even experience an adventure in good citizenship if you know why civil service exams are given.

B. WHY ARE CIVIL SERVICE EXAMINATIONS GIVEN?

Civil service examinations are important to you in two ways. As a citizen, you want public jobs filled by employees who know how to do their work. As a job seeker, you want a fair chance to compete for that job on an equal footing with other candidates. The best-known means of accomplishing this two-fold goal is the competitive examination.

Exams are widely publicized throughout the nation. They may be administered for jobs in federal, state, city, municipal, town or village governments or agencies.

Any citizen may apply, with some limitations, such as the age or residence of applicants. Your experience and education may be reviewed to see whether you meet the requirements for the particular examination. When these requirements exist, they are reasonable and applied consistently to all applicants. Thus, a competitive examination may cause you some uneasiness now, but it is your privilege and safeguard.

C. HOW ARE CIVIL SERVICE EXAMS DEVELOPED?

Examinations are carefully written by trained technicians who are specialists in the field known as "psychological measurement," in consultation with recognized authorities in the field of work that the test will cover. These experts recommend the subject matter areas or skills to be tested; only those knowledges or skills important to your success on the job are included. The most reliable books and source materials available are used as references. Together, the experts and technicians judge the difficulty level of the questions.

Test technicians know how to phrase questions so that the problem is clearly stated. Their ethics do not permit "trick" or "catch" questions. Questions may have been tried out on sample groups, or subjected to statistical analysis, to determine their usefulness.

Written tests are often used in combination with performance tests, ratings of training and experience, and oral interviews. All of these measures combine to form the best-known means of finding the right person for the right job.

II. HOW TO PASS THE WRITTEN TEST

A. NATURE OF THE EXAMINATION

To prepare intelligently for civil service examinations, you should know how they differ from school examinations you have taken. In school you were assigned certain definite pages to read or subjects to cover. The examination questions were quite detailed and usually emphasized memory. Civil service exams, on the other hand, try to discover your present ability to perform the duties of a position, plus your potentiality to learn these duties. In other words, a civil service exam attempts to predict how successful you will be. Questions cover such a broad area that they cannot be as minute and detailed as school exam questions.

In the public service similar kinds of work, or positions, are grouped together in one "class." This process is known as *position-classification*. All the positions in a class are paid according to the salary range for that class. One class title covers all of these positions, and they are all tested by the same examination.

B. FOUR BASIC STEPS

1) Study the announcement

How, then, can you know what subjects to study? Our best answer is: "Learn as much as possible about the class of positions for which you've applied." The exam will test the knowledge, skills and abilities needed to do the work.

Your most valuable source of information about the position you want is the official exam announcement. This announcement lists the training and experience qualifications. Check these standards and apply only if you come reasonably close to meeting them.

The brief description of the position in the examination announcement offers some clues to the subjects which will be tested. Think about the job itself. Review the duties in your mind. Can you perform them, or are there some in which you are rusty? Fill in the blank spots in your preparation.

Many jurisdictions preview the written test in the exam announcement by including a section called "Knowledge and Abilities Required," "Scope of the Examination," or some similar heading. Here you will find out specifically what fields will be tested.

2) Review your own background

Once you learn in general what the position is all about, and what you need to know to do the work, ask yourself which subjects you already know fairly well and which need improvement. You may wonder whether to concentrate on improving your strong areas or on building some background in your fields of weakness. When the announcement has specified "some knowledge" or "considerable knowledge," or has used adjectives like "beginning principles of..." or "advanced ... methods," you can get a clue as to the number and difficulty of questions to be asked in any given field. More questions, and hence broader coverage, would be included for those subjects which are more important in the work. Now weigh your strengths and weaknesses against the job requirements and prepare accordingly.

3) Determine the level of the position

Another way to tell how intensively you should prepare is to understand the level of the job for which you are applying. Is it the entering level? In other words, is this the position in which beginners in a field of work are hired? Or is it an intermediate or advanced level? Sometimes this is indicated by such words as "Junior" or "Senior" in the class title. Other jurisdictions use Roman numerals to designate the level – Clerk I, Clerk II, for example. The word "Supervisor" sometimes appears in the title. If the level is not indicated by the title, check the description of duties. Will you be working under very close supervision, or will you have responsibility for independent decisions in this work?

4) Choose appropriate study materials

Now that you know the subjects to be examined and the relative amount of each subject to be covered, you can choose suitable study materials. For beginning level jobs, or even advanced ones, if you have a pronounced weakness in some aspect of your training, read a modern, standard textbook in that field. Be sure it is up to date and has general coverage. Such books are normally available at your library, and the librarian will be glad to help you locate one. For entry-level positions, questions of appropriate difficulty are chosen – neither highly advanced questions, nor those too simple. Such questions require careful thought but not advanced training.

If the position for which you are applying is technical or advanced, you will read more advanced, specialized material. If you are already familiar with the basic principles of your field, elementary textbooks would waste your time. Concentrate on advanced textbooks and technical periodicals. Think through the concepts and review difficult problems in your field.

These are all general sources. You can get more ideas on your own initiative, following these leads. For example, training manuals and publications of the government agency which employs workers in your field can be useful, particularly for technical and professional positions. A letter or visit to the government department involved may result in more specific study suggestions, and certainly will provide you with a more definite idea of the exact nature of the position you are seeking.

III. KINDS OF TESTS

Tests are used for purposes other than measuring knowledge and ability to perform specified duties. For some positions, it is equally important to test ability to make adjustments to new situations or to profit from training. In others, basic mental abilities not dependent on information are essential. Questions which test these things may not appear as pertinent to the duties of the position as those which test for knowledge and information. Yet they are often highly important parts of a fair examination. For very general questions, it is almost impossible to help you direct your study efforts. What we can do is to point out some of the more common of these general abilities needed in public service positions and describe some typical questions.

1) General information

Broad, general information has been found useful for predicting job success in some kinds of work. This is tested in a variety of ways, from vocabulary lists to questions about current events. Basic background in some field of work, such as sociology or economics, may be sampled in a group of questions. Often these are principles which have become familiar to most persons through exposure rather than through formal training. It is difficult to advise you how to study for these questions; being alert to the world around you is our best suggestion.

2) Verbal ability

An example of an ability needed in many positions is verbal or language ability. Verbal ability is, in brief, the ability to use and understand words. Vocabulary and grammar tests are typical measures of this ability. Reading comprehension or paragraph interpretation questions are common in many kinds of civil service tests. You are given a paragraph of written material and asked to find its central meaning.

3) Numerical ability

Number skills can be tested by the familiar arithmetic problem, by checking paired lists of numbers to see which are alike and which are different, or by interpreting charts and graphs. In the latter test, a graph may be printed in the test booklet which you are asked to use as the basis for answering questions.

4) Observation

A popular test for law-enforcement positions is the observation test. A picture is shown to you for several minutes, then taken away. Questions about the picture test your ability to observe both details and larger elements.

5) Following directions

In many positions in the public service, the employee must be able to carry out written instructions dependably and accurately. You may be given a chart with several columns, each column listing a variety of information. The questions require you to carry out directions involving the information given in the chart.

6) Skills and aptitudes

Performance tests effectively measure some manual skills and aptitudes. When the skill is one in which you are trained, such as typing or shorthand, you can practice. These tests are often very much like those given in business school or high school courses. For many of the other skills and aptitudes, however, no short-time preparation can be made. Skills and abilities natural to you or that you have developed throughout your lifetime are being tested.

Many of the general questions just described provide all the data needed to answer the questions and ask you to use your reasoning ability to find the answers. Your best preparation for these tests, as well as for tests of facts and ideas, is to be at your physical and mental best. You, no doubt, have your own methods of getting into an exam-taking mood and keeping "in shape." The next section lists some ideas on this subject.

IV. KINDS OF QUESTIONS

Only rarely is the "essay" question, which you answer in narrative form, used in civil service tests. Civil service tests are usually of the short-answer type. Full instructions for answering these questions will be given to you at the examination. But in case this is your first experience with short-answer questions and separate answer sheets, here is what you need to know:

1) Multiple-choice Questions

Most popular of the short-answer questions is the "multiple choice" or "best answer" question. It can be used, for example, to test for factual knowledge, ability to solve problems or judgment in meeting situations found at work.

A multiple-choice question is normally one of three types—

- It can begin with an incomplete statement followed by several possible endings. You are to find the one ending which *best* completes the statement, although some of the others may not be entirely wrong.
- It can also be a complete statement in the form of a question which is answered by choosing one of the statements listed.

- It can be in the form of a problem – again you select the best answer.

Here is an example of a multiple-choice question with a discussion which should give you some clues as to the method for choosing the right answer:

When an employee has a complaint about his assignment, the action which will *best* help him overcome his difficulty is to

A. discuss his difficulty with his coworkers
B. take the problem to the head of the organization
C. take the problem to the person who gave him the assignment
D. say nothing to anyone about his complaint

In answering this question, you should study each of the choices to find which is best. Consider choice "A" – Certainly an employee may discuss his complaint with fellow employees, but no change or improvement can result, and the complaint remains unresolved. Choice "B" is a poor choice since the head of the organization probably does not know what assignment you have been given, and taking your problem to him is known as "going over the head" of the supervisor. The supervisor, or person who made the assignment, is the person who can clarify it or correct any injustice. Choice "C" is, therefore, correct. To say nothing, as in choice "D," is unwise. Supervisors have and interest in knowing the problems employees are facing, and the employee is seeking a solution to his problem.

2) True/False Questions

The "true/false" or "right/wrong" form of question is sometimes used. Here a complete statement is given. Your job is to decide whether the statement is right or wrong.

SAMPLE: A roaming cell-phone call to a nearby city costs less than a non-roaming call to a distant city.

This statement is wrong, or false, since roaming calls are more expensive.

This is not a complete list of all possible question forms, although most of the others are variations of these common types. You will always get complete directions for answering questions. Be sure you understand *how* to mark your answers – ask questions until you do.

V. RECORDING YOUR ANSWERS

Computer terminals are used more and more today for many different kinds of exams.

For an examination with very few applicants, you may be told to record your answers in the test booklet itself. Separate answer sheets are much more common. If this separate answer sheet is to be scored by machine – and this is often the case – it is highly important that you mark your answers correctly in order to get credit.

An electronic scoring machine is often used in civil service offices because of the speed with which papers can be scored. Machine-scored answer sheets must be marked with a pencil, which will be given to you. This pencil has a high graphite content which responds to the electronic scoring machine. As a matter of fact, stray dots may register as answers, so do not let your pencil rest on the answer sheet while you are pondering the correct answer. Also, if your pencil lead breaks or is otherwise defective, ask for another.

Since the answer sheet will be dropped in a slot in the scoring machine, be careful not to bend the corners or get the paper crumpled.

The answer sheet normally has five vertical columns of numbers, with 30 numbers to a column. These numbers correspond to the question numbers in your test booklet. After each number, going across the page are four or five pairs of dotted lines. These short dotted lines have small letters or numbers above them. The first two pairs may also have a "T" or "F" above the letters. This indicates that the first two pairs only are to be used if the questions are of the true-false type. If the questions are multiple choice, disregard the "T" and "F" and pay attention only to the small letters or numbers.

Answer your questions in the manner of the sample that follows:

32. The largest city in the United States is
    - A. Washington, D.C.
    - B. New York City
    - C. Chicago
    - D. Detroit
    - E. San Francisco

1) Choose the answer you think is best. (New York City is the largest, so "B" is correct.)
2) Find the row of dotted lines numbered the same as the question you are answering. (Find row number 32)
3) Find the pair of dotted lines corresponding to the answer. (Find the pair of lines under the mark "B.")
4) Make a solid black mark between the dotted lines.

VI. BEFORE THE TEST

Common sense will help you find procedures to follow to get ready for an examination. Too many of us, however, overlook these sensible measures. Indeed, nervousness and fatigue have been found to be the most serious reasons why applicants fail to do their best on civil service tests. Here is a list of reminders:

- Begin your preparation early – Don't wait until the last minute to go scurrying around for books and materials or to find out what the position is all about.
- Prepare continuously – An hour a night for a week is better than an all-night cram session. This has been definitely established. What is more, a night a week for a month will return better dividends than crowding your study into a shorter period of time.
- Locate the place of the exam – You have been sent a notice telling you when and where to report for the examination. If the location is in a different town or otherwise unfamiliar to you, it would be well to inquire the best route and learn something about the building.
- Relax the night before the test – Allow your mind to rest. Do not study at all that night. Plan some mild recreation or diversion; then go to bed early and get a good night's sleep.
- Get up early enough to make a leisurely trip to the place for the test – This way unforeseen events, traffic snarls, unfamiliar buildings, etc. will not upset you.
- Dress comfortably – A written test is not a fashion show. You will be known by number and not by name, so wear something comfortable.

- Leave excess paraphernalia at home – Shopping bags and odd bundles will get in your way. You need bring only the items mentioned in the official notice you received; usually everything you need is provided. Do not bring reference books to the exam. They will only confuse those last minutes and be taken away from you when in the test room.
- Arrive somewhat ahead of time – If because of transportation schedules you must get there very early, bring a newspaper or magazine to take your mind off yourself while waiting.
- Locate the examination room – When you have found the proper room, you will be directed to the seat or part of the room where you will sit. Sometimes you are given a sheet of instructions to read while you are waiting. Do not fill out any forms until you are told to do so; just read them and be prepared.
- Relax and prepare to listen to the instructions
- If you have any physical problem that may keep you from doing your best, be sure to tell the test administrator. If you are sick or in poor health, you really cannot do your best on the exam. You can come back and take the test some other time.

VII. AT THE TEST

The day of the test is here and you have the test booklet in your hand. The temptation to get going is very strong. Caution! There is more to success than knowing the right answers. You must know how to identify your papers and understand variations in the type of short-answer question used in this particular examination. Follow these suggestions for maximum results from your efforts:

1) Cooperate with the monitor

The test administrator has a duty to create a situation in which you can be as much at ease as possible. He will give instructions, tell you when to begin, check to see that you are marking your answer sheet correctly, and so on. He is not there to guard you, although he will see that your competitors do not take unfair advantage. He wants to help you do your best.

2) Listen to all instructions

Don't jump the gun! Wait until you understand all directions. In most civil service tests you get more time than you need to answer the questions. So don't be in a hurry. Read each word of instructions until you clearly understand the meaning. Study the examples, listen to all announcements and follow directions. Ask questions if you do not understand what to do.

3) Identify your papers

Civil service exams are usually identified by number only. You will be assigned a number; you must not put your name on your test papers. Be sure to copy your number correctly. Since more than one exam may be given, copy your exact examination title.

4) Plan your time

Unless you are told that a test is a "speed" or "rate of work" test, speed itself is usually not important. Time enough to answer all the questions will be provided, but this does not mean that you have all day. An overall time limit has been set. Divide the total time (in minutes) by the number of questions to determine the approximate time you have for each question.

5) Do not linger over difficult questions

If you come across a difficult question, mark it with a paper clip (useful to have along) and come back to it when you have been through the booklet. One caution if you do this – be sure to skip a number on your answer sheet as well. Check often to be sure that you have not lost your place and that you are marking in the row numbered the same as the question you are answering.

6) Read the questions

Be sure you know what the question asks! Many capable people are unsuccessful because they failed to *read* the questions correctly.

7) Answer all questions

Unless you have been instructed that a penalty will be deducted for incorrect answers, it is better to guess than to omit a question.

8) Speed tests

It is often better NOT to guess on speed tests. It has been found that on timed tests people are tempted to spend the last few seconds before time is called in marking answers at random – without even reading them – in the hope of picking up a few extra points. To discourage this practice, the instructions may warn you that your score will be "corrected" for guessing. That is, a penalty will be applied. The incorrect answers will be deducted from the correct ones, or some other penalty formula will be used.

9) Review your answers

If you finish before time is called, go back to the questions you guessed or omitted to give them further thought. Review other answers if you have time.

10) Return your test materials

If you are ready to leave before others have finished or time is called, take ALL your materials to the monitor and leave quietly. Never take any test material with you. The monitor can discover whose papers are not complete, and taking a test booklet may be grounds for disqualification.

VIII. EXAMINATION TECHNIQUES

1) Read the general instructions carefully. These are usually printed on the first page of the exam booklet. As a rule, these instructions refer to the timing of the examination; the fact that you should not start work until the signal and must stop work at a signal, etc. If there are any *special* instructions, such as a choice of questions to be answered, make sure that you note this instruction carefully.

2) When you are ready to start work on the examination, that is as soon as the signal has been given, read the instructions to each question booklet, underline any key words or phrases, such as *least, best, outline, describe* and the like. In this way you will tend to answer as requested rather than discover on reviewing your paper that you *listed without describing*, that you selected the *worst* choice rather than the *best* choice, etc.

3) If the examination is of the objective or multiple-choice type – that is, each question will also give a series of possible answers: A, B, C or D, and you are called upon to select the best answer and write the letter next to that answer on your answer paper – it is advisable to start answering each question in turn. There may be anywhere from 50 to 100 such questions in the three or four hours allotted and you can see how much time would be taken if you read through all the questions before beginning to answer any. Furthermore, if you come across a question or group of questions which you know would be difficult to answer, it would undoubtedly affect your handling of all the other questions.

4) If the examination is of the essay type and contains but a few questions, it is a moot point as to whether you should read all the questions before starting to answer any one. Of course, if you are given a choice – say five out of seven and the like – then it is essential to read all the questions so you can eliminate the two that are most difficult. If, however, you are asked to answer all the questions, there may be danger in trying to answer the easiest one first because you may find that you will spend too much time on it. The best technique is to answer the first question, then proceed to the second, etc.

5) Time your answers. Before the exam begins, write down the time it started, then add the time allowed for the examination and write down the time it must be completed, then divide the time available somewhat as follows:
    - If 3-1/2 hours are allowed, that would be 210 minutes. If you have 80 objective-type questions, that would be an average of 2-1/2 minutes per question. Allow yourself no more than 2 minutes per question, or a total of 160 minutes, which will permit about 50 minutes to review.
    - If for the time allotment of 210 minutes there are 7 essay questions to answer, that would average about 30 minutes a question. Give yourself only 25 minutes per question so that you have about 35 minutes to review.

6) The most important instruction is to *read each question* and make sure you know what is wanted. The second most important instruction is to *time yourself properly* so that you answer every question. The third most important instruction is to *answer every question.* Guess if you have to but include something for each question. Remember that you will receive no credit for a blank and will probably receive some credit if you write something in answer to an essay question. If you guess a letter – say "B" for a multiple-choice question – you may have guessed right. If you leave a blank as an answer to a multiple-choice question, the examiners may respect your feelings but it will not add a point to your score. Some exams may penalize you for wrong answers, so in such cases *only*, you may not want to guess unless you have some basis for your answer.

7) Suggestions
    a. Objective-type questions
        1. Examine the question booklet for proper sequence of pages and questions
        2. Read all instructions carefully
        3. Skip any question which seems too difficult; return to it after all other questions have been answered
        4. Apportion your time properly; do not spend too much time on any single question or group of questions

5. Note and underline key words – *all, most, fewest, least, best, worst, same, opposite,* etc.
6. Pay particular attention to negatives
7. Note unusual option, e.g., unduly long, short, complex, different or similar in content to the body of the question
8. Observe the use of "hedging" words – *probably, may, most likely,* etc.
9. Make sure that your answer is put next to the same number as the question
10. Do not second-guess unless you have good reason to believe the second answer is definitely more correct
11. Cross out original answer if you decide another answer is more accurate; do not erase until you are ready to hand your paper in
12. Answer all questions; guess unless instructed otherwise
13. Leave time for review

b. Essay questions
1. Read each question carefully
2. Determine exactly what is wanted. Underline key words or phrases.
3. Decide on outline or paragraph answer
4. Include many different points and elements unless asked to develop any one or two points or elements
5. Show impartiality by giving pros and cons unless directed to select one side only
6. Make and write down any assumptions you find necessary to answer the questions
7. Watch your English, grammar, punctuation and choice of words
8. Time your answers; don't crowd material

8) Answering the essay question

Most essay questions can be answered by framing the specific response around several key words or ideas. Here are a few such key words or ideas:

M's: manpower, materials, methods, money, management
P's: purpose, program, policy, plan, procedure, practice, problems, pitfalls, personnel, public relations

a. Six basic steps in handling problems:
1. Preliminary plan and background development
2. Collect information, data and facts
3. Analyze and interpret information, data and facts
4. Analyze and develop solutions as well as make recommendations
5. Prepare report and sell recommendations
6. Install recommendations and follow up effectiveness

b. Pitfalls to avoid
1. *Taking things for granted* – A statement of the situation does not necessarily imply that each of the elements is necessarily true; for example, a complaint may be invalid and biased so that all that can be taken for granted is that a complaint has been registered

2. *Considering only one side of a situation* – Wherever possible, indicate several alternatives and then point out the reasons you selected the best one
3. *Failing to indicate follow up* – Whenever your answer indicates action on your part, make certain that you will take proper follow-up action to see how successful your recommendations, procedures or actions turn out to be
4. *Taking too long in answering any single question* – Remember to time your answers properly

IX. AFTER THE TEST

Scoring procedures differ in detail among civil service jurisdictions although the general principles are the same. Whether the papers are hand-scored or graded by machine we have described, they are nearly always graded by number. That is, the person who marks the paper knows only the number – never the name – of the applicant. Not until all the papers have been graded will they be matched with names. If other tests, such as training and experience or oral interview ratings have been given, scores will be combined. Different parts of the examination usually have different weights. For example, the written test might count 60 percent of the final grade, and a rating of training and experience 40 percent. In many jurisdictions, veterans will have a certain number of points added to their grades.

After the final grade has been determined, the names are placed in grade order and an eligible list is established. There are various methods for resolving ties between those who get the same final grade – probably the most common is to place first the name of the person whose application was received first. Job offers are made from the eligible list in the order the names appear on it. You will be notified of your grade and your rank as soon as all these computations have been made. This will be done as rapidly as possible.

People who are found to meet the requirements in the announcement are called "eligibles." Their names are put on a list of eligible candidates. An eligible's chances of getting a job depend on how high he stands on this list and how fast agencies are filling jobs from the list.

When a job is to be filled from a list of eligibles, the agency asks for the names of people on the list of eligibles for that job. When the civil service commission receives this request, it sends to the agency the names of the three people highest on this list. Or, if the job to be filled has specialized requirements, the office sends the agency the names of the top three persons who meet these requirements from the general list.

The appointing officer makes a choice from among the three people whose names were sent to him. If the selected person accepts the appointment, the names of the others are put back on the list to be considered for future openings.

That is the rule in hiring from all kinds of eligible lists, whether they are for typist, carpenter, chemist, or something else. For every vacancy, the appointing officer has his choice of any one of the top three eligibles on the list. This explains why the person whose name is on top of the list sometimes does not get an appointment when some of the persons lower on the list do. If the appointing officer chooses the second or third eligible, the No. 1 eligible does not get a job at once, but stays on the list until he is appointed or the list is terminated.

X. HOW TO PASS THE INTERVIEW TEST

The examination for which you applied requires an oral interview test. You have already taken the written test and you are now being called for the interview test – the final part of the formal examination.

You may think that it is not possible to prepare for an interview test and that there are no procedures to follow during an interview. Our purpose is to point out some things you can do in advance that will help you and some good rules to follow and pitfalls to avoid while you are being interviewed.

What is an interview supposed to test?

The written examination is designed to test the technical knowledge and competence of the candidate; the oral is designed to evaluate intangible qualities, not readily measured otherwise, and to establish a list showing the relative fitness of each candidate – as measured against his competitors – for the position sought. Scoring is not on the basis of "right" and "wrong," but on a sliding scale of values ranging from "not passable" to "outstanding." As a matter of fact, it is possible to achieve a relatively low score without a single "incorrect" answer because of evident weakness in the qualities being measured.

Occasionally, an examination may consist entirely of an oral test – either an individual or a group oral. In such cases, information is sought concerning the technical knowledges and abilities of the candidate, since there has been no written examination for this purpose. More commonly, however, an oral test is used to supplement a written examination.

Who conducts interviews?

The composition of oral boards varies among different jurisdictions. In nearly all, a representative of the personnel department serves as chairman. One of the members of the board may be a representative of the department in which the candidate would work. In some cases, "outside experts" are used, and, frequently, a businessman or some other representative of the general public is asked to serve. Labor and management or other special groups may be represented. The aim is to secure the services of experts in the appropriate field.

However the board is composed, it is a good idea (and not at all improper or unethical) to ascertain in advance of the interview who the members are and what groups they represent. When you are introduced to them, you will have some idea of their backgrounds and interests, and at least you will not stutter and stammer over their names.

What should be done before the interview?

While knowledge about the board members is useful and takes some of the surprise element out of the interview, there is other preparation which is more substantive. It *is* possible to prepare for an oral interview – in several ways:

1) Keep a copy of your application and review it carefully before the interview

This may be the only document before the oral board, and the starting point of the interview. Know what education and experience you have listed there, and the sequence and dates of all of it. Sometimes the board will ask you to review the highlights of your experience for them; you should not have to hem and haw doing it.

2) Study the class specification and the examination announcement

Usually, the oral board has one or both of these to guide them. The qualities, characteristics or knowledges required by the position sought are stated in these documents. They offer valuable clues as to the nature of the oral interview. For example, if the job involves supervisory responsibilities, the announcement will usually indicate that knowledge of modern supervisory methods and the qualifications of the candidate as a supervisor will be tested. If so, you can expect such questions, frequently in the form of a hypothetical situation which you are expected to solve. NEVER go into an oral without knowledge of the duties and responsibilities of the job you seek.

3) Think through each qualification required

Try to visualize the kind of questions you would ask if you were a board member. How well could you answer them? Try especially to appraise your own knowledge and background in each area, *measured against the job sought*, and identify any areas in which you are weak. Be critical and realistic – do not flatter yourself.

4) Do some general reading in areas in which you feel you may be weak

For example, if the job involves supervision and your past experience has NOT, some general reading in supervisory methods and practices, particularly in the field of human relations, might be useful. Do NOT study agency procedures or detailed manuals. The oral board will be testing your understanding and capacity, not your memory.

5) Get a good night's sleep and watch your general health and mental attitude

You will want a clear head at the interview. Take care of a cold or any other minor ailment, and of course, no hangovers.

What should be done on the day of the interview?

Now comes the day of the interview itself. Give yourself plenty of time to get there. Plan to arrive somewhat ahead of the scheduled time, particularly if your appointment is in the fore part of the day. If a previous candidate fails to appear, the board might be ready for you a bit early. By early afternoon an oral board is almost invariably behind schedule if there are many candidates, and you may have to wait. Take along a book or magazine to read, or your application to review, but leave any extraneous material in the waiting room when you go in for your interview. In any event, relax and compose yourself.

The matter of dress is important. The board is forming impressions about you – from your experience, your manners, your attitude, and your appearance. Give your personal appearance careful attention. Dress your best, but not your flashiest. Choose conservative, appropriate clothing, and be sure it is immaculate. This is a business interview, and your appearance should indicate that you regard it as such. Besides, being well groomed and properly dressed will help boost your confidence.

Sooner or later, someone will call your name and escort you into the interview room. *This is it.* From here on you are on your own. It is too late for any more preparation. But remember, you asked for this opportunity to prove your fitness, and you are here because your request was granted.

What happens when you go in?

The usual sequence of events will be as follows: The clerk (who is often the board stenographer) will introduce you to the chairman of the oral board, who will introduce you to the other members of the board. Acknowledge the introductions before you sit down. Do not be surprised if you find a microphone facing you or a stenotypist sitting by. Oral interviews are usually recorded in the event of an appeal or other review.

Usually the chairman of the board will open the interview by reviewing the highlights of your education and work experience from your application – primarily for the benefit of the other members of the board, as well as to get the material into the record. Do not interrupt or comment unless there is an error or significant misinterpretation; if that is the case, do not hesitate. But do not quibble about insignificant matters. Also, he will usually ask you some question about your education, experience or your present job – partly to get you to start talking and to establish the interviewing "rapport." He may start the actual questioning, or turn it over to one of the other members. Frequently, each member undertakes the questioning on a particular area, one in which he is perhaps most competent, so you can expect each member to participate in the examination. Because time is limited, you may also expect some rather abrupt switches in the direction the questioning takes, so do not be upset by it. Normally, a board member will not pursue a single line of questioning unless he discovers a particular strength or weakness.

After each member has participated, the chairman will usually ask whether any member has any further questions, then will ask you if you have anything you wish to add. Unless you are expecting this question, it may floor you. Worse, it may start you off on an extended, extemporaneous speech. The board is not usually seeking more information. The question is principally to offer you a last opportunity to present further qualifications or to indicate that you have nothing to add. So, if you feel that a significant qualification or characteristic has been overlooked, it is proper to point it out in a sentence or so. Do not compliment the board on the thoroughness of their examination – they have been sketchy, and you know it. If you wish, merely say, "No thank you, I have nothing further to add." This is a point where you can "talk yourself out" of a good impression or fail to present an important bit of information. Remember, *you close the interview yourself.*

The chairman will then say, "That is all, Mr. _______, thank you." Do not be startled; the interview is over, and quicker than you think. Thank him, gather your belongings and take your leave. Save your sigh of relief for the other side of the door.

How to put your best foot forward

Throughout this entire process, you may feel that the board individually and collectively is trying to pierce your defenses, seek out your hidden weaknesses and embarrass and confuse you. Actually, this is not true. They are obliged to make an appraisal of your qualifications for the job you are seeking, and they want to see you in your best light. Remember, they must interview all candidates and a non-cooperative candidate may become a failure in spite of their best efforts to bring out his qualifications. Here are 15 suggestions that will help you:

1) Be natural – Keep your attitude confident, not cocky

If you are not confident that you can do the job, do not expect the board to be. Do not apologize for your weaknesses, try to bring out your strong points. The board is interested in a positive, not negative, presentation. Cockiness will antagonize any board member and make him wonder if you are covering up a weakness by a false show of strength.

2) Get comfortable, but don't lounge or sprawl

Sit erectly but not stiffly. A careless posture may lead the board to conclude that you are careless in other things, or at least that you are not impressed by the importance of the occasion. Either conclusion is natural, even if incorrect. Do not fuss with your clothing, a pencil or an ashtray. Your hands may occasionally be useful to emphasize a point; do not let them become a point of distraction.

3) Do not wisecrack or make small talk

This is a serious situation, and your attitude should show that you consider it as such. Further, the time of the board is limited – they do not want to waste it, and neither should you.

4) Do not exaggerate your experience or abilities

In the first place, from information in the application or other interviews and sources, the board may know more about you than you think. Secondly, you probably will not get away with it. An experienced board is rather adept at spotting such a situation, so do not take the chance.

5) If you know a board member, do not make a point of it, yet do not hide it

Certainly you are not fooling him, and probably not the other members of the board. Do not try to take advantage of your acquaintanceship – it will probably do you little good.

6) Do not dominate the interview

Let the board do that. They will give you the clues – do not assume that you have to do all the talking. Realize that the board has a number of questions to ask you, and do not try to take up all the interview time by showing off your extensive knowledge of the answer to the first one.

7) Be attentive

You only have 20 minutes or so, and you should keep your attention at its sharpest throughout. When a member is addressing a problem or question to you, give him your undivided attention. Address your reply principally to him, but do not exclude the other board members.

8) Do not interrupt

A board member may be stating a problem for you to analyze. He will ask you a question when the time comes. Let him state the problem, and wait for the question.

9) Make sure you understand the question

Do not try to answer until you are sure what the question is. If it is not clear, restate it in your own words or ask the board member to clarify it for you. However, do not haggle about minor elements.

10) Reply promptly but not hastily

A common entry on oral board rating sheets is "candidate responded readily," or "candidate hesitated in replies." Respond as promptly and quickly as you can, but do not jump to a hasty, ill-considered answer.

11) Do not be peremptory in your answers

A brief answer is proper – but do not fire your answer back. That is a losing game from your point of view. The board member can probably ask questions much faster than you can answer them.

12) Do not try to create the answer you think the board member wants

He is interested in what kind of mind you have and how it works – not in playing games. Furthermore, he can usually spot this practice and will actually grade you down on it.

13) Do not switch sides in your reply merely to agree with a board member

Frequently, a member will take a contrary position merely to draw you out and to see if you are willing and able to defend your point of view. Do not start a debate, yet do not surrender a good position. If a position is worth taking, it is worth defending.

14) Do not be afraid to admit an error in judgment if you are shown to be wrong

The board knows that you are forced to reply without any opportunity for careful consideration. Your answer may be demonstrably wrong. If so, admit it and get on with the interview.

15) Do not dwell at length on your present job

The opening question may relate to your present assignment. Answer the question but do not go into an extended discussion. You are being examined for a *new* job, not your present one. As a matter of fact, try to phrase ALL your answers in terms of the job for which you are being examined.

Basis of Rating

Probably you will forget most of these "do's" and "don'ts" when you walk into the oral interview room. Even remembering them all will not ensure you a passing grade. Perhaps you did not have the qualifications in the first place. But remembering them will help you to put your best foot forward, without treading on the toes of the board members.

Rumor and popular opinion to the contrary notwithstanding, an oral board wants you to make the best appearance possible. They know you are under pressure – but they also want to see how you respond to it as a guide to what your reaction would be under the pressures of the job you seek. They will be influenced by the degree of poise you display, the personal traits you show and the manner in which you respond.

ABOUT THIS BOOK

This book contains tests divided into Examination Sections. Go through each test, answering every question in the margin. We have also attached a sample answer sheet at the back of the book that can be removed and used. At the end of each test look at the answer key and check your answers. On the ones you got wrong, look at the right answer choice and learn. Do not fill in the answers first. Do not memorize the questions and answers, but understand the answer and principles involved. On your test, the questions will likely be different from the samples. Questions are changed and new ones added. If you understand these past questions you should have success with any changes that arise. Tests may consist of several types of questions. We have additional books on each subject should more study be advisable or necessary for you. Finally, the more you study, the better prepared you will be. This book is intended to be the last thing you study before you walk into the examination room. Prior study of relevant texts is also recommended. NLC publishes some of these in our Fundamental Series. Knowledge and good sense are important factors in passing your exam. Good luck also helps. So now study this Passbook, absorb the material contained within and take that knowledge into the examination. Then do your best to pass that exam.

EXAMINATION SECTION

EXAMINATION SECTION
TEST 1

DIRECTIONS: Each question or incomplete statement is followed by several suggested answers or completions. Select the one that BEST answers the question or completes the statement. *PRINT THE LETTER OF THE CORRECT ANSWER IN THE SPACE AT THE RIGHT.*

1. Of the following, the MOST important aim of community development is to assist a disadvantaged community to 1.____

   A. accomplish particular tasks within the service system
   B. evaluate its achievements in the light of pre-stated goals
   C. prepare itself to function as an organized, effective entity
   D. collect information about the network of social services

2. The goal of the reorganization of a human services agency is to provide services in the neighborhoods whenever feasible, in accordance with the needs of neighborhood residents. 2.____
   Of the following, a DESIRABLE result of this would be

   A. variation in the combination of services offered in each neighborhood
   B. uniformity of services offered in each neighborhood
   C. considerable variation in the amount of community participation in each neighborhood
   D. decrease in the need for utilization of existing community facilities

3. Appropriate division of functions and responsibilities between the communities and central headquarters is vital to the successful administration of a decentralized human services agency in a large urban center. The one of the following which is NOT an appropriate function to be performed at the community level is 3.____

   A. review of district plans for policy compliance
   B. stimulation of maximum use of both new and existing resources
   C. review of service program goals and relationships
   D. operation of community service teams

4. A new approach to the delivery of services being developed by the Department of Social Services is the Community Social Services Program. The one of the following which is NOT a major feature of this program is 4.____

   A. stationing of personnel in locations that are easily accessible to clients
   B. decentralization of authority to make decisions regarding services
   C. use of purchased services from private organizations to complement directly-delivered services
   D. preparation of a single annual Human Services Plan applicable to all Human Resources Districts

5. Representatives of a community organization which has an interest in developing a narcotics service program in a neighborhood with a high rate of narcotics addiction meet with you at the direction of the director of the human services center in order to ask you for assistance in developing this program. The MOST appropriate action for you to take FIRST would be to 5.____

A. assign a staff member to work with the group
B. inform the group that development of narcotics service programs is not a responsibility of the Department of Social Services
C. ask the Police Department to send a consultant to meet with you in order to develop a plan
D. refer the group back to the director of the human services center for consultation and clarification

6. Community participation is a key feature of the Community Social Services Program of the Department of Social Services. Of the following, a CORRECT statement with regard to the community participation facet of the program is that it 6.____

A. extends to the District level the consumer involvement aspect which was previously embodied in the client advisory committees of the citys social service centers
B. implements federal and state regulations which call for community control of planning and evaluation of services
C. emphasizes participation of local residents in service delivery rather than in planning and evaluation
D. makes evaluation the responsibility of consumers of social services

7. When the citizens of a disadvantaged community generally have a positive belief that they can work together in solving their problems, and thus achieve worthwhile goals, they are usually said to be working toward a community that is 7.____

A. complex
B. diverse
C. functional
D. underorganized

8. Which of the following is MOST likely to produce an initial positive response by local residents toward a community project? 8.____

A. Adoption of the cultural mannerisms and typical dress of local residents
B. Endorsement by a person or an institution trusted by local residents
C. Solution of a problem for the community to show good faith
D. Promising solutions for all the problems facing the community

9. Of the following, the MOST common mistake made by participants in social controversy is to 9.____

A. attribute a single point of view of all people of a certain group
B. try to understand all sides of the controversy
C. play down the controversy, in the hope that it will disappear
D. expect a cooperative resolution of the controversy

10. Of the following, the MOST probable result of citizen involvement in a community crisis situation is 10.____

A. stronger identification with community organizations and institutions
B. decreased effectiveness in the operation of community organizations
C. more accurate reporting of community events by mass media
D. loss of confidence in public agencies and private social services

11. Research in the form of fact finding constitutes a necessary foundation for community planning and action. 11.____
The one of the following which is LEAST likely to be a purpose of this type of research is to

A. evaluate services
B. determine needs
C. establish priorities
D. develop a theory

12. Administrative decentralization gives more authority to agency chiefs at the district level, as contrasted with political decentralization, which gives more decision-making power to local residents. 12.____
Of the following, the MOST important reason for emphasizing administrative decentralization would be to

A. remove decision-making power from local groups, because recent crises have shown that neighborhoods are not yet ready for community control
B. provide assurance that district chiefs of city agencies coordinate their actions with their central offices
C. encourage community participation in those neighborhoods where local residents have not taken the initiative to become involved in decision-making
D. provide essential administrative control at the neighborhood level in order to give community groups more assurance that their projects can be carried out

13. The *outreach* function provides a means of reaching out to disadvantaged community residents in order to become familiar with their needs and problems and to inform then of services available. 13.____
Which of the following would probably perform this function MOST effectively in their own neighborhoods?

A. Community leaders
B. Paraprofessionals
C. Small businessmen
D. School teachers

14. When people of a disadvantaged community are given the opportunity to gain satisfaction and self-confidence from small accomplishments, the MOST probable result is 14.____

A. discouragement of progress toward major goals
B. development of a false sense of achievement
C. progress toward overcoming more difficult problems
D. development of unrealistic and unachievable ambitions

15. At times, it is necessary for a community group to form a temporary work alliance with other self-interest community groups for the mutual support of programs. 15.____
Such a temporary work alliance is USUALLY called a

A. federation
B. coalition
C. union
D. society

16. The one of the following which accounts for the LARGEST portion of the budget of a human services agency is 16.____

A. personnel and support services
B. public assistance and medicaid
C. services to children and youth
D. community organization and development

17. According to the latest statistics published by the U.S. Department of Health, Education and Welfare, the state which spent the LARGEST amount of money per person for public assistance is 17.____

A. California
B. Massachusetts
C. Pennsylvania
D. New York

18. According to the most recent U.S. Census Bureau Report, the group living in New York City which has the LOWEST income level is the 18.____

A. Blacks
B. Puerto Ricans
C. Dominicans
D. Haitians

19. The group that contains the LARGEST number of individuals receiving public assistance is 19.____

A. children under working age
B. unemployed heads of families
C. the aged, disabled, and blind
D. unemployed single persons

20. A MAJOR difficulty faced by new arrivals to cities since 1950, which did not exist for earlier European immigrants, is the fact that the majority of present-day arrivals 20.____

A. must forfeit their native culture patterns
B. have an obviously darker skin color than most longtime residents
C. have little education
D. have few occupational skills

21. Generally speaking, low-income persons do not make maximum use of opportunities and services available to then, MAINLY because 21.____

A. most paraprofessional workers, while sincere in the desire to serve, are unable to reach the hard core
B. much of the routine paperwork in public assistance programs is now assigned to paraprofessional workers
C. they have become increasingly self-reliant and prefer to cope with their problems without help
D. they lack the confidence and know-how necessary to make their needs known to the proper persons or agencies

22. The one of the following problems which has MOST recently become a serious concern of the Youth Services Agency is the 22.____

A. increasing high school drop-out rate
B. resurgence of fighting youth gangs
C. spread of youth narcotics addiction
D. lack of recreation programs

23. Of the following, the MOST recent development with regard to welfare recipients is 23.____

A. introduction of the declaration of need instead of an investigation of elibibility
B. a major emphasis on employment programs
C. increased use of casework therapy and psychiatric counseling
D. acceptance of narcotics addicts for home relief

24. According to a recent decision by a Federal court, regular reporting at State Employment Service offices to pick up checks or accept work can NO longer be required of recipients of 24.____

A. Aid to the Disabled
B. Home Relief
C. Aid to Dependent Children
D. Medicaid

25. A BASIC objective of the proposal for revenue sharing is to provide 25.____

A. state and local governments with new sources of revenue from the federal government and greater control over how this revenue is spent
B. the federal government with greater control over spending of certain federally-raised tax revenues
C. safeguards against improper allocation of funds by state and local officials and incentives to states for reporting violations by local government
D. a method of sharing federal revenue with the states and localities in accordance with their required expenditures for public assistance and social welfare services

26. Acceptance of which of the following services provided by the Department of Social Services for public assistance clients is NOT voluntary on the part of the clients? 26.____

A. Home management
B. Family planning
C. Child protection
D. Educational counseling

27. The one of the following which is NOT part of the organization of the Youth Services Agency is the 27.____

A. Neighborhood Youth Corps
B. Recreation Support Program
C. Youth Development Centers
D. Youth Vocational Training Program

28. The one of the following which is NOT included under the organization of the Office of Special Services for Adults in the Department of Social Services is 28.____

A. senior citizen programs
B. Medicare
C. foster care for the aged and disabled
D. adult institutions

29. Several juvenile detention centers formerly run by the State Office of Probation are now operated by the 29.____

A. Youth Services Agency
B. Department of Social Services
C. Office of Child Development
D. Judicial Conference

30. Decentralized administration of the city's anti-poverty efforts is provided by the 30.____

A. Community Corporations
B. Council Against Poverty
C. Human Resources District Councils
D. Neighborhood Youth Corps

31. The Social Service Exchange is CORRECTLY described as a 31.____

A. recruitment center for the training and placement of volunteers for social and health agencies
B. center which maintains a central index of case records of families and individuals known to social and health agencies
C. center which provides information about and makes referrals to social and health agencies and proprietary nursing homes
D. confidential advisory service to help potential contributors evaluate local voluntary health and welfare agencies

32. Which one of the following is an IMPORTANT purpose of the formation of the Office of Special Services for Children in the Department of Social Services? 32.____

A. Greater programmatic integration of the protective and supportive services to children who are abused, neglected, dependent, delinquent or in need of services
B. More professional attention to child abuse cases and prompt court action to penalize parents of abused or neglected children
C. Separation of programs and facilities for children adjudged to be delinquent from special services for other dependent, abused or neglected children
D. Increased attention to home-finding and foster care and adoption services rather than institutional care for dependent children

33. The one of the following which is provided by the Department of Social Services for current, former, and potential assistance recipients ONLY is _____ services. 33.____

A. information
B. child welfare
C. referral
D. homemaker

34. A MAJOR goal of the Department of Social Services which is part of the reorganization and the separation of income maintenance from social services is to 34.____

A. limit the provision of public social services to those who are eligible for public assistance
B. make public social services available to all, whether or not they require financial assistance
C. refer clients who require social services to private agencies wherever possible
D. emphasize casework treatment and referral of clients for psychiatric services rather than programs to effect environmental change

35. Of the following, the MAIN functions of the Manpower and Career Development Agency (MCDA) of a human services agency are to 35.____

A. train the unskilled, upgrade existing skills, develop job opportunities, and place newly trained people in jobs
B. operate manpower, recruitment, and testing centers under contract with private organizations
C. provide remedial education and follow-up for disadvantaged potential college students and vocational testing and counseling for veterans and ex-addicts
D. provide job development, interviewing and placement, and manpower research services

---

KEY (CORRECT ANSWERS)

1.	C	16.	B
2.	A	17.	D
3.	A	18.	D
4.	D	19.	A
5.	A	20.	B
6.	A	21.	D
7.	C	22.	B
8.	B	23.	B
9.	A	24.	C
10.	A	25.	A
11.	D	26.	C
12.	D	27.	D
13.	B	28.	B
14.	C	29.	B
15.	B	30.	A

31.	B
32.	A
33.	D
34.	B
35.	A

TEST 2

DIRECTIONS: Each question or incomplete statement is followed by several suggested answers or completions. Select the one that BEST answers the question or completes the statement. *PRINT THE LETTER OF THE CORRECT ANSWER IN THE SPACE AT THE RIGHT.*

Questions 1-6.

DIRECTIONS: Questions 1 through 6 are to be answered SOLELY on the basis of the following passage.

Too often in the past society has accepted the existing social welfare programs, preferring to tinker with refinements when fundamental reform was in order. It has been a demeaning, degrading welfare system in which the instrument of government was wrongfully and ineptly used. It has been a system which has only alienated those forced to benefit from it and demoralized those who had to administer it at the level where the pain was clearly visible.

There is a need to put this nation on a course in which cash benefits, providing a basic level of support, are conferred in such a way as to intrude as little as possible into privacy and self-respect. It is difficult to define a basic level of support, no matter how high or low it might be set. In the end, however, the decision is not determined so much by how much is truly adequate for a family to meet all of its needs, but by the resources available to carry out the promise. That may be a harsh fact of life but it is also just that – a fact of life.

1. Of the following, the MOST suitable title for the foregoing passage would be: 1.____

   A. The Need for Government Control of Welfare
   B. Determining the Basic Level of Support
   C. The Need for Welfare Reform
   D. The Elimination of Welfare Programs

2. In this passage, the authors GREATEST criticism of the welfare system is that it is too 2.____

   A. disrespectful of recipients
   B. expensive to administer
   C. limited by regulations
   D. widespread in application

3. According to the passage, the BASIC level of support is actually determined by 3.____

   A. how much is required for a family to meet all of its needs
   B. the age of the recipients
   C. how difficult it is to administer the program
   D. the economic resources of the nation

4. In this passage, the author does NOT argue for 4.____

   A. a work incentive system
   B. a basic level of support
   C. cash benefits
   D. the privacy of recipients

5. As used in the foregoing passage, the underlined word *demeaning* means MOST NEARLY 5.____

   A. ineffective
   B. expensive
   C. overburdened
   D. humiliating

6. As used in the foregoing passage, the underlined word *ineptly* means MOST NEARLY 6.____

   A. foolishly
   B. unsuccessfully
   C. unskillfully
   D. unhappily

Questions 7-10.

DIRECTIONS: Questions 7 through 10 are to be answered SOLELY on the basis of the following paragraph.

The unemployment rate, which counts those unemployed in the sense that they are actively looking for work and unable to find it, gives a relatively superficial index of economic conditions in a community. A better index is the sub employment rate which includes the unemployment rate and also includes those working part-time while they are trying to get full-time work; those heads of households under 65 years of age who earn less than $360 per week working full-time, and those individuals under 65 who are not heads of households and earn less than $336 per week in a full-time job; and an estimate of the males "not counted," which is a very real concern in ghetto areas.

7. Of the following, the MOST suitable title for the foregoing paragraph would be 7.____

   A. Employment in the United States
   B. Part-time Workers and the Economy
   C. The Labor Market and the Community
   D. Two Indicators of Economic Conditions

8. On the basis of the paragraph, which of the following statements is CORRECT? 8.____

   A. The *unemployment* rate includes everyone who is not fully employed.
   B. The *subemployment* rate is higher than the unemployment rate.
   C. The *unemployment* rate gives a more complete picture of the economic situation than the subemployment rate.
   D. The *subemployment* rate indicates how many part-time workers are dissatisfied with the number of hours they work per week.

9. As used in the foregoing paragraph, the underlined word *superficial* means MOST NEARLY 9.____

   A. exaggerated
   B. official
   C. surface
   D. current

10. According to the paragraph, which of the following is included in the subemployment rate? 10.____

    A. Everyone who is unemployed
    B. All part-time workers
    C. Everyone under 65 who earns less than $336 per week in a full-time job
    D. All heads of households who earn less than $360 per week in a full-time job

Questions 11-15.

DIRECTIONS: Questions 11 through 15 are to be answered SOLELY on the basis of the diagram presented below.

HOW THE INNER-CITY FAMILY IN URBANVILLE SPENDS ITS MONEY

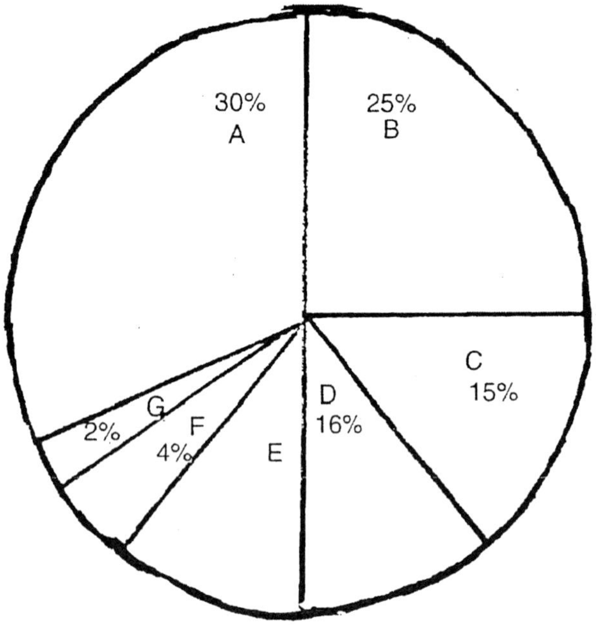

A. Food

B. Shelter

C. Clothing

D. Household Operation

E. Medical Care

F. Transportation

G. Miscellaneous

11. According to the diagram, the percentage spent on medical care is 11.____

A. 7% B. 8% C. 16% D. 18%

12. According to the diagram, the total percentage spent on food, shelter, and clothing is 12.____

A. 55% B. 60% C. 70% D. 75%

13. In a typical period, if the family spent $60 on transportation, how much did it spend on household operation? 13.____

A. $240 B. $384 C. $600 D. $960

14. If the family income is $250 a week, how much does it spend on transportation each year? 14.____

A. $120 B. $520 C. $1200 D. $5,200

15. Assume that the annual income of a family was $10,800 for several years. Last year, the income went up 5%, and the family then tripled the typical percentage for household operation. The amount spent on this item last year was MOST NEARLY 15.____

A. $1782 B. $2268 C. $2592 D. $5442

Questions 16-20.

DIRECTIONS: Questions 16 through 20 are to be answered SOLELY on the basis of the table presented below.

AFDC FAMILY MEMBERS IN URBANVILLE

Referred to and Enrolled in WIN Program, 1999-2001

	REFERRED		ENROLLED	
FAMILY MEMBER	1999	2001	1999	2001
Mother	1,091	1,306	730	877
Father	743	950	520	731
Child, age 16 and over	170	222	150	184

16. According to the table, how many AFDC family members were referred to WIN in 2001? 16.____

A. 1,792 B. 2,004 C. 2,388 D. 2,478

17. According to the table, the number of AFDC children, 16 and over, who were enrolled in WIN in 2001, was greater than the number enrolled in 1999 by 17.____

A. 12 B. 34 C. 38 D. 52

18. According to the table, the number of AFDC mothers who were enrolled in 2001 increased over the number enrolled in 1999 by MOST NEARLY 18.____

A. 20% B. 32% C. 54% D. 83%

19. In 2002, if the number of AFDC mothers referred to WIN increases 5% over 2001, the number of fathers referred increases 8% over 2001, and the number of children referred increases 5% over 2001, the total number of AFDC family members that will be referred in 2002 is MOST NEARLY 19.____

A. 1,424 B. 1,524 C. 3,130 D. 3,990

20. According to the table, the percentage of AFDC fathers NOT enrolled in WIN in 2001 of the number referred that year is MOST NEARLY 20.____

A. 23% B. 25% C. 71% D. 77%

KEY (CORRECT ANSWERS)

1. C
2. A
3. D
4. A
5. D

6. C
7. D
8. B
9. C
10. C

11. B
12. C
13. A
14. B
15. D

16. D
17. B
18. A
19. C
20. A

EXAMINATION SECTION
TEST 1

DIRECTIONS: Each question or incomplete statement is followed by several suggested answers or completions. Select the one that BEST answers the question or completes the statement. *PRINT THE LETTER OF THE CORRECT ANSWER IN THE SPACE AT THE RIGHT.*

1. During an interview with a tenant at your office, he confides to you that he would rather find his own apartment for his family than move into public housing. He asks for your advice in this matter. 1._____
The BEST thing you can do is

   A. advise that he look only to public housing since these are the best apartments
   B. tell him that you cannot advise him in such personal matters and then refer him to Social Services
   C. discuss with him the different ways he might find an apartment, including one in public housing
   D. suggest that he talk over his decision more carefully with his family

2. While inspecting conditions around a site, you notice that some of the garbage cans are not covered. 2._____
Which of the following BEST explains why this condition should be corrected? To

   A. prevent the garbage cans from getting lost
   B. prevent garbage from cans spreading onto the street
   C. allow sanitation men to handle the cans without spillage
   D. keep dogs and cats from knocking garbage cans over

3. While interviewing tenants, an assistant may find that a tenant will be silent for a short time before answering questions. 3._____
In order to get the required information from the tenant when this happens, the assistant should GENERALLY

   A. repeat the same question to make the tenant stop hesitating
   B. ask the tenant to write out his answer
   C. ask the tenant to answer quickly because other tenants are waiting to see you
   D. wait patiently and not pressure the tenant into quick, undeveloped answers

4. A tenant that you have been trying to encourage to apply for public housing comes to your desk at the site office. He is talking in a very angry and excited way about the lack of heat in his apartment. He says he will not pay his rent until there is heat. 4._____
The BEST thing for you to do at this time is to

   A. tell him that he should have applied for public housing as you suggested
   B. immediately let your supervisor know that he is refusing to pay his rent
   C. let him talk until he finishes and then discuss his problem with him
   D. tell him that you will not talk to him until he stops yelling

5. You have been informed that no determination has yet been made on the eligibility of a certain tenant for public housing. The decision will depend upon further checking. When you see the tenant, he seems to be quite worried, and he asks you whether his application has been accepted. 5.____
What would be BEST for you to do under these circumstances? Tell him

A. you can't talk to him because there is no definite information and you are very busy
B. to put his question in writing and send it to your manager so that it will be on record
C. you don't know yet but that he should not worry since you are quite sure he will be accepted
D. his application is being checked, and you will let him know the final result

6. An assistant is interviewing a high priority applicant who, contrary to usual experience, is extremely well-prepared and supplied with all the information the assistant is seeking. Which of the following possible actions by the assistant is MOST suitable under these circumstances? 6.____

A. Directly showing a willingness to review the information carefully and promptly
B. Exercising extreme caution about the credibility of the facts presented
C. Showing his awareness that the applicant is trying to trick him with false information
D. Accepting all of the candidate's information because of his obviously high level of intelligence

7. One of the tenants to be relocated is an extremely alert but elderly man who resists your every attempt to discuss with him the necessity for moving. He has lived in this building for almost thirty years, and he states flatly that he will NOT move. 7.____
Of the following, the MOST acceptable action for you to take is to

A. tell him he is being unreasonable and selfish
B. forcibly have him removed from the premises
C. refer his case to a social worker
D. advise him to take his case to the Legal Aid Society

8. Suppose you telephone to set up an important appointment with a tenant for a specific day on your calendar. He refuses to meet with you on that day because he claims the day is his religious holiday. 8.____
What is the BEST way of handling this situation?

A. Tell him it is against his interest not to meet with you on that day
B. Give up any idea now of meeting with him and go on to arranging your next appointment
C. Ask when he will be able to meet with you and indicate to him what the subject is
D. Indicate to him that you know the holiday cannot be important since city employees do not officially have that day off

9. In a building slated for demolition but still inhabited by tenants, an assistant sees some children of tenants pulling on a pipe in the hall. He tells them to stop but they say that the building is being torn down anyway. What should the assistant do FIRST? 9.____

A. Explain to the children that although this is true, they are causing danger to tenants still in the building.

B. Go immediately to the parents and tell them to punish their children for their misbehavior.
C. Say nothing else to the children but go to the site office and report the problem to his supervisor.
D. Go outside and call a policeman but tell the policeman to treat the children gently.

10. When interviewing a tenant who is to be relocated, the FIRST of the following actions for you to take is to 10.____

A. inform the tenant that your office will help only if he cooperates
B. advise the tenant that you must see proof for all statements he makes
C. assure the tenant that every effort will be made to find suitable housing
D. tell the tenant he will have no trouble finding new housing facilities

11. During interviews, people give information about themselves in several ways. 11.____
Of the following, which would usually give the LEAST amount of information about the person being questioned? His

A. spoken words
B. tone of voice
C. facial expression
D. body position

12. Suppose that while you are interviewing a tenant about the condition of his apartment, he becomes angered by your questioning and begins to use abusive language. Which of the following is the BEST way for you to react to him? 12.____

A. Use the same kind of language as he does to show him that you are neither impressed nor upset by his speech.
B. Interrupt him and tell him that you are not required to listen to such language.
C. Lower your voice and speak more slowly in an attempt to set an example that will calm him.
D. Let him continue to use abusive language but insist that he answer your questions at once.

13. Of the following characteristics, the one which would be MOST helpful for an assistant when helping an angry applicant understand why he has been turned down for public housing would be the ability to 13.____

A. state the rules exactly as they are written
B. show examples of other cases where the same thing happened
C. remain patient and understanding of the person's position
D. remain uninvolved and cold to individual personal problems

Questions 14-19.

DIRECTIONS: Answer Questions 14 through 19 on the basis of the information given in the paragraphs below.

Three year's ago, a city introduced a program of reduced transit rates for the elderly. It was hoped that this program would increase the travel of the elderly and help them maintain a greater measure of independence. About 600,000 of the 800,000 eligible residents are currently enrolled in the program. To be eligible, a person must be 65 years of age or older and not employed full-time. Riding for reduced fare is permitted between 10:00 M. and 4:00 P.M. and between 7:00 P.M. and midnight on weekdays and 24 hours a day on Saturdays, Sundays, and holidays.

In a city university study based on a sampling of 728 enrollees interviewed, it was learned that 51 percent are able to travel more, and 30.8 percent had been able to save enough money to make a noticeable difference in their budgets as a result of the reduced-fare program.

It has been recommended that reduced-fare programs be extended to encourage the use of transit Lines in off-hours by other groups such as the poor, the very young, housewives, and the physically handicapped. To implement this recommendation, it would be necessary for the Federal government to increase transit subsidies.

14. Which one of the following would be the BEST title for the passage above? 14.___

A. *A Program of Reduced Transit Rates for the Elderly*
B. *Recommendations for Extending Programs for the Elderly*
C. *City University Study on the Relationship of Age and Travel*
D. *Eligibility Requirements for the Reduced Rate Program*

15. *Approximately* what percentage of the eligible residents is currently enrolled in the reduced-fare program? 15.___

A. 25% B. 50% C. 65% D. 75%

16. Which one of the following persons is NOT eligible for the reduced-fare program? A 16.___

A. Woman, age *67,* employed part-time as a stenographer
B. Handicapped man, age 62
C. Blind man, age 66, employed part-time as a transcribing typist
D. Housewife, age 70

17. At which one of the following times would the reduced-fare NOT be permitted for an eligible elderly person? 17.___

A. Sunday, 6:00 P.M. B. Christmas Day, 2:00 M.
C. Tuesday, 9:00 M. D. Thursday, 8:00 P.M.

18. Of the 728 enrollees interviewed in a city university study of the reduced-fare program, it was found that 18.___

A. the majority traveled more and saved money at the same time
B. more than half traveled less and therefore saved money
C. about half traveled more and. about one-third saved money
D. the majority saved money but traveled the same rate as before

19. According to the passage above, what would be necessary to extend the reduced-fare program to other groups of people? 19.____

A. Increasing the eligible age to 68
B. Reducing the hours when half-fare is permitted
C. Increasing the fare for other riders
D. Increasing the transit subsidies by the Federal government

20. Reports are made MOST often in order to 20.____

A. suggest new ideas
B. give information
C. issue orders to workers
D. show that work is being done

21. An assistant is reporting a loose floor board in a certain apartment building on the site. The MOST important thing he should report in order to get immediate repairs is 21.____

A. how the floor board became loose
B. when the floor board became loose
C. the type of material and the number of men needed to make the repair
D. in which apartment the loose floor board is located

22. Suppose you receive a phone call from a tenant about a problem that requires you to look up the information and call her back. Although the tenant had given you her name earlier and you can say the name, you are not sure that you can spell it correctly. Which of the following would be MOST likely to insure that you spell the name correctly? 22.____

A. Say the name slowly and ask her if you are saying it correctly.
B. Spell her name as you have been saying it.
C. Ask her to spell the name so that you can write it.
D. Look through your files for a similar name and copy the spelling.

23. When tenants relocate, a report is made. This report is in the form of a standard form instead of a fully written report. 23.____
The MOST important advantage of using a standard form for certain information is that

A. one can be sure that the report will be sent in as soon as possible
B. anyone can write out the report without directions from a supervisor
C. needed information is less likely to be left out of the report
D. information that is written up this way is less likely to be false

24. Suppose you are filling out a section of a form to describe an incident which will be read by a social worker but you run out of space before finishing. It would be BEST for you to 24.____

A. leave out whatever information you consider unimportant
B. write what you can on the form and attach another sheet with the rest of the information
C. cross out what you wrote on the form and write on a separate sheet of paper which you attach to the form
D. write what you can on the form and tell your supervisor or the social worker the rest of it

25. It is part of an assistant's job to help a manager enter various items of information on a monthly report. This information may be, for example, the number of tenants relocated to different types of housing and the number of tenants left on the site. 25.____
The assistant must be careful NOT to make mistakes on his entries about tenants because

A. mistakes will show his supervisor that his work is poor
B. records must not be too difficult to read
C. these mistakes are hard to notice and correct
D. correct records are needed for the department to operate smoothly

26. For tenants who are not eligible for public housing and who are unable to find a new apartment, the relocation agency 26.____

A. refers the case to the Human Rights Commission
B. seeks to obtain private housing for the family
C. advises the family to move in with relatives and friends
D. arranges sleeping quarters at the site office

27. The MAXIMUM amount of money a relocated family can receive for moving expenses is 27.____

A. under $500
B. $500 - 750
C. $751 - 1000
D. $1001 - 1500

28. Of the following conditions that are often present in slum buildings, the one which is MOST likely to cause lead poisoning in children is 28.____

A. exposed rusty nails in floors
B. uncovered garbage cans containing old pencils
C. paint flaking off walls and window sills
D. the escape of fumes from faulty oil burners

29. An assistant would be correct to advise a tenant that it is ILLEGAL to throw which of the following into an incinerator? 29.____

A. Compactly wrapped bundles
B. Empty plastic bags
C. Loose vacuum or carpet sweepings
D. Soapy rags

30. A housing project is being built on Site X. 30.____
Of the following, the people who are given priority for apartments in the project if they meet eligibility requirements are

A. former tenants of Site X
B. welfare recipients
C. minority groups with the lowest income
D. families with the most children

31. A family which occupied a 4 1/2 room apartment at an urban renewal site moved to an off-site 5-room apartment. They were eligible for a 6-room apartment, but it was unavailable . 31.____
The family is now entitled to reimbursement for moving expenses based on

A. a 4-room apartment
B. a 5-room apartment
C. a 6-room apartment
D. actual cost of the move in an unlimited amount

32. During inspection of a tenant's apartment, you observe that the grids and burners of the stove are greasy and heavily caked with spilled food. Because of this, the burners do not produce an even flame from all the ga.s openings. 32.____
Of the following, the BEST thing to tell the tenant FIRST is that she should

A. scrape off the caked-on drippings and then poke open all the clogged openings so the gas. will burn evenly
B. remove the soiled parts of the burner and soak them in hot water with a mild cleaner to remove the dirt
C. learn how to use the stove properly so that her food does not boil over or splatter onto the grids
D. stop using the range until someone from the management office comes to adjust the flame

33. While inspecting a tenant's apartment, one of the things you should check is the drainage of the sinks. In testing the kitchen sink, you observe that there are coffee grinds and a film of grease in the drain basket. 33.____
Of the following, the BEST instructions to give the tenant are to

A. throw coffee grinds in the garbage and wash oils down the drain
B. collect oil in a can and put it in the garbage, but wash coffee grinds down with cold water
C. avoid clogging, wash both coffee grinds and oil down the sink with hot, soapy water
D. collect and dispose of coffee grinds and oils by putting them in the garbage and not in the sink

34. Mrs. Mary Jones and her family live in a 5-room apartment in a building on an urban renewal site. A public housing development is planned for this site. You are interviewing her with regard to relocation. During the interview, you learn that Mrs. Jones is divorced, unemployed, and receiving public assistance. Her four children are all under eight years of age, she is from a. small town in North Carolina, and she has lived in the city for over 2 1/2 years. 34.____
From 'your questions, what should you *immediately* know regarding relocation possibilities?
She is

A. *eligible* for high priority in a public housing development
B. *eligible* for public housing but not for another two months
C. *not eligible* for public housing
D. *not eligible* for public housing for another six months

35. You are about to visit a tenant to encourage him to move from the site when a neighbor tells you that for the last week the tenant has been quarreling loudly and constantly with his wife and children. When you knock on his door, he tells you to go away. You try several times to visit this apartment, but with no success. 35.____
What is the BEST thing to do in an effort to solve this problem?

A. Ask the neighbor to encourage him to let you in since he probably has confidence in the neighbor
B. Report the problem to your supervisor since the services of a social worker may be needed
C. Leave a note in the door telling the tenant to come to the site office
D. Call the police and tell them of the unusual difficulty you are having with this man

36. Which one of the following is the BEST kind of evidence presented by a tenant to prove that he actually lives at his current address? 36.____

A. change-of-address form that the tenant has filled out for a creditor
B. letter with the tenant's name and present address on it
C. library card
D. receipt

37. As an assistant, you could be asked to make a recommendation regarding the type of lighting fixtures a tenant should use. 37.____
If you were concerned with not overburdening the present electrical circuits, a recommendation to use fluorescent lights rather than incandescent lights would be

A. *good,* because fluorescent lights flicker less than , incandescent bulbs
B. *good,* because fluorescent lights draw less current than incandescent bulbs
C. *poor,* because fluorescent lights are very hard to install in a system designed for incandescent lights
D. *poor,* because incandescent lights use less current than fluorescent lights

38. If a tenant had to move more than one time, moving expenses would be paid for all of the following combinations of moves EXCEPT 38.____

A. an intrasite move and a subsequent move to a tenant-found apartment
B. a move to another site and a subsequent move to public housing
C. two moves to another site and a subsequent move to a tenant-found apartment
D. a move-out to a tenant-found apartment and a subsequent move to public housing

39. The step of eviction of an on-site tenant is *generally* considered 39.____

A. when a tenant has failed to pay a month's rent
B. only when a tenant has refused to move into public housing
C. as a last step in solving any housing problems of a tenant
D. as a warning to an on-site tenant who is allowing more relatives to live with him than is noted on the S.O.R. card

40. Suppose that a tenant tells you her moving expenses will come to more than the amount she is eligible to receive. You WOULD tell her to 40.____

A. pay the extra expense herself
B. ask the Social Service Department for help
C. submit a moving bill from the mover
D. leave behind all broken furniture

KEY (CORRECT ANSWERS)

1.	C	11.	D	21.	D	31.	A
2.	B	12.	C	22.	C	32.	B
3.	D	13.	C	23.	C	33.	D
4.	C	14.	A	24.	D	34.	A
5.	D	15.	D	25.	B	35.	B
6.	A	16.	B	26.	B	36.	D
7.	C	17.	C	27.	A	37.	B
8.	C	18.	C	28.	C	38.	D
9.	A	19.	D	29.	C	39.	C
10.	C	20.	B	30.	A	40.	C

TEST 2

DIRECTIONS: Each question or incomplete statement is followed by several suggested answers or completions. Select the one that BEST answers the question or completes the statement. *PRINT THE LETTER OF THE CORRECT ANSWER IN THE SPACE AT THE RIGHT.*

1. Housing officials and experts have long suggested changing slum tenements into cooperatives. 1.____
The PROBABLE reason that the advocates of tenement cooperatives feel that tenant-owners would be more likely than absentee landlords to keep buildings in good condition is that

    A. the tenant-owners would be living there while an absentee landlord would not
    B. the tenants in cooperatives want to demonstrate the advantages of cooperative living
    C. absentee landlords do not understand inner city problems
    D. absentee landlords have no reason to provide .good maintenance

2. A three-part plan to control the loss of an estimated sixty million dollars a year in welfare monies has been proposed. 2.____
Which one of the following proposals would LEAST likely be part of this plan?

    A. Identification cards with photographs of the welfare client
    B. Face-to-face interviews with the welfare clients
    C. Computerized processing of welfare money records
    D. Individual cash payments to each member of a family

3. Which one of the following statements describes the purpose of the Equal Rights Amendment which was passed by Congress but was not ratified by the required number of states? 3.____
To

    A. eliminate state-enforced racial discrimination in public schools through extensive use of busing
    B. guarantee to aliens living in the United States the right to hold Civil Service jobs
    C. prohibit sex discrimination by any law or action of the government
    D. extend the right to vote to those previously ineligible by requiring only thirty days residency in a state

4. In dealing with members of different ethnic groups in the area he serves, the assistant should give 4.____

    A. individuals the services required by his agency
    B. less service to those he judges to be more advantaged
    C. better service to groups with which he sympathizes most
    D. better service to groups with political *muscle*

5. The MAJOR reason for joining a professional group such as The National Association of Housing and Redevelopment Officials, The Citizens Housing and Planning Council, or The National Housing Conference is to 5.____

A. keep yourself informed about current ideas and
B. directions in the housing field · put it on your resume
C. get promoted
D. gain respect from fellow workers

6. Suppose you are interviewing a tenant whose clothing is sloppy, strange, or out of fashion. 6.____
Which of the following is MOST certain to be an appropriate action taken toward this tenant?

A. Tell him he will get better service when he dresses better.
B. Refer him to the Department of Social Services for help.
C. Refer his children to the Bureau of Child Welfare.
D. Treat him as respectfully as you treat other tenants.

7. An assistant may initiate an order that a tenant's welfare check be *rent-restricted* if that tenant has mismanaged his welfare check and not paid his rent. 7.____
Taking this action assures that

A. all of the tenant's next welfare checks will be sent to the Urban Renewal Site as payment on account
B. the Urban Renewal Site will receive a certain portion of the tenant's next welfare check and the tenant will receive the remainder
C. the welfare center will send the Urban Renewal Site full payment for the rent and will require that the tenant repay this amount
D. the welfare center will hold payment of checks from the tenant until they are notified by the assistant that the rent has been paid

8. For six months, a family lived in a 4-room apartment where they paid $376 a month. They made an intrasite move to a 4-room apartment where they paid $92 per room a month for six months. 8.____
Comparing the two six-month periods, the TOTAL amount of money the family saved by making the intrasite move was

A. $48 B. $58 C. $86 D. $118

9. To calculate a tenant's usable income, you should ma.ke tax deductions of 4.4 percent on salary up to a maximum of $9,000 and state disability deductions of .5 percent on salary up to $3,000. 9.____
What does a tenant's COMBINED deduction amount to if his annual salary is $6,700?

A. $228.00 B. $284.30 C. $309.80 D. $350.00

10. If the temporary relocation expenses for housing are set at $27 per day for one adult and $15 per day for each additional person in a room, how much money is allowed for a woman and four children temporarily relocated in one room for a period of six days? 10.____

A. $252 B. $522 C. $567 D. $777

11. According to relocation policy, a family relocating to private housing from federally-aided or certain other sites will be granted a relocation payment. This payment equals the difference between 1/5 of the family's yearly income and the scheduled yearly rent for a standard apartment for their size family. 11.____
Suppose a two-person family whose yearly income is $6,450 has been unable to obtain public housing and so finds a one-bedroom private apartment. The scheduled rent for a one-bedroom apartment appropriate for their occupancy is $120 a month. What payment will they receive?

A. $120 B. $144 C. $150 D. $205

12. A family on a housing relocation site is paying $240 per month for rent. This represents 25% of their gross monthly income. 12.____
If the husband earns 4/5 of their total combined monthly income, how much does the WIFE earn per month?

A. $192 B. $324 C. $768 D. $960

13. In a nearly vacant building, there are only a few tenants left who are waiting to move into public housing. When you visit them to check their present conditions, you notice that some of the *tinned-up* apartments have the sheet metal partly pulled off the doors. The tenants tell you that they think that the many men who come and go frequently are drug addicts. 13.____
The BEST action for you to take is to

A. ignore the incident since all tenants will be moving out soon
B. visit the site when you think someone might actually be selling drugs
C. put up a sign warning these men that the building will be knocked down shortly
D. report all your observations and the reports of the tenants to your supervisor

Questions 14-19.

DIRECTIONS: Answer Questions 14 through 19 on the basis of the information given in the passage below.

The City of X has set up a Maximum Base Rent Program for all rent-controlled apartments. The objective is to insure that the landlord will get a fair, but not excessive, profit on his building to stem the great tide of buildings being abandoned by their owners and to encourage landlords to continue the upkeep of their property. The Maximum Base Rent Program permits the landlord to raise rents under carefully devised standards, while practically no raises in rents in this City were permitted under previous guidelines.

Under this plan, the City determines a Maximum Ease Rent amount by means of a formula which takes into account the age of the building, the number of apartments, total rents received from the building, the amount of expenses, and labor costs. The Maximum Base Rent amount is to be recomputed every two years to allow for increases or decreases in building costs.

The Maximum Base Rent, which will allow the landlord to make a "fair return" on his investment, may not be collected immediately, however, since no rent increases over 7.5 percent will be permitted in any one year. The highest actual rent for each apartment during a given year will be called the Maximum Collectible Rent. This will be computed so that the increase over the present rent is not more . than 7.5 percent ($7.50 on every $100.00). Sometimes it may be less. Therefore, collectible rents will increase each year until the Maximum Base Rent is reached.

14. According to the above passage, the Maximum Base Rent is determined by the 14.____

A. landlord B. Mayor
C. Rent Commissioner D. City

15. Which of the following, according to the passage, permits a *fair return* on the landlord's investment? 15.____
The _____ Rent Program.

A. Minimum Base B. Maximum Base
C. Minimum Collectible D. Maximum Collectible

16. It may be concluded from the passage that the City of X hopes that insuring fair profits for landlords will be followed by 16.____

A. good upkeep of apartment buildings
B. decreased interest rates on home mortgages
C. lower rents in the future
D. a better formula for determining rents

17. According to the passage, guidelines for determining rents previous to the Maximum Base Rent Program resulted in 17.____

A. practically no raises in rents being made
B. rent increases of approximately 10 percent a year
C. a *fair return* to landlords from most rents
D. landlords making too much money on their property

18. Based on the above passage, which is the MOST correct description of the kinds of facts that are taken into consideration when determining the Maximum Base Rent? Facts about 18.____

A. labor costs and politics
B. the landlord and labor costs
C. the building and labor costs
D. the building and the landlord

19. According to the above passage, the MAXIMUM annual increase in rent for a tenant in rent-controlled housing under the Maximum Base Rent Program is 19.____

A. 7.5 percent each year for ten years
B. 7.5 percent each year until the Maximum Base Rent is reached
C. always under 7.5 percent a year
D. $7.50 each year until it reaches $100.00

Questions 20-25.

DIRECTIONS: Answer Questions 20 through 25 on the basis of the information in the following form.

METROPOLITAN CITY		
Last Name Smith	First Name John	Middle Initial G.
Street 758 Reason Street		Apartment 1C
Borough or Town Bronx	State New York	Zip Code 10403
Monthly Rent $110.00	Number of Rooms 5	

E.

FAMILY COMPOSITION

	Name	Relation to Head	Birth Date Mo. /Yr.	Annual Income	Employer or School
1.	Smith , John G.	Head	7/58	$10,400	Harris Chemical
2.	Smith , Ethel S.	Wife	3/61	0	
3.	Smith, Lucy M.	Daughter	4/81	0	P.S. 172
4.	Smith, John G. , Jr .	Son	8/83	0	P.S. 172
5.	Smith, Susan F.	Daughter	1/88	0	
6.	Simmons , Sylvia T.	Mother-in- law	4/40	$4,680	F.W. Woolworth (part-time)
7.					

Total Annual Income $15,080

Total Assets: Small Savings Accounts. $5,000 life insurance on Mr. Smith.

Additional Information

20. The occupants of the Smith apartment are Mr. Smith, Mrs. Smith, ____ mother, their ____ and ____. 20.____

A. her; son; daughters
B. his; son; daughters
C. her; sons; daughter
D. her; sons; daughters

21. The income of the Smith household comes from the earnings of the father, the 21.____

A. mother, the mother-in-law, and the children
B. mother, and the children, but not the mother-in-law
C. mother-in-law, and the children, but not the mother
D. mother-in-law, but not the mother and children

22. From the information given about the Smith family, their apartment seems to be 22.____

A. too small
B. the right size
C. a little large
D. much too large

23. If an assistant goes to the Smiths' apartment to discuss their relocation and everyone is home except Mr. Smith, with whom should the assistant talk about relocation? 23.____

A. John Jr. and Ethel Smith
B. Ethel Smith and Sylvia Simmons
C. Lucy and Ethel Smith
D. John Smith, Jr. and Sylvia Simmons

24. The reason why the last column was left blank for Susan Smith is PROBABLY that 24.____

A. the assistant forgot to ask for this information
B. Susan's parents would not give this information
C. Susan is too young to go to school
D. Susan does not live at home

25. The section for Additional Information was left blank MOST probably because 25.____

A. the assistant did not have time to ask for more information
B. the Smith family is sufficiently well-described by the other information on the form
C. the Additional Information section is not an important part of the form
D. unfavorable facts have been purposely left out

26. Whenever a tenant moves into a private apartment for which a finder's fee is to be paid, this fee is payable to the 26.____

A. landlord or broker
B. tenant
C. local site office
D. Housing and Development Administration

27. When a relocated tenant moves into public housing in the city, all rents must be paid DIRECTLY to the 27.____

A. Relocation and Management Services Office
B. Housing and Redevelopment Administration

C. Model Cities Administration
D. City Housing Authority

28. According to relocation rules and regulations, in order for an apartment to be considered *standard,* it is LEAST important that the apartment 28.____

A. not be overcrowded
B. have a bathroom with a shower
C. have hot and cold running water
D. be free of hazardous violations

29. The PRIMARY purpose of the Finder's Fee Program is to 29.____

A. provide a listing of private home owners willing to take in tenants during emergencies
B. establish a link between private contractors and public housing
C. arrange housing for those forced to vacate because of boiler breakdowns
D. provide a listing of housing facilities in private housing

30. Which one of the following would MOST likely cause the GREATEST amount of damage to the asphalt tiles on apartment floors? 30.____

A. Protective furniture casters
B. Wet mopping
C. Liquid wax
D. Grease

31. The rents for three families in a relocation site come to a total of $0,720 per year. If Family A pays $3,480 per year and Family B pays $2,400 per year, how much does Family C pay? 31.____

A. $2,760 B. $3,840 C. $4,200 D. $5,800

32. Of 180 families that relocated in a given month, one-fifth moved into Finder's Fee apartments, one-quarter moved into tenant-found apartments, one-third moved into public housing, and the rest moved out of the city. How many moved out of the city? 32.____

A. 36 B. 39 C. 45 D. 60

33. If a tenant earns $5,280 a year and his rent is 25% of his annual income, the amount of rent he pays each month is 33.____

A. $110 B. $115 C. $120 D. $135

34. The word *recycling* has become a popular one as used by those who are concerned with saving the environment. This word USUALLY refers to an interest in 34.____

A. using bicycles again instead of automobiles for transportation
B. the chemical treatment of rain water for drinking purposes
C. collecting used bottles, cans, and newspaper which will be sold, treated, and re-used
D. reorganizing public transportation routes in the city so that noise and traffic will be reduced

35. Recent accusations of fraud involving FHA-insured mortgages in various American cities have brought to light the fact that 35.____

A. blockbusting has become the favorite tactic of real estate brokers
B. families with incomes of $16,000 - $20,000 have been prevented from obtaining mortgages
C. homes bought through false credit ratings at inflated prices were quickly lost by low income owners
D. the bad design of homes involved has helped pollute the urban environment

---

KEY (CORRECT ANSWERS)

1. A
2. D
3. C
4. A
5. A

6. D
7. B
8. A
9. C
10. B

11. C
12. A
13. D
14. D
15. B

16. A
17. A
18. C
19. B
20. A

21. D
22. A
23. B
24. C
25. B

26. A
27. D
28. B
29. D
30. D

31. B
32. B
33. A
34. C
35. C

EXAMINATION SECTION
TEST 1

DIRECTIONS: Each question or incomplete statement is followed by several suggested answers or completions. Select the one that BEST answers the question or completes the statement. *PRINT THE LETTER OF THE CORRECT ANSWER IN THE SPACE AT THE RIGHT.*

1. While interviewing tenants, an assistant should use the technique of interruption, beginning to speak when a tenant has temporarily paused at the end of a phrase or sentence, in order to 1.____

   A. limit the tenant's ability to voice his objection or complaints
   B. shorten, terminate, or redirect a tenant's response
   C. assert authority when he feels that the tenant is too conceited
   D. demonstrate to the tenant that pauses in speech should be avoided

2. An assistant might gain background information about a tenant by being aware of the person's speech during an interview. 2.____
   Which one of the following patterns of speech would offer the LEAST accurate information about a tenant?
   The

   A. number of slang expressions and the level of vocabulary
   B. presence and degree of an accent
   C. rate of speech and the audibility level
   D. presence of a physical speech defect

3. Suppose that you are interviewing a distressed tenant who claims that he was just laid off from his job and has no money to pay his rent. 3.____
   Your FIRST action should be to

   A. ask if he has sought other employment or has other sources of income
   B. express your sympathy but explain that he must pay the rent on time
   C. inquire about the reasons he was laid off from work
   D. try to transfer him to a smaller apartment which he can afford

4. Suppose you have some background information on an applicant whom you are interviewing. During the interview, it appears that the applicant is giving you false information. 4.____
   The BEST thing for you to do at that point is to

   A. pretend that you are not aware of the written facts and let him continue
   B. tell him what you already know and discuss the discrepancies with him
   C. terminate the interview and make a note that the applicant is untrustworthy
   D. tell him that because he is making false statements, he will not be eligible for an appointment

5. Since at present there are not many Spanish-speaking assistants, a Spanish-speaking applicant may want to bring his bilingual child with him to an interview to act as an interpreter. 5.____
   Which of the following would be LEAST likely to affect the value of an interview in which an applicant's child has acted as interpreter?

A. It may make it undesirable for the assistant to ask certain questions.
B. A child may do an inadequate job of interpretation.
C. A child's answers may indicate his feelings toward his parents.
D. The applicant may not want to reveal all information in front of his child.

6. While you are showing families around a new project which will be ready for occupancy in a month, you are asked many questions concerning the present state of disorder in the halls and grounds of the buildings. These families are concerned that this condition will exist when they move in. 6.____
Of the following, the BEST way to handle this situation would be for you to

A. assure the tenants that the buildings will all be clean and tidy when they are due to move in
B. explain that almost everything will be completed when the tenants move in, but that temporary inconveniences tend to exist when one moves into a new project
C. avoid answering the questions since the condition will exist, but emphasize the advantage of moving into a new project
D. explain that because this is a low-income project, efficiency is reduced and it will, therefore, take more time to get the building ready

7. Assume that you are responsible for making apartment inspections. 7.____
To make a practice of setting up appointments with tenants before visiting is

A. *good,* mainly because it allows the tenant time to become acquainted with household safety procedures
B. *good,* mainly because it is demeaning and disrespectful of tenant's privacy to appear at the apartment unannounced
C. *poor,* mainly because it will give the tenant an opportunity to clean the house, thus not giving a picture of normal conditions
D. *poor,* mainly because tenants should be available at all times for inspections

8. Assume that you are approached by a tenant who seeks your help in dealing with her 12-year-old son, Joe. He apparently leaves for school each morning, but another child has just informed her that Joe has not been in school for a month. She is very upset and does not know what action to take. 8.____
The one of the following actions which you should recommend that she take as a FIRST step is to

A. report the truancy to the school immediately so they can take action
B. discuss the situation with Joe, inquiring as to the truth of the matter
C. reprimand Joe or deprive him of something he wants to get him to go to school
D. tell Joe to report to you to discuss an important matter

9. Suppose you have been informed by your supervisor that he has checked the applications that you have submitted and he found that you have categorized a disproportionate number of minority applicants as ineligible. You feel that you have impartially evaluated all of the applications. 9.____
Of the following, the MOST appropriate action for you to take is to

A. request that he review the application forms with you to discuss the eligibility of specific applications
B. tell him that you will look over the applications and change them to eligible

C. tell him that you will try to be more careful in the future when interviewing and qualifying applicants
D. provide as much evidence as possible showing your good treatment of members of minority groups in other situations

10. Suppose you have placed in an apartment a family that has recently arrived from a distant country. Other tenants have mentioned to you that they are puzzled by the new tenants' strange culture and wonder when they will adapt to our society. 10.____
Of the following, which aspect of their culture is MOST conducive to change?

A. Religious beliefs
B. Parent-child relationships
C. Use of household appliances
D. Customs observed at meal-time

11. Suppose a tenant, Mr. X, complains to you that the occupants of the apartment directly below his apartment play their boom box . very loudly, although he has repeatedly asked them to lower it. 11.____
Of the following, the BEST action for you to take is to

A. suggest that Mr. X also play loud music in his apartment to show how annoying it can be
B. inform Mr. X that there is nothing that you can do-Mr. X must deal with the tenants directly
C. post a sign in the building lobby stating the Noise Abatement Laws
D. speak with the other tenant and discuss the situation with him

12. Suppose one of your duties includes inspecting the apartments of all new tenants and suggesting proper care of equipment. A family you are visiting appears to be quite hostile to you, although you have explained the purpose of your visit. You notice that the stove is covered with grease and the sink drain is clogged with coffee grounds. Of the following, what is the BEST thing for you to do in this situation? 12.____

A. Refrain from making comments on the situation at this time, but remember to report the conditions to your supervisor
B. Describe the dangers or possible results of the clogged drain and greasy stove, and suggest easy ways to correct these conditions
C. Offer to help clean the stove and sink drain and enumerate, on paper, the ways to take care of the equipment properly
D. Make an appointment for the tenants to speak with you about the situation in your office

13. Assume you are assigned to interview applicants for low-rent apartments. 13.____
Of the following, which is the BEST attitude for you to take in dealing with applicants for apartments?

A. Assume they will enjoy being interviewed because they believe that you, as a representative of the landlord, will get them an apartment
B. Expect that they have had a history of anti-social behavior in the family, and probe deeply into the social development of family members
C. Expect that they will try to control the interview, thus you should keep them on the defensive

D. Assume that they will be polite and cooperative and attempt to secure the information you need in a business-like manner

14. Assume that the following problem of a tenant family has come to your attention. The tenant, who is the main support of his family, has developed a health problem which prevents him from driving a car or traveling to work by subway. He can, however, walk up to a mile or travel by surface transportation. Because of the problem of traveling to work, he may lose his job. 14.____
Which of the following courses of action should you take FIRST?

A. Put the tenant in touch with the department of social services. They may be able to arrange public assistance payments for him.
B. Find out whether any housing projects meeting the new transportation restrictions of the tenant have any apartments available.
C. Arrange a visit by a social worker. If the man stays home and his wife goes to work, they may be able to maintain their income.
D. Send the man for employment counseling. He may have skills that are in demand, close to his present apartment.

15. Assume that an elderly single tenant who has habitually paid her rent on time is now two weeks late with her current month's rent. You have sent her an official notice of delinquency. 15.____
Assuming that you have taken no other action to collect the rent, the NEXT thing you should do is to

A. send her a strong personal note demanding payment of her rent
B. send a polite note to her daughter, who is listed on your records as next of kin, asking her to speak to her mother about her delinquency
C. send her a note asking her to telephone you immediately
D. telephone or visit her apartment because illness may be the cause of the late rent payment

16. Assume that you are working at a project and a tenant tells you that some equipment left on the grounds poses a hazard to the tenants and their children. She suggests that this equipment be surrounded by barricades and signs. 16.____
Of the following, the BEST response for you to make is to tell the tenant

A. to route her complaint and suggestion through the tenants' association
B. that you will pass her complaint and suggestion on to the manager of the project for consideration
C. to be careful in making complaints; she may be labeled as a troublemaker
D. suggest that she put her complaint and suggestion into writing so that it will be easier to understand

17. Assume that, in a public housing project, a tenant complains that the interior of the elevator has recently been defaced by graffiti. She claims that for the past two days, at about 3 P.M., she has seen a few teenage boys running from the building and suspects they are the culprits. 17.____
The FIRST thing that you should do is to

A. station a housing patrolman by the elevator for the next few days to observe any unusual incidents
B. explain to her that the incidents appear to be totally unrelated

C. have a housing patrolman patrol the outside of the building at 3 P.M. to watch for the boys
D. ask her why she feels the boys are responsible for the graffiti

Questions 18-20.

DIRECTIONS: Questions 18 through 20 each list various duties that you are to perform on a particular day. Assuming that you have arrived at the office at 9:00 A.M., indicate for each question which of the four duties listed should be taken care of FIRST.

18. A. You are informed that an elderly tenant has just been taken to the hospital and you must call his son, whose telephone number you have on file. 18.____
B. Two tenants whose children have been involved in a series of complaints concerning damage to housing authority property are waiting to see you.
C. You have a message from the central office of the housing authority requesting clarification of a single point in a report you prepared.
D. A tenant who was already served with an eviction notice for non-payment of rent is waiting with a large back-rent check.

19. A. A tenant who is about to be evicted because of non-payment of rent is waiting to see you. 19.____
B. A housing patrolman who must leave for court wants to speak to you about a tenant's child he has just arrested.
C. It will take only ten minutes to finish your monthly activities report which is overdue.
D. An insurance investigator is waiting to see you concerning an injury suffered by a tenant in his building's elevator.

20. A. The receptionist tells you that a woman is waiting to see you with a complaint about a repair to a toilet. The woman says she must leave for work by 9:30 A.M. 20.____
B. You have an unfinished report in your desk which requires about 15 minutes to complete,
C. A tenant is early for a 9:15 appointment for an interview that should take approximately 15 minutes.
D. There is a note to you from the project manager which says, *Please see me as soon as you can spare 15 minutes.*

KEY (CORRECT ANSWERS)

1. B	6. B	11. D	16. B
2. C	7. B	12. B	17. D
3. A	8. B	13. D	18. A
4. B	9. A	14. B	19. B
5. C	10. C	15. D	20. A

TEST 2

DIRECTIONS: Each question or incomplete statement is followed by several suggested answers or completions. Select the one that BEST answers the question or completes the statement. *PRINT THE LETTER OF THE CORRECT ANSWER IN THE SPACE AT THE RIGHT.*

Questions 1-5.

DIRECTIONS: Questions 1 through 5 are to be answered SOLELY on the basis of the following passage.

At one time people thought that in the interview designed primarily to obtain information, the interviewer had to resort to clever and subtle lines of questioning in order to accomplish his ends. Some people still believe that this is necessary, but it is not so. An example of the "tricky" approach may be seen in the work of a recent study. The study deals with materials likely to be buried beneath deep defenses. Interviewers utilized methods of questioning which, in effect, trapped the interviewee and destroyed his defenses. Doubtless these methods succeeded in bringing out items of information which straightforward questions would have missed. Whether they missed more information than they obtained and whether they obtained the most important facts must remain unanswered questions. In defense of the "clever" approach, it is often said that, in many situations, the interviewee is motivated to conceal information or to distort what he chooses to report.

Technically, it is likely that a highly skilled interviewer can, given the time and the inclination, penetrate the interviewee's defenses and get information which the latter intended to keep hidden. It is unlikely that the interviewer can successfully elicit all of the information that might be relevant. If, for example, he found that an applicant for financial assistance was heavily in debt to gamblers, he might not care about getting any other information. There are situations in which one item, if answered in the "wrong" way, is enough. Ordinarily, this is not true. The usual situation is that there are many considerations and that the plus and minus features must be weighed before a decision may be made. It is, therefore, important to obtain complete information.

1. According to the above passage, it was generally believed that an interviewer would have difficulty in obtaining the information he sought from a person if he 1.____

   A. were tricky in his methods
   B. were open and frank in his approach
   C. were clever in his questioning
   D. utilized carefully prepared questions

2. The passage does NOT reveal whether the type of questions used 2.____

   A. trapped those being interviewed
   B. elicited facts which an open method of questioning might miss
   C. elicited the most important facts that were sought
   D. covered matters which those interviewed were reluctant to talk about openly

3. An argument in favor of the *tricky* or *clever* interviewing technique is that, unless this approach is used, the person interviewed will NOT 3.____

   A. offer to furnish all pertinent information
   B. answer questions concerning routine data

C. clearly understand what is being sought
D. want to continue the interview

4. According to the above passage, in favorable circumstances, a talented interviewer would be able to obtain from the person interviewed information 4.____

A. which the person regards as irrelevant
B. which the person intends to conceal
C. about the person's family background
D. which the person would normally have forgotten

5. According to the above passage, a highly skilled interviewer should concentrate, in most cases, on getting 5.____

A. one outstanding fact about the interviewee which would do away with the need for prolonged questioning
B. facts which the interviewee wanted to conceal because these would be the most relevant in making a decision
C. all the facts so that he can consider their relative values before reaching any conclusion
D. information about any bad habits of the interviewee, such as gambling, which would make further questioning

Questions 6-8.

DIRECTIONS: Questions 6 through 8 are to be answered SOLELY on the basis of the following passage.

City governments have long had building codes which set minimum standards for building and for human occupancy. The code (or series of codes) makes provisions for standards of lighting and ventilation sanitation, fire prevention and protection. As a result of demands from manufacturers, builders, real estate people, tenement owners, and building-trades unions, these codes often have established minimum standards well below those that the contemporary society would accept as a rock-bottom minimum. Codes often become outdated, so that meager standards in one era become seriously inadequate a few decades later as society's concept of a minimum standard of living changes. Out-of-date codes, when still in use, have sometimes prevented the introduction of new devices and modern building techniques. Thus, it is extremely important that building codes keep pace with changes in the accepted concept of a minimum standard of living.

6. According to the above passage, all of the following considerations in building planning would probably be covered in a building code EXCEPT 6.____

A. closet space as a percentage of total floor area
B. size and number of windows required for rooms of differing sizes
C. placement of fire escapes in each line of apartments
D. type of garbage disposal units to be installed

7. According to the above passage, if an ideal building code were to be created, how would the established minimum standards in it compare to the ones that are presently set by city governments? 7.____
They would

A. be lower than they are at present
B. be higher than they are at present
C. be comparable to the present minimum standards
D. vary according to the economic group that sets them

8. On the basis of the above passage, what is the reason for difficulties in introducing new building techniques? 8.____

A. Builders prefer techniques which represent the rock-bottom minimum desired by society.
B. Certain manufacturers have obtained patents on various building methods to the exclusion of new techniques.
C. The government does not want to invest money in techniques that will soon be outdated,
D. New techniques are not provided for in building codes which are not up to date.

Questions 9-11.

DIRECTIONS: Questions 9 through 11 are to be answered SOLELY on the basis of the following passage.

The agreement under which a tenant rents property from a landlord is known as a lease. Generally speaking, leases are classified as either short-term or long-term in duration. They are further subdivided according to the method used to determine the amount of periodic rent payments. Of the following types of leases in use, the more commonly used ones are the following;

1. *The straight or fixed lease is one in which rent may be paid in equal amounts throughout the duration of the lease. These are usually restricted to short-term leasing, or somewhat longer-term if clauses in the lease provide for periodic escalation of payments as the economy shifts.*
2. *Percentage leasing, used for short-term commercial leasing, provides the landlord with a stipulated percentage of a tenant's gross sales from goods and services sold on the premises, in addition to a fixed amount of rent.*
3. *The net lease, generally long-term (ten years or more), requires the tenant to pay all operating costs, including real estate taxes and insurance. In a net-net lease, the tenant further agrees to meet mortgage interest and principal payments.*
4. *An escalated lease, which is a long-term lease, requires rent to be of a stipulated base amount which periodically is subject to escalation in accordance with cost-of-living index scales, or in direct proportion to taxes, insurance, and operating costs.*

9. Based on the information given in the passage, which type of lease is MOST likely to be advantageous to a landlord if there is a high rate of inflation? ______ lease. 9.____

A. Fixed
B. Percentage
C. Net
D. Escalated

10. On the basis of the above passage, which types of lease would generally be MOST suitable for a well-established textile company which requires permanent facilities for its large operations? 10.____
______ lease and______ lease.

A. Percentage; escalated
B. Escalated; net
C. Straight; net
D. Straight; percentage

11. According to the above passage, the ONLY type of lease which assures the same amount of rent throughout a specified interval is the ______ lease. 11.____

A. straight B. percentage C. net-net D. escalated

Questions 12-14.

DIRECTIONS: Questions 12 through 14 are to be answered SOLELY on the basis of the following passage.

Physical design plays a very significant role in crime rate. Crime rate has been found to increase almost proportionately with building height. The average number of crimes is much greater in higher buildings than in lower ones (equal or less than six stories). What is most interesting is that in buildings of six stories or less, the project size or total number of units does not make a difference. It seems that although larger projects encourage crime by fostering feelings of anonymity, isolation, irresponsibility, and lack of identity with surroundings, evidence indicates that larger projects encompassed in low buildings seem to offset what we may assume to be factors conducive to high crime rates. High-rise projects not only experience a higher rate of crime within the buildings, but a greater proportion of the crime occurs in the interior public spaces of these buildings as compared with those of the lower buildings. Lower buildings have more limited public space than higher ones. A criminal probably perceives that the interior public areas of buildings are where his victims are most vulnerable and where the possibility of his being seen or apprehended is minimal. Placement of elevators, entrance lobbies, fire stairs, and secondary exits all are factors related to the likelihood of crimes taking place in buildings. The study of all of these elements should bear some weight in the planning of new projects.

12. According to the above passage, which of the following BEST describes the relationship between building size and crime? 12.____

A. Larger projects lead to a greater crime rate.
B. Higher buildings tend to increase the crime rate.
C. The smaller the number of project apartments in low buildings, the higher the crime rate.
D. Anonymity and isolation serve to lower the crime rate in small buildings.

13. According to the passage, the likelihood of a criminal attempting a mugging in the interior public portions of a high-rise building is GOOD because 13.____

A. tenants will be constantly flowing in and out of the area
B. there is easy access to fire stairs and secondary exits
C. there is a good chance that no one will see him
D. tenants may not recognize the victims of crime as their neighbors

14. Which of the following is IMPLIED by the passage as an explanation for the fact that the crime rate is lower in large low-rise housing projects than in large high-rise projects? 14.____

A. Tenants know each other better and take a greater interest in what happens in the project.
B. There is more public space where tenants are likely to gather together.
C. The total number of units in a low-rise project is fewer than the total number of units in a high-rise project.

D. Elevators in low-rise buildings travel quickly, thus limiting the amount of time in which a criminal can act.

Questions 15-19.

DIRECTIONS: Questions 15 through 19 are to be answered SOLELY on the basis of the following *total annual income adjustment* rules for household income.

The basic annual income is to be calculated by multiplying the total of the current weekly salaries of all adults (age 21 or over) by 52.

Upward and downward adjustments must be made to the basic annual salary to arrive at the *total adjusted annual income* for the household.

UPWARD ADJUSTMENTS

1. Add one-half of total overtime payments in the previous two years.
2. Add that part of the earnings of any minor in the household that exceeded $2,000 in the previous 12 months.

DOWNWARD ADJUSTMENTS

1. Deduct one-third of all educational tuition payments for household members in the previous 12 months.
2. Deduct the expense of going to and from work in excess of $20 per week per household member. This adjustment is made on the basis of the previous 12 months and should be computed for each household member individually for each week in which excess travel expenses were incurred.
3. Deduct that part of child care expenses which exceeded $1000 in the previous 12 months.

15. In household A, the husband has a weekly salary of $390 and the wife has just had her salary increased from $260 to $280 per week. In the previous 12 months, each had a paid continuous vacation of four weeks; the husband had to travel to a secondary work location every fourth week. His travel costs during those weeks were $28 per week. In the previous 12 months, they had child care costs of $980. What is the total annual adjusted income for the household? 15.____

A. $34,744 B. $34,736 C. $34,552 D. $34,156

16. In household B, the husband has a weekly salary of $360. In the past year, he received overtime payments of $170. In the year before that he received overtime payments of $814. His wife has just begun a job with a weekly salary of $220. As a result of this, annual child care expenses will be $1420. What is the total annual adjusted income for the household? 16.____

A. $30,160 B. $30,232 C. $30,652 D. $31,216

17. In household C, the husband has a weekly salary of $370, The wife has a weekly salary of $260. They each had expenses of $22 per week when traveling to and from work in the previous 12 months. The husband had an annual paid vacation of five weeks, and the wife had an annual paid vacation of three weeks in the previous year. There is a daughter in college for whom annual tuition payments of $1140 were made in the previous 12 months.
What is the total annual adjusted income for the household? 17.____

A. $32,172 B. $32,188 C. $32,760 D. $33,348

18. In household D, the husband has a weekly salary of $310, the wife has a weekly salary of $220, and an adult daughter has a weekly salary of $190. The husband received overtime payments of $1260 in the past year. In the year before that, he received no overtime payments. In the past year, there were weekly child care expenses of $140 per week for 47 weeks.
What is the total annual adjusted income for the household? 18.____

A. $38;070 B. $32,490 C. $31,490 D. $31,230

19. In household E, the husband has a weekly salary of $410. The wife has a weekly salary of $130. During the past year, there were tuition payments of $170 per month for 10 months per year for children in grade school and annual tuition payments of $1540 for a boy in high school.
What is the total annual adjusted income for the household? 19.____

A. $26,380 B. $26,400 C. $27,000 D. $28,080

20. In the writing of reports or letters, the ideas presented in a paragraph are usually of unequal importance and require varying degrees of emphasis.
All of the following are methods of placing extra stress on an idea EXCEPT 20.____

A. repeating it in a number of forms
B. placing it in the middle of the paragraph
C. placing it either at the beginning or at the end of the paragraph
D. underlining it

KEY (CORRECT ANSWERS)

1. B	6. A	11. A	16. C
2. C	7. B	12. B	17. B
3. A	8. D	13. C	18. B
4. B	9. D	14. A	19. C
5. C	10. B	15. A	20. B

TEST 3

DIRECTIONS: Each question or incomplete statement is followed by several suggested answers or completions. Select the one that BEST answers the question or completes the statement. *PRINT THE LETTER OF THE CORRECT ANSWER IN THE SPACE AT THE RIGHT.*

Questions 1-2.

DIRECTIONS: Questions 1 and 2 are to be answered SOLELY on the basis of the following paragraph.

A housing development has 450 apartments. The average monthly rent is $269 per apartment. The average amount of subsidy money added to the average monthly rent (to meet the total operating costs) is $136. Since the time when the amount of the subsidy was determined, operating costs for the development have increased by $7920.00 per month.

1. If the subsidy is increased by 6%, what increase in the average monthly rental will be necessary to meet monthly operating costs? 1.____

   A. $6.80
   B. $9.44
   C. $17.60
   D. No increase

2. What is the NEW total monthly operating cost per apartment? 2.____

   A. $153.60
   B. $286.60
   C. $422.60
   D. $484.20

3. In a certain housing project, the average income of tenant families is $18,400 per annum and the average rent per apartment is $360 per month. 3.____
   If the average income increases 12% in a year while the average rent of an apartment increases 15%, how much more money will the average family have in a year after paying rent?

   A. $677.60
   B. $1560.00
   C. $2241.60
   D. $4968.00

4. A certain housing project has 1860 tenant families. It has two playgrounds, both rectangular in shape. One measures 104 feet by 45 feet; the other is 74 feet by 53 feet. 4.____
   The number of square feet of playground space per family in this project is MOST NEARLY

   A. 3
   B. 5
   C. 7
   D. 9

5. A particular housing project has 1460 occupied apartments. If there are 12 new tenants in January, 14 in February, and 16 in March, the turnover rate for the first quarter of the year is MOST NEARLY 5.____

   A. 2.9%
   B. 3.2%
   C. 3.5%
   D. 3.8%

Questions 6-7.

DIRECTIONS: Questions 6 and 7 are to be answered SOLELY on the basis of the following paragraph.

A tenant in a housing development receives a semi-monthly public assistance check of $234 and pays a monthly rental of $142 from the proceeds. The tenant is about to begin paying $18 additional per month toward total rent arrears of $272. At the same time that the arrears payments begin, his semi-monthly check increases to $242.

6. What will be the TOTAL change in monthly net income after all rent payments. 6._____

A. $6 B. $4 C. $2 D. No change

7. If, instead of paying only $18 per month toward the arrears, the total increase in public assistance payments is used to increase arrears payments, how many months will it take the tenant to pay off the arrears? 7._____

_______ months.

A. 8 B. 10 C. 12 D. 14

8. A tenant is offered two options in renewing a lease: (1) a one-year lease at a 10% increase in rent, or (2) a three-year lease at an 18% increase in rent. The tenant's current rent is $440 monthly. 8._____

If the tenant takes the first option and continues to live in the apartment for three years with a 10% increase in rent each year, what would be the difference between the total rent he would pay and the rent he would have paid had he chosen the three-year lease?

A. $533.28 B. $553.28 C. $2,851.20 D. $3,384.48

9. A certain task that an assistant performs takes approximately 45 minutes per unit of work. Seventy-five percent of his work day is spent on this task. 9._____

Assuming that he works seven hours per day, how many work-days will it take him to finish 1,470 units of work?

A. 153 B. 210 C. 240 D. 270

10. It takes 5 1/2 gallons of paint to paint an average apartment, and it requires 18 man-hours. 10._____

If the price of paint increases 24 cents per gallon and the pay of the painters increases 26.5 cents per hour, what is the INCREASE in the cost of painting an apartment?

A. $4.99 B. $5.09 C. $5.99 D. $6.09

11. A government employee can process a certain type of report in 23 minutes. 11._____

How many such reports could he finish processing in a work day from 9:00 A.M. to 5:00 P.M., with a 45-minute lunch break and two 10-minute coffee breaks?

A. 16 B. 17 C. 18 D. 19

12. The income of a tenant family is as follows: The husband has a gross income of $280 per week; the wife has a gross income of $220 per week. Deductions from gross family income total $116 per week, plus an allowable child care expense of $56 per week. What is the net annual income of the family after deductions and allowable child care expenses? 12._____

A. $16,656 B. $17,056 C. $18,656 D. $19,056

Questions 13-15

DIRECTIONS: Questions 13 through 15 are to be answered on the basis of the following information and schedule.

Assume that, after having been appointed as an assistant at the Rumsey Housing Project, you are now ready to assume the same duties being performed by the other two assistants, X and Y, Their daily work schedules have already been prepared, and you are asked to work out a schedule which will be compatible with theirs and which will conform to the following stipulations:

a. At least one assistant is to be in the project office at all times between 9 A.M. and 5 P.M. Monday through Friday.
b. No more than two assistants are to conduct office interviews at one time.
c. All assistants must be in the project office between the hours of 4 P.M. and 5 P.M.
d. Each assistant is to take one hour for lunch between 11:30 A.M. and 2 P.M.

Following is the Monday schedule for assistants X and Y.

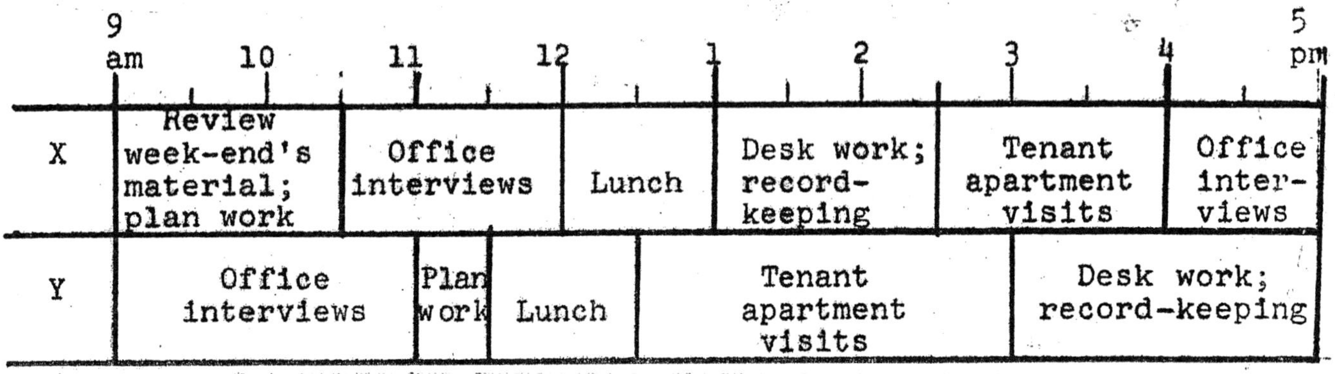

13. Which one of the following blocks of time would be BEST for you to plan 2 1/2 hours of office interviewing? 13.____

A. 9:00-11:30 B. 11:00-1:30
C. 1:30-4:00 D. 2:00-4:30

14. During what hours would it be BEST for you to schedule tenant apartment visits covering a two-hour block of time? 14.____

A. 9:00-11:00 B. 10:30-12:30
C. 1:00-3:00 D. 3:00-5:00

15. Of the following suggestions for scheduling your day's assignments, which one would NOT be acceptable? 15.____

A. Desk work including weekly plans from 9:00-11:00 and 2:00-3:00
B. Interviews from 11:00-1:00
C. Lunch from 1:00-2:00
D. Tenant apartment visits from 3:00-5:00

Questions 16-20.

DIRECTIONS: Questions 16 through 20 are to be answered SOLELY on the basis of the information contained in the following table of apartment availabilities and explanation of *Priority Codes for Admission* column.

PRIORITY CODES AND MAXIMUM ANNUAL INCOME FOR ADMISSION TO PROJECTS

			Maximum Annual Income for Admission			
Division	*Projects*	*Priority Codes for Admission*	*One Bedroom*	*Two Bedrooms*	*Three Bedrooms*	*Four Bedrooms*
Northern	*Allan*	*1-3Cs 4B*	*$18,200*	*$20,000*	*$21,400*	*$ 23,000*
	Boston	*1-2C; 3-4A*	*13, 600*	*15,800*	*18,000*	*19,800*
	Danton	*1-2C; 3Bs 4 A*	*14, 800*	*16,400*	*18,200*	*20,200*
	Miller	*1-3B; 4 A*	*13,600*	*15,800*	*18, 000*	*19,800*
	Preston	*1-2C, 3B; 4A*	*16, 600*	*18,800*	*20,400*	*22,000*
Central	*Andrews*	*1-2D; SB; 4 A*	*13,600*	*15,800*	*18, 000*	*19,800*
	Clayton	*1-2D, SB, 4 A*	*13,600*	*15,800*	*18,000*	*19, 800*
	Ivy Hill	*1-3C; 4B*	*14,800*	*16,400*	*18, 200*	*20, 200*
	Montrose	*1-2B, 3-4A*	*18,200*	*20,000*	*21,400*	*23, 000*
Eastern	*Bryan*	*1B; 2-4 A*	*16,600*	*18,800*	*20,400*	*22, 000*
	Farrar	*1C; 2-4A*	*18,200*	*20,000*	*21, 400*	*28, 000*
	Golden	*1-2B; 3-4A*	*13,600*	*15,800*	*18, 000*	*19,800*
	Wagner	*1B; 2-4A*	*18,200*	*20,000*	*21,400*	*23, 000*
Western	*Colfax*	*1-3C; 4B*	*18,200*	*20,000*	*21, 400*	*23, 000*
	Drexel	*1-3B, 4 A*	*14,800*	*16,400*	*18, 200*	*20, 200*
	Foxton	*1-3C; 4A*	*13,600*	*15,800*	*18, 000*	*19,800*

EXPLANATION OF PRIORITY CODES FOR ADMISSION COLUMN

The letters A, B, C, and D represent four levels of priority for admission to a project. Level A priority is the most restrictive of the four priority levels and represents the highest level of need; level D priority is the least restrictive of the four priority levels and represents the lowest level of need. An applicant can be admitted only to an apartment with the same level of priority or to an apartment with a lower level of priority. For example, an applicant with a C priority can be admitted to an apartment with a C or D priority but not to an apartment with an A or B priority.

The numbers 1, 2, 3, and 4 represent the number of bedrooms in the apartments. For example, the notation after the Allan project, 1-3C; 4B, means that apartments with from one to three bedrooms have priority level C and apartments with four bedrooms have priority level In the Allan project, only applicants with a priority level of C or higher (levels A and B) can be admitted to apartments with one, two, or three bedrooms and only applicants with a priority level of B or higher (level A) can be admitted to a four-bedroom apartment.

16. An applicant with an annual income of $16,400 needs an apartment with two bedrooms. The applicant has a level B priority. Those projects in the Eastern and Central Divisions which have two-bedroom apartments for which the applicant is eligible are 16.____

A. Allan and Ivy Hill
B. Montrose, Bryan, and Golden
C. Ivy Hill and Montrose
D. Ivy Hill, Montrose, and Farrar

17. What is the LOWEST level of priority an applicant may have in order to be eligible for a three-bedroom apartment in the Western Division if he has an income of $18,200 a year? 17.____
Level

A. A B. B C. C D. D

18. Which division is MOST restrictive as to the level of priority required for three-bedroom apartments? 18.____

A. Northern B. Central C. Eastern D. Western

19. Which division contains the GREATEST number of projects with two-bedroom apartments in the LEAST restrictive level of priority? 19.____

A. Northern B. Central C. Eastern D. Western

20. How many projects have four-bedroom apartments available to an applicant with an A priority and an income of $22,000? 20.____

A. 3 B. 5 C. 7 D. 12

KEY (CORRECT ANSWERS)

1.	B	6.	C	11.	C	16.	C
2.	C	7.	A	12.	B	17.	C
3.	B	8.	A	13.	D	18.	C
4.	B	9.	B	14.	A	19.	B
5.	A	10.	D	15.	D	20.	C

TEST 4

DIRECTIONS: Each question or incomplete statement is followed by several suggested answers or completions. Select the one that BEST answers the question or completes the statement. *PRINT THE LETTER OF THE CORRECT ANSWER IN THE SPACE AT THE RIGHT.*

Questions 1-4.

DIRECTIONS: Questions 1 through 4 are to be answered SOLELY on the basis of the following information and hypothetical schedule for the granting of priority points. These points determine the applicant's place on a waiting list for an apartment. The applicants may be awarded points for condition of present housing, for children, for veteran status, and for space falling below the minimum space standard. Categories not listed get no points. Points in all categories are added together to determine total number of priority points.

	Priority Points
Condition of Present Housing (choose one)	
Extremely substandard housing	5
Moderately substandard housing	3
Minimally substandard housing	1
Children (choose as many as apply)	
Two children over age eight, of different sexes, sleeping in same room	2
Two children of different sexes, one over age eight, the other under age eight, sleeping in same room	1
Family with child over age 18 months sleeping in same bedroom with parents	2
Veteran Status	
Veteran of Vietnam War in household	1
Minimum Space Standard	
For each 75 square feet or part thereof below minimum space standard, computed by totaling the following: 110 square feet for each person over age 18 90 square feet for each person age 18 or under	1

1. A husband, wife, six-year-old son, and nine-year-old daughter live in a moderately substandard apartment of 280 square feet. The son and daughter sleep in the same bedroom. There are no war veterans in the household. How many priority points should be given? 1.____

   A. 6 B. 5 C. 4 D. 3

2. A husband, wife, wife's father, 16-year-old daughter, 14-year-old son, and 12-year-old son live in an extremely substandard apartment of 450 square feet. The daughter sleeps in her own room. The sons have their own room. The wife's father is a World War II veteran. 2.____
   How many priority points should be given?

   A. 9 B. 8 C. 7 D. 6

3. A widow, age 50, who is not a war veteran, lives with her son, age 15, in a minimally substandard two-bedroom apartment with 290 square feet of living space. 3.____
How many priority points should be given?

A. 3 B. 2 C. 1 D. 0

4. A family has had to leave their former apartment because of fire damage. They are presently living in an extremely substandard storefront which is one room of 320 square feet, without partitions. The family consists of a father who is a Vietnam war veteran, a mother, and their two children: a girl, age 5; and a boy, age 7. 4.____
How many priority points should be given?

A. 10 B. 9 C. 8 D. 7

Questions 5-8.

DIRECTIONS: In Questions 5 through 8, choose the sentence which contains NO errors in grammar, punctuation, or spelling.

5. 5.____
A. Certain changes in family income must be reported as they occur.
B. When certain changes in family income occur, it must be reported.
C. Certain family income changes must be reported as they occur.
D. Certain changes in family income must be reported as they have been occuring.

6. 6.____
A. Each tenant has to complete the application themselves.
B. Each of the tenants have to complete the application by himself.
C. Each of the tenants has to complete the application himself.
D. Each of the tenants has to complete the application by themselves.

7. 7.____
A. Yours is the only building that the construction will effect.
B. Your's is the only building affected by the construction.
C. The construction will only effect your building.
D. Yours is the only building that will be affected by the construction.

8. 8.____
A. A copy of the lease, in addition to the Rules and Regulations, are to be given to each tenant.
B. The Rules and Regulations and a copy of the lease is being given to each tenant.
C. A copy of the lease, in addition to the Rules and Regulations, is to be given to each tenant.
D. A copy of the lease, in addition to the Rules and Regulations, are being given to each tenant.

Questions 9-10.

DIRECTIONS: Each of Questions 9 and 10 consists of four numbered sentences which constitute a paragraph in a report. They are not in the right order. Choose the numbered arrangement appearing after letter A, B, C, or D which is MOST logical and which BEST expresses the thought of the paragraph.

9. I. Congress made the commitment explicit in the Housing Act of 1949, establishing as a national goal the realization of *a decent home and suitable environment for every American family.* 9.____
II. The result has been that the goal of decent home and suitable environment is still as far distant as ever for the disadvantaged urban family.
III. In spite of this action by Congress, federal housing programs have continued to be fragmented and grossly underfunded.
IV. The passage of the National Housing Act signalled a new federal commitment to provide housing for the nation's citizens,

A. I, IV, III, II
B. IV, I, III, II
C. IV, I, II, III
D. II, IV, I, III

10. I. The greater expense does not necessarily involve *exploitation,* but it is often perceived as exploitative and unfair by those who are aware of the price differences involved, but unaware of operating costs. 10.____
II. Ghetto residents believe they are *exploited* by local merchants and evidence substantiates some of these beliefs.
III. However, stores in low-income areas were more likely to be small independents, which could not achieve the economies available to supermarket chains and were, therefore, more likely to charge higher prices, and the customers were more likely to buy smaller-sized packages which are more expensive per unit of measure.
IV. A study conducted in one city showed that distinctly higher prices were charged for goods sold in ghetto stores than in other areas.

A. IV, II, I, III
B. IV, I, III, II
C. II, IV, III, I
D. II, III, IV, I

11. If an assistant is writing to an applicant who is a minority group member in reference to his eligibility for an apartment, it would be BEST for him to use language that is 11.____

A. informal, using ethnic expressions known to the applicant
B. technical, using the expressions commonly used in the housing authority
C. simple, using words and phrases which laymen understand
D. formal, to remind the applicant that he is dealing with a government agency

12. Assume that you have just informed an applicant for an apartment that he has a low priority and that it is unlikely that he will be assigned an apartment within the next two years. When informed of this, he becomes angry and abusive. 12.____
Of the following, the MOST effective action you can take is to

A. tell the applicant that you will do your best to get him a higher priority
B. let him know he cannot intimidate you
C. tell him to submit a new application that has greater emotional appeal
D. keep your self-control and try to calm the applicant

13. When interviewing an applicant to determine his eligibility for public housing, it is MOST important to 13.____

A. have a prior mental picture of the typical eligible applicant
B. conduct the interview strictly according to a previously prepared script
C. keep in mind the goal of the interview, which is to determine eligibility
D. get an accurate and detailed account of the applicant's life history

14. The practice of trying to imagine yourself in the applicant's place during an interview is 14.____

A. *good,* mainly because you will be able to evaluate his responses better
B. *good,* mainly because it will enable you to treat him as a friend rather than an applicant
C. *poor,* mainly because it is important for the applicant to see you as an impartial person
D. *poor,* mainly because it is too time-consuming to do this with each applicant

15. When dealing with tenants from different ethnic backgrounds, an assistant should be aware of certain tendencies toward prejudice. 15.____
Which of the following statements is LEAST likely to be valid?

A. Whites prejudiced against Blacks are more likely to be prejudiced against Puerto Ricans than whites not prejudiced against Blacks.
B. The less a white is in competition with Blacks, the less likely he is to be prejudiced against them.
C. Persons who have moved from one social group to another are likely to retain the attitudes and prejudices of their original social group.
D. When there are few Blacks or Puerto Ricans in a project, whites are less likely to be prejudiced against them than when there are many.

16. Mr. Smith asks the assistant why his rent is higher than his neighbor's, although he claims that both apartments are the same size, and that his neighbor's income is the same as his. The assistant is aware of this but is also aware that the neighbor is allowed several deductions in computing income that are not available to Mr. Smith. 16.____
The assistant should explain to Mr. Smith that

A. the amount of his neighbor's rent is really no concern of his, but that the neighbor's rent will be raised if Mr. Smith can prove that the neighbor is not reporting income
B. his neighbor receives more deductions in computing income
C. he cannot discuss complaints presented by Mr. Smith concerning the rent of other tenants
D. the amount of rent is based on the rules for computing rent and that there may be individual circumstances of which Mr. Smith is not aware

17. Of the following, the assistant who is MOST likely to be a good interviewer of people seeking low-rent housing from a public agency is one who 17.____

A. tries to get applicants to seek private housing instead
B. believes that it is necessary to get as much pertinent information as possible in order to determine the applicant's real needs
C. believes that people who seek public housing are likely to have persons with a history of irresponsible behavior in their households
D. is convinced that there is no need for public housing

18. An assistant must be familiar with the policies of both federal and state agencies which regulate public housing as well as with the many rules, regulations, and procedures of the housing authority. 18.____
The MOST important reason for an assistant to have a thorough knowledge and understanding of these policies and procedures is that he

A. will know when to tell an applicant that his request for a particular project cannot be granted
B. will be able to back up his actions by referring to the relevant rule or policy when making a report
C. can give the best possible service to tenants and applicants
D. will be able to show that he has the knowledge needed for his job

Questions 19-20.

DIRECTIONS: Questions 19 and 20 must be answered SOLELY on the basis of the following passage.

The new suburbia that is currently being built does not look much different from the old; there has, however, been an increase in the class and race polarization that has been developing between the suburbs and the cities for several generations now. The suburbs have become the home for an ever larger proportion of working-class, middle-class, and upper-class whitest the oities, for an even larger proportion of poor and non-white people. A great number of cities are 30 to 50 percent non-white in population, with more and larger ghettos than cities have ever had. Now, there is greater urban poverty on the one hand, and stronger suburban opposition to open housing and related policies to solve the cities' problems on the other hand. The urban crisis will worsen, and although there is no shortage of rational solutions, nothing much will be done about the crisis unless white America permits a radical change of public policy and undergoes a miraculous change of attitude towards it cities and their populations.

19. Which of the following statements is IMPLIED by the above passage? 19.____

A. The percentage of non-whites in the suburbs is increasing.
B. The policies of suburbanites have contributed to the seriousness of the urban crisis.
C. The problems of the cities defy rational solutions.
D. There has been a radical change in the appearance of both suburbia and the cities in the past few years.

20. Of the following, the title which BEST describes the passage's main them is: 20.____

A. The New Suburbia
B. Urban Poverty
C. Urban-Suburban Polarization
D. Why Americans Want to Live in the Suburbs

KEY (CORRECT ANSWERS)

1.	A	6.	C	11.	C	16.	D
2.	C	7.	D	12.	D	17.	B
3.	C	8.	C	13.	C	18.	C
4.	A	9.	B	14.	A	19.	B
5.	A	10.	C	15.	C	20.	C

EXAMINATION SECTION

TEST 1

DIRECTIONS: Each question or incomplete statement is followed by several suggested answers or completions. Select the one that BEST answers the question or completes the statement. *PRINT THE LETTER OF THE CORRECT ANSWER IN THE SPACE AT THE RIGHT.*

1. Because of the severe housing shortage, the state legislature has decided that, notwithstanding statutory limits for continuing occupancy, a public housing authority may permit a family to remain in occupancy if it finds that the family is genuinely unable to find adequate and affordable local housing. The legislation provides that the rent of such a family remaining in occupancy shall be increased on the basis of the 1.______
   A. family's composition
   B. family's income
   C. age of the head of household
   D. number of wage earners

2. In federally aided projects having fixed rent, excess income families who are eligible for continued occupancy because they qualify for transfer to a larger apartment in the project are 2.______
   A. required to pay the same rent while awaiting transfer as charged for the apartment to which they are moving
   B. subject to a designated fractional rent increase while awaiting transfer
   C. not subject to a rent increase before or after transfer
   D. not subject to a rent increase while awaiting transfer

3. A residual single person who refuses to transfer to an apartment of appropriate size should generally have his tenancy terminated on the ground of 3.______
   A. breach of rules and regulations
   B. excess income
   C. non-desirability
   D. residual single-person occupancy

4. The Housing Authority sometimes uses Herculite K glass rather than ordinary glass PRIMARILY because it can 4.______
   A. be installed with special low-cost materials other than putty and clips
   B. withstand greater impact
   C. be cut to size at the project
   D. resist yellowing which is typical of ordinary glass

5. A tenant whose apartment is to be painted is responsible for 5.______
   A. moving all furniture to the center of the room
   B. taping electric switch and receptacle plates
   C. washing ceiling fixtures free of grease and grime
   D. washing all walls prior to the application of paint

6. When a project painting contract is completed, the Housing Manager may attach to the final request for payment a memorandum to the Chief of Maintenance recommending that a certain portion of payment be withheld in order to 6.______
   A. pay the required premiums to the covering bonding company
   B. meet unpaid wage claims filed against the painting contractor by his employees
   C. cover all outstanding tenant and Housing Authority claims for property damage against the painting contractor
   D. pay the mandatory fees incurred in meeting federal affirmative action requirements

7. Housing Authority project staff have, at times, been asked to reveal confidential information about tenants on the telephone to persons who have misrepresented themselves as members of the central office staff. To avoid divulging confidential information to unauthorized persons, project staff should 7.______
   A. ask the caller several technical questions concerning the Housing Authority to determine if he is an imposter
   B. ask the caller to put his inquiry in writing and submit it through prescribed office channels
   C. inform the caller that he should communicate directly with any tenant about whom he desires information
   D. inform the caller that his call will be returned, and then verify the number and name the caller has given

8. Project personnel are NOT to become involved in opening a tenant's door for a marshal or a sheriff in connection with a civil suit UNLESS 8.______
   A. the marshal or sheriff agrees in writing to reimburse the Housing Authority for damage to the door
   B. the marshal or sheriff specifically orders them to do so
   C. the Housing Authority itself is a party in an action to repossess the project apartment
   D. the tenant refuses admittance after being shown a court-issued writ or warrant

9. Whenever a dangerous weapon is found by a project staff member in a project apartment, public space or on the project grounds, the staff member should notify the project's Housing Patrolmen or security department, and should 9.______
   A. notify the local precinct of the Police Department
   B. question anyone who looks suspicious
   C. safeguard the weapon without disturbing it in any way
   D. take the weapon to the project office for safekeeping

10. Public assistance payment checks issued by the Department of Social Services are usually payable on the 10.______
   A. 1st and 16th of each month
   B. 5th and 20th of each month
   C. 8th and 23rd of each month
   D. 10th and 25th of each month

11. The better supervisor sees that the work for which he is responsible is done efficiently by 11.______
    A. delegating to his subordinates as much authority as possible
    B. handling as many details of the job as possible himself
    C. keeping for himself authority over all important parts of the job
    D. maintaining close supervision over all his subordinates

12. A person who inquires at a project or site about applying for public housing should be referred to the 12.______
    A. Applications Information Section
    B. Department of Community and Social Services
    C. local Community Corporation
    D. Tenant Selection Division

13. At the renting interview for an apartment available for immediate occupancy, the new tenant asks for an allowance of time, in order to make necessary moving arrangements, before her occupancy begins. Without special approval from the Chief Manager, the project manager may grant up to 13.______
    A. 3 days B. 5 days C. 10 days D. 15 days

14. A termination-of-tenancy interview may properly be conducted by a Housing Assistant if the reason for termination is 14.______
    A. excess income
    B. misrepresentation
    C. non-desirability
    D. residual single-person occupancy

15. The primary purpose of an annual apartment visit to a tenant by a Housing Assistant is to 15.______
    A. determine tenant desirability
    B. discover faulty housekeeping
    C. improve tenant-management cooperation
    D. prepare necessary work orders

16. When a Housing Assistant conducts an annual apartment visit, if the tenant has no record of poor housekeeping and the apartment appears to be in reasonably good condition, it would usually be most suitable for the Housing Assistant, as the next step, to 16.______
    A. check for possible rodent or insect infestation
    B. inquire about unauthorized occupancy
    C. inspect the range and the refrigerator for cleanliness
    D. prepare requested work orders, if any

17. Potential problem families should be referred to public or voluntary agencies for specialized assistance if the project staff is unable to remedy the problem within a reasonable time. The main purpose of making these referrals is to 17.______
    A. justify referral to the Tenant Review Board
    B. prevent or correct situations that could result in termination of tenancy
    C. develop sufficient data on the family to justify termination of tenancy
    D. reduce the amount of crime taking place on Housing Authority property

18. Home relief recipients who are Public Works Project Assignees may be assigned to lobby and stairwell duties in a project where a tenant patrol is functioning provided that their assignment is acceptable to the tenant patrol and 18.______
    A. their duties can be performed between the hours of 9:00 a.m. and 5:00 p.m.
    B. the Public Works Project Assignees are eligible for the customary surety bond
    C. such home relief recipients have had previous experience in performing similar duties
    D. their assignment will not tend to undermine tenant patrol interest and activity

19. All of the following statements concerning Public Works Project Assignees (home relief recipients) are correct EXCEPT: 19.______
    A. Assignees are not, in legal terms, employees of the Housing Authority or the city
    B. Assignees may perform any kind of work ordinarily and actually performed by regular employees
    C. Assignees may be accorded some benefits equal to those received by a regular employee with equal length of service
    D. Assignees may be assigned to duties other than those suggested by the title in which the Assignee is referred

20. Of the following notices, the one considered desirable for display on a project bulletin board is the one which 20.______
    A. gives tenants information abut the process of voter registration and elections
    B. informs tenants that the Housing Authority has endorsed a community candidate who is an Authority tenant
    C. presents the views on public housing of a candidate seeking reelection
    D. urges an affirmative vote for a bipartisan housing construction bond proposition

21. A project included in its communications a listing of some local physicians, dentists, optometrists and pharmacists. This practice should be considered 21.______
    A. advisable, mainly because it shows that the Authority is concerned with the well-being of tenants
    B. advisable, mainly because it provides essential information
    C. inadvisable, mainly because it raises ethical questions
    D. inadvisable, mainly because tenants tend to resent this paternalistic approach

22. The one of the following which is correct regarding the keeping of records of the race, color or ethnic background of tenants who have rented apartments and signed leases with the Housing Authority is that such records should be kept 22.______
    A. only for tenants who were not born in the state
    B. only for multi-problem families
    C. only for tenants receiving public assistance
    D. for all tenants

23. Housing Assistants who are on a promotion eligible list for Assistant Housing Manager and who are likely to be promoted within one year should be given the opportunity to learn the duties of this higher position before their appointment. All of the following are considered to be proper in accomplishing this EXCEPT: 23.______
    A. Give such Housing Assistants supervisory authority over other Housing Assistants at the work location
    B. Make arrangements to minimize interference with regular project activities performed by such Housing Assistants
    C. Permit such Housing Assistants to carry out some of the duties of an Assistant Housing Manager
    D. Schedule a weekly time period for such Housing Assistants to study with, and observe, an Assistant Housing Manager

24. The one of the following employees who may be employed at a project where he or she is a tenant is a(n) 24.______
    A. housing guard
    B. housing supplyman
    C. assistant accountant
    D. assistant housing manager

25. A Housing Assistant asks permission to use the project garage for his car. He points out that he regularly transports several of his coworkers to the project. His request should be 25.______
    A. granted; he may use the garage if he signs a statement relieving the Housing Authority from responsibility for damage caused by his car
    B. granted; he may use the garage as long as he does not violate internal parking regulations
    C. denied; the garage may be used only by resident employees
    D. denied; the garage may be used only for Housing Authority equipment

26. A major research finding regarding employee absenteeism is that 26.______
   A. absenteeism is likely to be higher on hot days
   B. male employees tend to be absent more than female employees
   C. the way an employee is treated has a definite bearing on absenteeism
   D. the distance employees have to travel is one of the most important factors in absenteeism

27. "The 'unguided interview' technique permits the interviewee to talk about anything that happens to be on his mind. When using this technique the interviewer avoids asking direct questions." Of the following, the main criticism of the unguided interview is that, generally, 27.______
   A. interviewees resist giving information to interviewers
   B. it is too time-consuming
   C. it reveals too many personal details about the interviewee
   D. interviewers, to be effective, must be trained psychologists

28. In interviewing, the tendency to judge the total personality of the interviewee on the basis of a single trait is known as the 28.______
   A. halo effect
   B. objective factor
   C. rapport ratio
   D. suggestibility quotient

29. Of the following, the supervisory behavior that is of greatest benefit to the organization is exhibited by supervisors who 29.______
   A. are strict with subordinates about following rules and regulations
   B. encourage subordinates to be interested in the work
   C. are willing to assist with subordinates' work on most occasions
   D. get the most done with available staff and resources

30. Before making a definite decision where group problems were involved, an Assistant Housing Manager frequently asked his subordinates for their opinions and recommendations. When the situation warranted he suggested to his subordinates that they make their own decisions. This approach to supervision is called "participative management." Of the following, probably the greatest benefit the Assistant Housing Manager gains from the use of "participative management" is that it 30.______
   A. permits him to pass the responsibility for faulty decisions on to his subordinates
   B. eliminates friction among his subordinates
   C. reduces the demands made on his time and attention
   D. enables him to achieve broader acceptance of agreed-upon goals and greater unity of purpose

KEY (CORRECT ANSWERS)

1. B	11. A	21. C
2. D	12. A	22. D
3. A	13. B	23. A
4. B	14. A	24. B
5. A	15. C	25. D
6. C	16. D	26. C
7. D	17. B	27. B
8. C	18. D	28. A
9. C	19. B	29. D
10. A	20. A	30. D

TEST 2

DIRECTIONS: Each question or incomplete statement is followed by several suggested answers or completions. Select the one that BEST answers the question or completes the statement. *PRINT THE LETTER OF THE CORRECT ANSWER IN THE SPACE AT THE RIGHT.*

1. Every public agency should adequately inform the public of its work, since public opinion affects public agencies. Of the following, which is usually the single greatest barrier to effective communications by public agencies? 1.______
   A. The inborn tendency to place too much faith in the printed word
   B. Giving too much attention to persons holding opposing views
   C. Professionally developed public information campaigns containing information which is repetitious in character are often relied upon by the agencies
   D. Lack of appropriate skill and insight on the part of the communicators

2. In order to develop effective public relations, a public agency must identify the feelings and beliefs of the groups it seeks to reach. The MAIN reason for carefully studying such groups is to 2.______
   A. be able to counteract negative group attitudes regarding the future of public employment
   B. facilitate selecting the means, context and timing of informational efforts
   C. create a strong impression that public opinion is important to the agency
   D. demonstrate openly the abilities and skills of competent public relations people

3. "Communications research strongly indicates that persuasive mass communication is, in general, more likely to reinforce the existing opinions of its audience than it is to change such opinions." For a public agency wishing to communicate effectively and to influence public opinion, the major implication of this statement is that 3.______
   A. most people tend to ignore a message if it is presented in an unusual manner
   B. the prestige of the source determines whether information will be accepted wholly or only in part
   C. public information campaigns should, if possible, begin by stressing widely accepted beliefs in order to strengthen the credibility of the agency's message
   D. an audience low in self-esteem is easily persuaded because it lacks self-confidence

4. A public agency's public relations efforts should not only be honest but should also clearly appear to be honest primarily because 4.______
   A. an audience develops resistance when it perceives communications as being manipulative
   B. communications are usually interpreted in a greatly different manner by each recipient
   C. government agencies, more than private advertisers, have a low public image which they must overcome
   D. many persons have private economic interests in the outcome of a public relations campaign

5. A public relations program of a governmental agency should be designed primarily to 5.______
   A. build good human relations in order to improve the agency's ability to serve
   B. increase the agency's activities for the purpose of gaining recognition
   C. persuade various media to provide free or low-cost exposure
   D. reduce the public's resistance to new or increased taxes

6. The managements of some large organizations encourage lower-level supervisors to take necessary risks in decision-making, especially when immediate decisions must be made in the absence of complete information. The one of the following which is most likely to discourage such decision-making is 6.______
   A. management's expectation that necessary decisions be made with promptness
   B. lack of policy guidelines to provide insight into past experiences
   C. the unwillingness of employees to follow special or unusual instructions issued by lower-level supervisors
   D. the lower-level supervisor's fear of making mistakes

7. Of the following, the most effective way for an Assistant Housing Manager to gain the cooperation of Housing Assistants is for him to give them instructions 7.______
   A. exactly as given to him by higher officials
   B. which emphasize competitive standards
   C. in the form of suggestions or requests
   D. as much as possible in private

8. "Since each person sees things in his own way, even 'factual' things may be seen differently. Relevance to a person's needs is the most important determinant of his view of the world." Of the following, the most logical conclusion to be drawn from this quotation is that most subordinates 8.______
   A. alter their behavior for reasons which cannot be understood
   B. oppose organizational policies which are based on reasons beyond their understanding
   C. respond most favorably when communications with them are uniform and forceful
   D. tend to pay attention to things which they feel relate to them

9. A newly appointed employee, Mr. Jones, was added to the staff of a supervisor who, because of pressure of other work, turned him over to an experienced subordinate by saying, "Show Mr. Jones around and give him something to do." On the basis of this experience, Mr. Jones' first impression of his new position was most likely to have been 9.______
   A. negative, mainly because it appeared that his job was not worth his supervisor's attention
   B. negative, mainly because the more experienced subordinate would tend to emphasize the unpleasant aspects of the work
   C. positive, mainly because the supervisor wasted no time in assigning him to a subordinate
   D. positive, mainly because he saw himself working for a dynamic supervisor who expected immediate results

10. An employee who stays in one assignment for a number of years often develops a feeling of possessiveness concerning his knowledge of the job which may develop into a problem. Of the following, the best way for a supervisor to remedy this difficulty is to 10.______
    A. give the employee less important work to do
    B. point out minor errors as often as possible
    C. raise performance standards for all employees
    D. rotate the employee to a different assignment

11. A supervisor who tends to be supportive of his subordinates, in contrast to a supervisor who relies upon an authoritarian style of leadership, is more likely, in dealing with his staff, to have to listen to complaints, tolerate emotionally upset employees and even hear unreasonable and insulting remarks. Compared to the authoritarian supervisor, he is more likely to 11.______
    A. be unconsciously fearful of failure
    B. have an overriding interest in production
    C. have subordinates who are better educated
    D. receive accurate feedback information

12. Assume that you are an Assistant Housing Manager and have been assigned to assist the head of a large agency unit. He asks you to prepare a simple, functional organization chart of the unit. Such a chart would be useful for 12.______
    A. favorably impressing members of the public with the important nature of the agency's work
    B. graphically presenting staff relationships which may indicate previously unknown duplications, overlaps and gaps in job duties
    C. motivating all employees toward better performance because they will have a better understanding of job procedures
    D. subtly and inoffensively making known to the staff in the unit that you are now in a position of responsibility

13. In some large organizations, management's traditional means of learning about employee dissatisfaction has been the "open door policy." This policy usually means that 13.______
    A. management lets it be known that a management representative is generally available to discuss employees' questions, suggestions and complaints
    B. management sets up an informal employee organization to establish a democratic procedure for orderly representation of employees
    C. employees are encouraged to attempt to resolve dissatisfactions at the lowest possible level of authority
    D. employees are provided with an address or box so that they may safely and anonymously register complaints

14. Recent research shows that some lower-level professional employees feel that they accomplish little in their work that is worthwhile. Management experts usually say that the one of the following which best explains such feelings is 14.______
    A. dissatisfaction among employees provoked by the activities of labor unions
    B. frequent salary increases unmatched by any significant increase in productivity
    C. the failure to properly develop in these employees an understanding of the significance of their work
    D. the almost total indifference of employees to the vital issues of the times

15. One way to get maximum effort from employees is for management to give employees the maximum possible personal freedom in accomplishing agency objectives. This encourages a feeling of self-management which is most basic to 15.______
    A. high levels of motivation
    B. tightly coordinated team effort
    C. an impartial approach to work
    D. uniformity of action

16. "In an organization where each supervisor has only three or four subordinates, the result may be over-management and a tendency to stifle creativity." Such over-management is most likely to result from 16.______
    A. the desire on the part of competent supervisors to delegate responsibility too soon when subordinates show promise
    B. the over-training of supervisors in office routines and procedures
    C. the supervisors' having so few subordinates that supervisors are free to direct nearly all the actions of their subordinates
    D. the general tendency of organizations to regard strict supervisors as being efficient

17. It has been said, "In a democratic administrative climate, employees are often encouraged, within reasonable limits, to learn by their own errors. The unfailing benefit of this is the growth of both human abilities and organizational capabilities." 17.______
The development of employees as described in this passage takes place in most organizations mainly by means of appropriate
   A. committee assignments
   B. delegation of authority
   C. training publications
   D. close and careful supervision

18. An effective system of evaluating employees' suggestions should provide for evaluation without the evaluators knowing the identities of suggesters. 18.______
The MAIN purpose of maintaining such anonymity is to
   A. concentrate attention on the needs of the organization, not on the rewarding of suggesters
   B. reduce the normal, but potentially harmful, urge for individual recognition
   C. encourage a spirit of competition among employees
   D. increase the probability that ideas are judged on their merits

19. Of the following forms of training, the one that is usually most similar to an actual work situation is the 19.______
   A. case-study method
   B. training conference technique
   C. lecture method
   D. role-playing method

20. Assume that you are an Assistant Housing Manager and that you have been attempting to improve the work performance of one of your subordinates by providing informal on-the-job training. He is making satisfactory, although slow, progress. In these circumstances, in order to further his progress, it would be best for you to 20.______
   A. avoid praise except when he implicitly asks for it
   B. imply approval by not criticizing his mistakes
   C. withhold praise until he has reached the final desired level of skill
   D. tell him he is doing well as his performance improves

21. One of the best ways of finding out whether training or retraining of employees is needed is to use 21.______
   A. confidential questionnaires directed to taxpayer groups
   B. employee questionnaires
   C. performance appraisals
   D. standardized intelligence tests

22. Within every organization, policies on most matters exist, either in written or oral form. A unique advantage of having policies expressed in writing is that it 22.______
    A. raises employee morale by creating the feeling that management has recognized employees' feelings
    B. increases employee confidence by reducing confusion, since management's positions are on record
    C. inhibits individual employees from asking for special treatment based on personal circumstances
    D. bridges the understanding gap between management and the less educated employees

23. An Assistant Housing Manager who believes that one of his subordinates has a mental health problem should consider taking, or recommending, appropriate referral action primarily when the problem 23.______
    A. affects the employee's job performance or adjustment to his work environment
    B. appears trivial on the surface but may have an underlying cause
    C. involves behavior which generally is different from prevailing social customs
    D. is of such nature that the supervisor is in danger of becoming personally involved

Answer questions 24 though 28 on the basis of the following paragraph:

"It is probable that supervisors who arouse anxiety in employees with early threats of low ratings and failure interfere with learning instead of *facilitating* it. It may well be that such threats serve to increase the employees' concern, but there is no guarantee that they will increase learning. In fact, experimental evidence gained from studies of college students suggests that, with very simple tasks, learning is enhanced by conditions of high motivation; but with complex tasks, the most efficient learning condition is one of low motivation. Moreover, when the motivation of the learner is raised artificially, as by a threat of failure, in the face of a complex task, there often occurs irrelevant learning not under the control of the supervisor, such as learning to worry. This emotional learning is likely to interfere with learning the task at hand."

24. According to the passage, studies have indicated that persons who attempt to learn difficult tasks 24.______
    A. are motivated most efficiently by an indirect approach despite the danger of unwanted side effects
    B. are more likely to learn if they are not especially concerned about learning
    C. usually begin in a state of tension provoked by supervisory intervention
    D. cannot learn efficiently unless motivated by a moderate fear of failure

25. Of the following, the most appropriate title for the passage is 25.______
    A. Blocks to Learning
    B. How to Prepare Employees for Advancement
    C. Experimentation in Training
    D. The Role of Psychology in Human Relations

26. Of the following, the most reasonable conclusion to be drawn from the passage is that 26.______
    A. learning progress should be measured by a single standard
    B. college graduates are relatively easily motivated to perform difficult tasks
    C. inexperienced supervisors generally rely upon threats in order to facilitate learning
    D. employee training requires that employees be appropriately motivated

27. The underlined word, facilitating, as used in the passage means, most nearly, 27.______
    A. establishing B. assuring C. assisting D. evaluating

28. According to the passage, a supervisor who causes an employee to be strongly motivated in connection with the learning of a task of low complexity is most likely to 28.______
    A. decrease anxiety
    B. facilitate learning
    C. prevent worrying
    D. reduce motivation

29. The majority of public housing tenants in the nation are classified, socio-economically, as 29.______
    A. a downwardly mobile, highly stable, lower-class population
    B. a lower-income, stable-family, upper-working-class population
    C. a poverty-afflicted, non-mobile, lower-class population
    D. an upwardly mobile, intact-family, working-class population

30. Although 17% of the area of a given city consists of parks and recreation space, most of the space is underutilized, inaccessible, peripheral or even underwater; the rest is unevenly distributed. The immediate remedy usually proposed for this maldistribution of space is to 30.______
    A. decrease facilities in the over-utilized parks
    B. create additional small parks
    C. divide large parks into community sections
    D. establish a unified system of user fees

KEY (CORRECT ANSWERS)

1. D	11. D	21. C
2. B	12. B	22. B
3. C	13. A	23. A
4. A	14. C	24. B
5. A	15. A	25. A
6. D	16. C	26. D
7. C	17. B	27. C
8. D	18. D	28. B
9. A	19. D	29. C
10. D	20. D	30. B

TEST 3

DIRECTIONS: Each question or incomplete statement is followed by several suggested answers or completions. Select the one that BEST answers the question or completes the statement. *PRINT THE LETTER OF THE CORRECT ANSWER IN THE SPACE AT THE RIGHT.*

1. Modular housing refers most specifically to housing that 1.______
   A. is partly pre-fabricated
   B. is covered by an insured mortgage
   C. uses electricity exclusively as a power and heat source
   D. stresses uniform interior decoration

2. In a rehabilitation program, rundown buildings are being turned into modernized units for low-income and moderate-income families. A common courtyard in the block's interior will feature trees, benches and a landscaped play area. A major reason for having such a courtyard, rather than a vacant area, is to reduce 2.______
   A. garbage throwing from windows facing the courtyard
   B. initial construction costs
   C. area-wide air pollution
   D. the rent levels of all the buildings

3. In connection with housing construction, "economies of scale" would most likely result from 3.______
   A. allowing purchasers of condominiums to specify individual modifications prior to construction
   B. constructing small, low-cost frame houses of different layouts based on age and the family composition of prospective purchasers
   C. erecting several high-rise buildings at the same time on one plot of land
   D. permitting cooperators to vote on the architectural design of their building

4. In many parts of the United States, the poor have been prevented from residing in the suburbs by 4.______
   A. low-density residential zoning
   B. large business organizations relocating to the suburbs
   C. lack of vacant suburban land
   D. low property taxes

Questions 5 through 7 are to be answered solely on the basis of the following passage:

"In the early 1900's, the two major ingredients of slums (overcrowding and physical obsolescence and deterioration) were increasingly evident in the core of most of our major cities. Other ingredients of slums were: poor original construction, lack of facilities, inadequate city services, unplanned development and overcrowding.

"The widespread incidence of these abject living conditions became a matter of concern among students of our social structure, progressive legislators and many apprehensive public officials. For example, in England, a Labor Government was in control after World War I and a serious housing shortage resulted from the urbanization drives being manifested by the people. Parliament passed a law in 1919 providing for state-assistance in the creation of new housing, which was the forerunner to our own housing legislation.

"The complete and unfettered right of private ownership was a part of the American creed. People were loath to sponsor or promote public action which would violate these rights. The first tenement house law was enacted in 1867 in New York and further legislation was passed in the year 1901. However, the continuing consumer pressure for housing made old, obsolete and substandard buildings a scarce commodity and hence preserved their earning power and their value. As in all cities, these old buildings were too valuable an 'asset' to destroy. Only recently have U.S. cities tightened up their enforcement programs as well as their housing and building codes."

5. Of the following, the most suitable title for the passage would be — 5.______
   - A. Government Action to Deal With Slums
   - B. Maximizing Profits From Slum Growth
   - C. Parliamentary Interest in Slums
   - D. The Focus on Tenant Responsibility for Slum Conditions

6. Of the following factors, which was probably the most important in eventually bringing about housing legislation in England in 1919? — 6.______
   - A. A desire on the part of the public to improve the physical appearance of slum areas
   - B. A pledge by the Labor Government to repair and renovate deteriorated housing
   - C. The movement of people from rural areas to urban areas
   - D. The new enlightenment of land owners

7. According to the above passage, at one time most Americans generally believed that, with regard to real estate, — 7.______
   - A. a man had a right to put his land to use in whatever way he wished
   - B. limiting owner's profits from slums would also prevent the creation of slums
   - C. slums could be largely eliminated by concentrating on the enforcement of existing housing legislation
   - D. the worst features of slums could be remedied by insisting that tenants maintain the property they had leased

Answer questions 8 and 9 solely on the basis of the following paragraph:

"Public housing planners are caught in a dilemma. They want to rid the cities of the most deteriorated housing, which are unsightly and sometimes dangerous. They want to reduce crowding, improve the physical environment, admit light and air, and bring trees and grass to the heart of the city. But their aspirations are usually frustrated by the scarcity and high cost of land that dictate intensive use and dense occupancy. Public housing, therefore, tends to increase the number of persons per acre even though the amount of space between buildings is greater than before the slums were cleared."

8. Based on the paragraph, it would be most reasonable to conclude that public housing, compared to the housing which it replaces, usually — 8.______
   A. fails to increase the total supply of housing
   B. has a longer economic life
   C. increases gross rental profits
   D. provides more open areas

9. According to the paragraph, public housing planners are often unable to achieve their goals because they generally — 9.______
   A. are forced to increase the concentration of tenants
   B. advocate public rather than private housing
   C. select sites located in unreceptive communities
   D. fail to take into account tenant wishes

Questions 10 through 14 consist of short paragraphs. Each paragraph contains one word which is INCORRECTLY used because it is not in keeping with the meaning of the paragraph. Find the word in each paragraph which is incorrectly used and then select as your answer the suggested word which should be substituted for the incorrect word.

SAMPLE: "One of your lowest responsibilities is to assign work so that it is fairly distributed and that everyone uses his best talents."
A. complain B. exclude C. important D. return

The word not in keeping with the meaning of the paragraph is <u>lowest</u>. The suggested word most in keeping with the meaning is <u>important</u> and should therefore be substituted. Thus, the correct answer is "C."

10. "Careful proofreading of all reports and correspondence is always necessary, since errors can have reductions ranging from simple embarrassment to serious misunderstanding. Common errors include omissions, transpositions, confused syntax and misspellings." — 10.______
   A. emotions B. requirements
   C. overly D. consequences

11. "The assumption that the average person dislikes work and will seek to avoid it has been shown to be wrong. And the companion assumption that most employees must be coerced, controlled and threatened before they will avoid effort toward organizational goals is equally in error. Scientific research has demonstrated that the opposite concepts are true." 11.______

A. establish B. exert C. identify D. verify

12. "The administrative climate – the lines of authority, the confidence in staff, the minimizing of status or class, the style of executive direction – should be sufficiently motivating and supportive that it evaluates the release of human energies and ideas in the interest of the public service." 12.______

A. ceases B. discusses C. modernizes D. stimulates

13. "H.L. Menken once said: 'There is always an easy solution to every human problem – neat, plausible and wrong.' If this bit of cynicism means that we should be wary of simplistic formulas to solve human problems, it is worthwhile. If, on the other hand, it means to encourage our having any guideposts, it is seriously overdrawn." 13.______

A. aversion B. disparage C. hesitate D. speculate

14. "Public employees, like any other group of employees, deserve being regarded by their employer not only as workers performing essential services but as human beings worthy of care and cultivation. Of all those organizations in our civilization that examine the services of people, the government can least justify disregard for the welfare of its employees." 14.______

A. accumulate B. employ C. predict D. restrict

15. In order for a supervisor to employ the system of democratic leadership in his supervision, it would generally be best for him to 15.______

A. allow his subordinates to assist in deciding on methods of work performance and job assignments but only in those areas where decisions have not been made on higher administrative levels
B. allow his subordinates to decide how to do the required work, interposing his authority when work is not completed on schedule or is improperly completed
C. attempt to make assignments of work to individuals only of the type which they enjoy doing
D. maintain control over the job assignments and work production, but allow the subordinates to select methods of work and internal conditions of work at democratically conducted staff conferences

16. In an office in which supervision has been considered quite effective, it has become necessary to press for above-normal production for a limited period to achieve a required goal. The one of the following which is a LEAST likely result of this pressure is that 16.______

A. there will be more griping by employees
B. some workers will do both more and better work than has been normal for them
C. there will be an enhanced feeling of group unity
D. there will be increased absenteeism

17. The practice whereby the Assistant Housing Manager at a large site with many Housing Assistants delegates to one of them who is highly competent and experienced the task of initially training a newly employed Housing Assistant in the routines and procedures of the site office is one which should be followed 17.______
    A. frequently, since the experienced Housing Assistant will himself learn by the act of teacing and the time of the Assistant Manager will be free for other work
    B. very frequently, since it enhances the status of the experienced Housing Assistant and sets a pattern for continuing differentiation between the more experienced and less experienced Housing Assistants
    C. rarely, since the newly employed Housing Assistant is likely to feel resentful that the Assistant Manager does not think him important enough to do the training personally
    D. very rarely, since it delegates to a non-supervisory employee supervisory functions over someone on his own level and with whom he will later have to work on an equal basis

18. Assume that you are an Assistant Housing Manager in charge of a staff of three Housing Assistants: "A," who is a very competent individual; "B," who is very experienced but only of average ability; and "C," who has been recently assigned to you, although he has been employed at another location for about a year. Your operation is currently going through a slack period. You are given a job to be done of a type requiring work by only one individual. It is a rather difficult and complex job. "A" has not done this job before but has competently done similar work. "B" has done this job before but only with the moderate competence that he does all jobs. "C" has no experience with this job or a similar one. To accomplish this task while at the same time accomplishing other supervisory aims, it would generally be best that you assign it to 18.______
    A. "A," since he has experience with similar work and can be expected to do this task competently
    B. "B," since his work is acceptable even though not outstanding, and he has already had experience with this job
    C. "C," since the slack period will give you a good opportunity to train him in the job and to form your own evaluation of his competence
    D. yourself, since it is a slack period and the job is a difficult and complex one

19. An Assistant Housing Manager happens to be passing by when one of his experienced Housing Assistants is interviewing a tenant, asking questions concerning pertinent and important matters. The Assistant Manager becomes aware that the questions are being asked in a way that is annoying the tenant, a way that the Assistant Manager believes can be improved upon. It would generally be best for the Assistant Manager to 19.______

A. introduce himself to the tenant, explain that there is no intention of annoying her, that the questions asked are necessary and important, and that the Housing Assistant is just doing his job
B. introduce himself to the tenant and join in the conversation, asking the questions in an improved way, and, at an early opportunity, discuss interviewing techniques with the Housing Assistant
C. pass by without comment but, at an early opportunity, discuss with the Housing Assistant some methods which may improve his interviewing techniques
D. take no action in the matter at this time, with the intention of discussing methods of improving interviewing techniques in some later in-service training conferences

20. It is the practice of some supervisors, when they believe that it would be desirable for a subordinate to take a particular action in a case, to inform the subordinate of this in the form of a suggestion rather than in the form of a direct order. In general, this method of getting a subordinate to take the desired action is 20.______

A. inadvisable; it may create in the mind of the subordinate the impression that the supervisor is uncertain about the efficacy of his plan and is trying to avoid whatever responsibility he may have in resolving the case
B. advisable; it provides the subordinate with the maximum opportunity to use his own judgment in handling the case
C. inadvisable; it provides the subordinate with no clear-cut direction and, therefore, is likely to leave him with a feeling of uncertainty and frustration
D. advisable; it presents the supervisor's view in a manner which will be most likely to evoke the subordinate's cooperation

21. At a group training conference of Housing Assistants conducted by an Assistant Housing Manager, one of the Housing Assistants asks a question which is only partially related to the subject under discussion. The Assistant Manager does not know the answer to the question and believes the question was asked to embarrass him since he recently reprimanded the Housing Assistant for inattention to his work. Under the circumstances, it would generally be best for the Assistant Manager to 21.______
    A. pointedly ignore the question and the questioner and go on to other matters
    B. request the questioner to remain after the group session, at which time the question and the questioner's attitude will be considered
    C. state that he does not know the answer and ask for a volunteer to give a brief answer, because the question is only partially relevant
    D. tell the questioner that the question is not pertinent, show wherein it is not pertinent and state that the time of the group should not be wasted on it

22. The one of the following circumstances when it would generally be most proper for a supervisor to do a job himself rather than train a subordinate to do the job is when it is 22.______
    A. a job which the supervisor enjoys doing and does well
    B. not a very time-consuming job but an important one
    C. difficult to train another to do the job yet is not difficult for the supervisor to do
    D. unlikely that this or any similar job will have to be done again at any future time

23. Effective training of subordinates requires that the supervisor understand certain facts about learning and forgetting processes. Among these is the fact that people generally 23.______
    A. both learn and forget at a relatively constant rate and this rate is dependent upon their general intellectual capacity
    B. forget what they learned at a much greater rate during the first day than during subsequent periods
    C. learn at a relatively constant rate except for periods of assimilation when the quantity of retained learning decreases while information is becoming firmly fixed in the mind
    D. learn very slowly at first when introduced to a new topic, after which there is a great increase in the rate of learning

24. It has been suggested that a subordinate who likes his supervisor tends to do better work than one who does not. According to the most widely held theories of supervision, this suggestion is a 24.______
    A. bad one, since personal relationships tend to interfere with proper professional relationships
    B. bad one, since the strongest motivating factors are fear and uncertainty
    C. good one, since liking one's supervisor is a motivating factor for good work performance
    D. good one, since liking one's supervisor is the most important factor in employee performance

25. An Assistant Housing Manager is supervising a Housing Assistant who is very soon to complete his six-months' probationary period. The Assistant Housing Manager finds him to be slow, to make many errors, to do work poorly, to be antagonistic toward the Assistant Housing Manager and to be disliked by many of his co-workers. The Assistant Manager is aware that he is the sole support of his wife and two children. He has never been late or absent during his service with the Housing Authority. If he is terminated, there will be considerable delay before a replacement arrives. It would generally be best for the Assistant Housing Manager to recommend that this Housing Assistant be 25.______
    A. transferred to work with another supervisor and other staff members with whom he may get along better
    B. retained but be very closely supervised until his work shows marked improvement
    C. retained since his services are needed with the expectation that he be terminated at some later date when a replacement is readily available
    D. terminated

26. Assume that you are an Assistant Housing Manager recently assigned to a new unit. You notice that, for the past few days, one of the Housing Assistants in your unit whose work is about average has been stopping work at about 4:00 and has been spending the rest of the afternoon relaxing at his desk. The best of the following actions for you to take in this situation is to 26.______
    A. assign more work to this Housing Assistant since it is apparent that he does not have enough work to keep him busy
    B. observe the Housing Assistant's conduct more closely for about ten days before taking any more positive action
    C. discuss the matter with the Housing Assistant, pointing out to him how he can use the extra hour daily to raise the level of his job performance
    D. question the previous supervisor in charge of the unit in order to determine whether he had sanctioned such conduct when he supervised that unit

27. It has long been recognized that relationships exist between worker morale and working conditions. The one of the following which best clarifies these existing relationships is that morale is 27.______
    A. affected for better or worse in direct relationship to the magnitude of the changes in working conditions for better or worse
    B. better when working conditions are better
    C. little affected by working conditions so long as the working conditions do not approach the intolerable
    D. more affected by the degree of interest shown in providing good working conditions than in the actual conditions, and may, perversely, be highest when working conditions are worst

28. An Assistant Housing Manager, newly assigned in charge of a small project, discovers that the previous Assistant Housing Manger and one of the Housing Assistants supervised by him put all their business communications with each other in written form. The newly assigned Assistant Housing Manager finds that the Housing Assistant is continuing to put his communications in writing and has requested that the Manager do the same in order to prevent misunderstandings. It would generally be best for the Assistant Housing Manager to 28.______

A. accede to the request since the likelihood of misunderstandings will be reduced and since, as a newly assigned supervisor, he should not make changes until he is well established and accepted
B. allow the Housing Assistant to communicate with him in the way in which he chooses but refuse to communicate back to him in writing except in cases where he would generally consider written communications to be desirable, on the grounds that too much of the Assistant Housing Manager's time would be wasted thereby
C. inform the Housing Assistant that neither one of them is to use written communications excessively in order to reduce the time consumed by communication but with the understanding that the Housing Assistant may resort to writing in cases where he has serious reason to fear a misunderstanding
D. instruct the Housing Assistant to cease the use of written communications in excess of the use of them by the other Housing Assistants and refuse to accede to his request since the result would be excessive waste of time

29. A policy of direct crosswise communication at a project between a member of the management staff and a member of the maintenance staff of equal or superior status rather than following the chain of command upward through the manager and down through the top maintenance supervisors is a policy to be 29.______

A. discouraged, primarily because it places responsibility where it does not belong and makes the quality of communication erratic and undependable
B. discouraged, primarily because the manager and upper-level supervisors will fail to receive the full information they need to make policy and administrative decisions
C. encouraged, primarily because it results in decision making at the lowest practical level
D. encouraged, primarily because it shortens the communication time and improves the quality of communication

30. Assume that a tenant has made a claim against the Housing Authority which is being handled by an Authority insurance carrier. Further, assume that you are aware of certain information in the tenant's folder which would be helpful in determining the merits of the claim. With regard to releasing this information to the insurance carrier, it would generally be considered best 30.______
   A. to refer the matter to the central office because of its effect on tenant relations and its legal implications
   B. not to reveal the information because of the legal requirement that tenant folder information be considered confidential
   C. not to reveal the information because of the likelihood that tenants will conceal or falsify information which they believe might in future be used to their detriment
   D. to reveal the information so as to increase the amount of information upon which the decision on the claim will be based

---

KEY (CORRECT ANSWERS)

1. A	11. B	21. C
2. A	12. D	22. D
3. C	13. B	23. B
4. A	14. B	24. C
5. A	15. A	25. D
6. C	16. D	26. C
7. A	17. A	27. D
8. D	18. C	28. C
9. A	19. C	29. D
10. D	20. D	30. D

TEST 4

DIRECTIONS: Each question or incomplete statement is followed by several suggested answers or completions. Select the one that BEST answers the question or completes the statement. *PRINT THE LETTER OF THE CORRECT ANSWER IN THE SPACE AT THE RIGHT.*

1. The director of the community center in a housing project has asked the Housing Manager for any information he may have about the character and interests of a certain boy living in the project. The tenant folder contains information about several infractions of rules and incidents involving this boy. For the Housing Manager to give the director of the center a summary of this information about the boy would generally be 1.______
   A. improper, if the director is not an employee of the Housing Authority, since information in tenant folders is confidential
   B. improper, since the boy might be stigmatized at the center by the revealed information, which in turn might cause a worsening in his attitude and actions
   C. proper, because of the help it gives the director in justifying the elimination from the center of a disturbing or disruptive influence
   D. proper, because of the help it might give the director in understanding the boy and improving ways in which to handle him

2. The one of the following which most fully and accurately describes the attitude which would be best for project management to maintain toward door-to-door fund solicitations by well-known reputable charitable organizations is to 2.______
   A. allow the solicitation but without assisting the operation
   B. allow the solicitation, giving minor assistance by such methods as suggesting the names of reliable tenants who might be interested in soliciting for a worthy cause within the project
   C. allow the solicitation, assisting the operation where possible by encouraging the staff to make collections after working hours
   D. ignore the matter unless a complaint is received from a tenant after which the solicitors must be politely informed that it will be necessary to enforce the laws against trespass if they visit tenants without appointments

3. A project tenant requests permission from the Assistant Housing Manager to post on the management office bulletin board in the rent collection office a notice to other tenants that she is available for hire as a babysitter. It would generally be best for the Assistant Housing Manager to 3.______
   A. deny the request because it might be considered as implying Housing Authority approval of the caliber of the service advertised
   B. deny the request because the use of this bulletin board should be restricted to those official matters which the management wishes to bring to the attention of the tenants
   C. grant the request because it is a service not only to the tenant making the request but also to other tenants with children
   D. grant the request in order to encourage the development of community living and the building of meaningful inter-relationships among the tenants

4. Housing Assistants should be instructed that in timing initial apartment inspection and orientation visits to new tenants, it is generally best to make the first visit 4.______
   A. within 24 hours after the tenant moves in
   B. about two days after the tenant moves in
   C. about two weeks after the tenant moves in
   D. about two months after the tenant moves in

5. On the 30th day of the month, a Housing Assistant visits a chronic rent delinquent in his apartment to discuss the rent for that month which has not yet been paid. The tenant, cash in hand, offers to pay the rent money to the Housing Assistant, in the apartment, explaining that she cannot leave the apartment until she gets someone to baby-sit for her ill two-month-old son. The Housing Assistant is aware that on previous occasions, when he refused to accept rent offered in the apartment, the money was not brought to the office for many days. In such an instance, the Housing Assistant should 5.______
   A. accept the money, giving a handwritten receipt, with instructions to the tenant to return this receipt when she next comes to the office to be replaced by the regulation machine entry in her rent book
   B. call in a neighbor to be a witness, accept the money and the rent book and return the latter after a regulation machine entry has been made in the rent book
   C. refuse to accept the money but offer to baby-sit while the mother brings the rent to the rent office, impressing upon her the importance of paying the money immediately
   D. refuse to accept the money, insisting that the mother make payment in the normal way, and warning her of the serious consequences of continued rent delinquencies

6. The Housing Authority has certain policies concerning the use of community space for dances sponsored by private, non-profit agencies. Dances may be of the invitation type, wherein admission is by invitation or ticket procured in advance, or of the open-type, wherein there is no limit on admission of non-members of the community center. According to these policies, 6.______
   A. both open dances and invitation dances are permitted so long as no admission fees are charged and proper arrangements for control of behavior are made and enforced
   B. both open and invitation dances are permitted and admission fees may be charged
   C. open dances are not permitted but invitation dances are permitted and admission fees may be charged
   D. open dances are not permitted but invitation dances are permitted as long as no admission fees are charged

7. The one of the following conditions under which it is necessary to make an interim change in income and rent for a tenant in federal or state subsidized housing is a condition wherein 7.______
   A. a non-welfare family contains a member who had been receiving welfare assistance which has now been terminated
   B. a member of the tenant household has graduated from high school and secured a permanent full-time job
   C. a regularly employed tenant has left his full-time job in one industry and received a full-time job in another industry at a substantial increase in salary
   D. a tenant with non-fixed employment in an industry characterized by long-term unemployment during slack seasons has now been without work for over three months during such a slack period

8. The one of the following which is the most complete and accurate description of the information contained in the Tenants' Charges and Credits Book (TCC Book) is that this book contains 8.______
   A. daily entries and monthly summaries of retroactive surcharges and credits broken down into categories by months to which attributed
   B. daily entries of total charges or debits, all the credits to the tenants' accounts, and all cash receipts broken down into categories of charges or credits but not by tenant or apartment account numbers
   C. monthly entries of total miscellaneous charges or debits, credits and receipts broken down into categories of such charges and credits and by tenant account number
   D. monthly summaries of all charges or debits and credits to tenants other than minimum or basic rent, broken down into categories of such charges and credits and by tenant account number

9. Assume that interest is paid on security deposits at the rate of 2% per annum, compounded annually, and paid to the nearest quarter of a year. A tenant who paid a security deposit of $100 on January 2, 1997 moved out with a charge-through date of February 10, 2001. He should have refunded to him, most nearly (assuming that there are no charges to be deducted from the security deposit), 9.______
   A. $107 B. $108 C. $109 D. $110
   E. $111

10. The peculiarities of the payment system of a particular employer have resulted in payments during a particular year of 53 weekly paychecks although only 52 paychecks were earned during the year. Assuming that there has been no change in salary during the year and that a tenant working for this employer has a statement of income for that year of $5,550 (covering 53 payments), his year's income for 52 weeks is most nearly 10.______
   A. $5,442 B. $5,445 C. $5,456 D. $5,495
   E. $5,549

Questions 11 through 15 are to be answered on the basis of the following graphs:

TENANT ELIGIBILITY STATUS IN STATE AND FEDERALLY AIDED PROJECTS
(MONTHS ENDING JANUARY 31 THROUGH JULY 31)

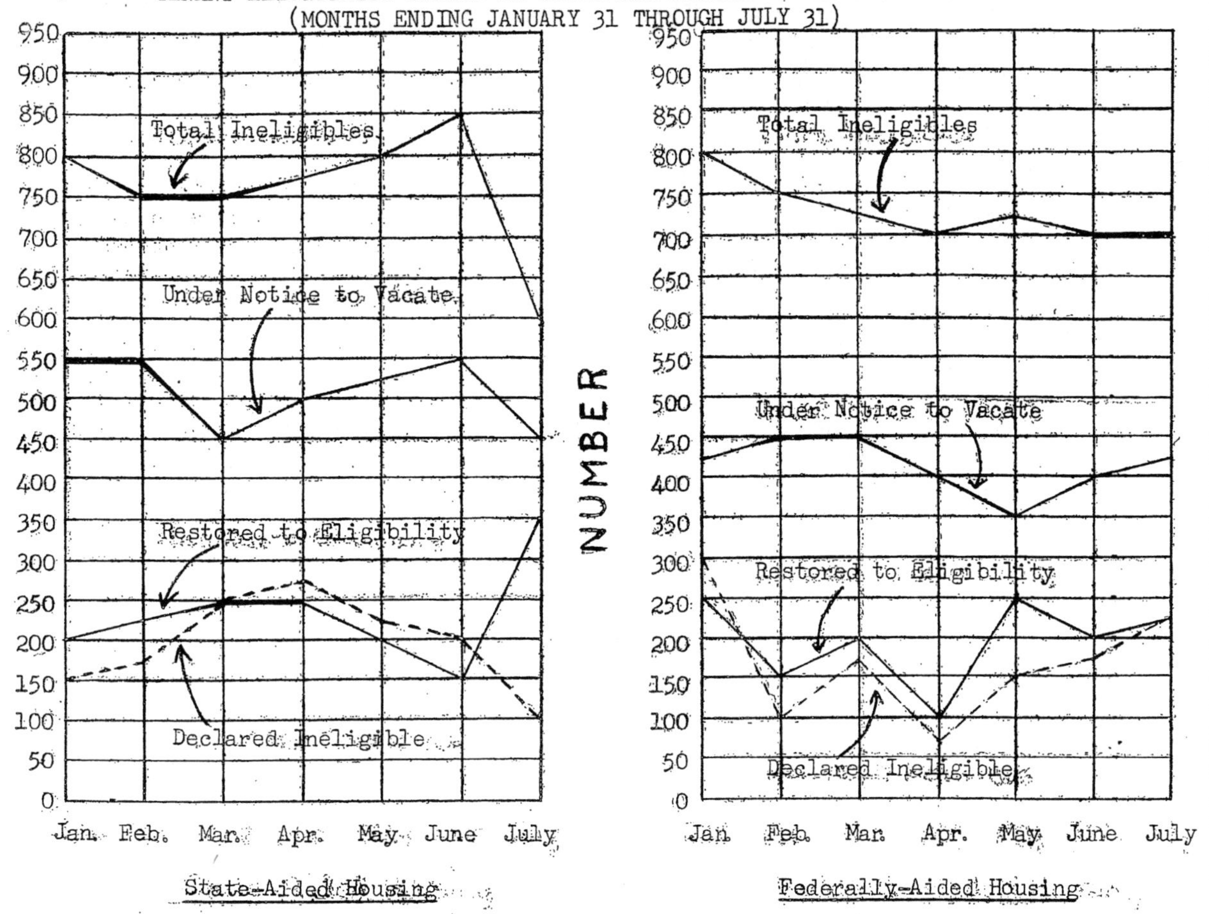

Note: Figures for "Restored to Eligibility" and "Declared Ineligible" show total activity for the month as compiled as of the end of each month. Figures for "Total Ineligibles" and "Under Notice to Vacate" show the total situation including that of past months.

11. In Federally-aided housing, the average number of tenants restored to eligibility during the first six months of the year is, most nearly 11.______
    A. 100
    B. 188
    C. 192
    D. 196
    E. 200

12. For the months covered by the graphs, in State-aided housing, the ratio of the average number of total ineligibles to the average number under notice to vacate is, most nearly 12.______
    A. 1:2
    B. 2:3
    C. 3:2
    D. 2:1
    E. 3:1

13. For State-aided housing, assume that it has been decided to predict figures for the end of August and the end of September on the basis that the number of tenants expected to be declared ineligible in each future month will be 30% less than the average for the previous three months. The number of tenants expected to be declared ineligible during the month of September is expected to be, most nearly 13.______
   A. 100   B. 122   C. 141   D. 158
   E. 175

14. Of the four categories of tenant status in the graph, the number of categories in which, at the end of May as compared with the end of April, there was a greater numerical increase in State-aided housing as compared with the same category in Federally-aided housing, is 14.______
   A. 0   B. 1   C. 2   D. 3
   E. 4

15. Assume that, at the end of March, in State-aided housing, the total number of ineligibles was 10% greater than shown on the graph, and that this 10% increase was due entirely to a greater number of tenants being declared ineligible in that month than is shown on the graph. Under this assumption, the percentage increase in the number *declared ineligible*, as compared with the figure in the graph would be, most nearly 15.______
   A. 3%   B. 10%   C. 17%   D. 23%
   E. 30%

16. In a housing project, the term hatch door is generally used to describe a door 16.______
   A. between the outdoors and the basement
   B. giving access from the boiler room to the fire tubes of a boiler
   C. giving access to the roof from the top of the stairway
   D. giving entrance from the hallway to the elevator shaft

17. A parapet is 17.______
   A. a device through which a fine spray of oil enters the firebox of an oil burner
   B. a hot water drain used in mornings to bleed off cold water which has accumulated overnight
   C. a protective low wall at the edge of a roof
   D. the primary support of an arch

18. 2-4-D is used to designate 18.______
   A. an oil mixture used to start an oil burner in operation
   B. a size of threaded pipe of the type used to carry waste water
   C. a type of weed killer for use on lawns
   D. a type of pre-mixed cement for patching walks

19. A condenser is part of a 19.______
   A, boiler where the oil is preheated
   B. fertilizer spreader where concentrated fertilizer is mixed with water
   C. radiator where the return water forms from steam
   D. refrigerator where the refrigerant takes liquid form

20. In a housing project, a low water cut-off is usually a device to 20.______
    A. close the waste line opening when the waste has flushed out of the toilet bowl
    B. shut down the automatic lawn-watering system when the moisture level in the lawn reaches a pre-determined level of saturation
    C. stop a sum pump when the water level is below floor level in the sump wall
    D. stop an oil burner motor when the water level in the system falls below a pre-determined level

21. The purpose of a check valve is to 21.______
    A. interrupt the flow of electricity in an overloaded circuit
    B. limit the amount of electrical current which can flow from a main line into a branch circuit
    C. prevent water from flowing in a pipe system in a direction opposite to that desired
    D. stop the flow of water when the water in a system reaches a pre-determined level

22. In deteriorating slum neighborhoods which have high rates of crime and juvenile delinquency, the attitude of the majority of the residents toward the neighborhood is that it is 22.______
    A. a neighborhood which they understand and which understands them, so that it is to be preferred over any neighborhood except one with much better physical amenities
    B. a neighborhood with faults, but as good a neighborhood as most
    C. a bad place to live, one they would like to be able to leave
    D. a fine place to live and one which meets their needs

23. The one of the following which is NOT considered an *essential* criterion in the determination that an apartment is standard is that 23.______
    A. heat be provided centrally
    B. there be a fully enclosed bath in the apartment
    C. it have a kitchen or kitchenette
    D. there be a window in every room

24. The one of the following circumstances under which it would be proper for the Assistant Housing Manager at a project to unlock the door to a tenant's apartment for a law enforcement official without first contacting the Legal Department for an opinion is when 24.______
    A. an agent of the FBI, without a warrant, wishes to further an investigation by searching an apartment where, he states, he has reason to believe a crime is being committed
    B. a city patrolman wants to enter an apartment at night to make an arrest pursuant to a warrant in which the crime specified is a misdemeanor and the warrant makes no specification as to the time when it may be served
    C. a city patrolman, without a warrant, wishes to enter an apartment where he is in hot pursuit of someone whom, he states, he saw commit a felony
    D. a United States Army military policeman has a warrant for the arrest of a deserter whom, he states, he has just seen entering the apartment

25. The Assistant Manager of a large project becomes aware that two of the Housing Assistants do not get along with each other and have not gotten along for some time. In view of this fact, it would be best for the Assistant Manager to 25.______
    A. arrange assignments in such a way that these two assistants have as little contact with each other as possible
    B. call a staff meeting and emphasize the need for teamwork
    C. suggest that both assistants apply for transfers
    D. try to determine which of the two is at fault and insist that the one at fault correct his attitude

26. On the basis of a complaint by a site tenant that a certain Housing Assistant had refused to listen to her complaint about a lack of services, an Assistant Housing Manager has reprimanded the Housing Assistant. The Assistant Manager later becomes aware that the assistant reprimanded is not the one who was at fault. It would be best for the Assistant Manager to 26.______
    A. apologize privately to the assistant as soon as possible
    B. give the assistant certain desirable assignments in partial redress of the past error
    C. make a public apology at the next staff meeting
    D. say nothing about this incident but investigate such complaints much more carefully in the future

27. The manager called one of the Housing Assistants into his office and told him that his work was very unsatisfactory and pointed out exactly wherein it was so poor. He also stated that an improvement was expected. This method of approaching the situation is generally 27.______
    A. desirable; the discussion and criticism was carried on in private
    B. desirable; the Housing Assistant knows exactly where he stands
    C. poor; some praise or favorable comment should also be made if possible
    D. poor; a better approach would be to ask the Housing Assistant to explain why his work is unsatisfactory

28. Assume that you are the manager of a project. You have found it necessary to successively warn, reprimand and then severely reprimand a Housing Assistant for failure to carry out your orders. If the Housing Assistant again does not carry out your orders, it would be best for you to 28.______
    A. confer with the assistant privately, again explain the reason for the orders, and in most serious terms indicate the necessity for carrying them out
    B. bring the assistant up on charges of failure to perform his duties properly
    C. recommend that the assistant be transferred elsewhere
    D. severely reprimand the assistant again and warn him that more drastic action will be taken if it happens again

29. A junior accountant requests a transfer from the project where he is presently working to another project where he would be doing the same type of work. This transfer would be of no apparent advantage either to the Housing Authority or to the junior accountant. It would be best for the manager of the project to 29.______
    A. base his approval or rejection of the request on whether the junior accountant will be acceptable in the other project
    B. recommend the transfer if there is no apparent disadvantage to the Housing Authority
    C. refer the matter to the supervising manager without recommendation
    D. refuse the request and explain to the junior accountant that it is not in his best interest

30. A typist at a Housing Authority site comes to the Assistant Manager with a request that she be transferred to a project because she does not like site work, which she defines as making families move from their homes. It would be best for the Assistant Manager to 30.______
    A. explain to the typist the need for making families move in order to accomplish the slum clearance job of the Housing Authority and ask her to reconsider the request
    B. explain to the typist the need for making families move in order to accomplish the slum clearance job of the Housing Authority and refuse the request since it was based on a misunderstanding of the situation
    C. grant the request
    D. point out to the typist that the responsibility for making families move is not hers and ask her to reconsider the request

KEY (CORRECT ANSWERS)

1. D	11. C	21. C
2. A	12. C	22. C
3. A	13. A	23. D
4. C	14. B	24. C
5. D	15. E	25. A
6. C	16. D	26. A
7. B	17. C	27. C
8. B	18. C	28. B
9. B	19. D	29. A
10. B	20. D	30. A

READING COMPREHENSION
UNDERSTANDING AND INTERPRETING WRITTEN MATERIAL
EXAMINATION SECTION
TEST 1

DIRECTIONS: Each question or incomplete statement is followed by several suggested answers or completions. Select the one that BEST answers the question or completes the statement. *PRINT THE LETTER OF THE CORRECT ANSWER IN THE SPACE AT THE RIGHT.*

Questions 1-3.

DIRECTIONS: Questions 1 through 3 are to be answered SOLELY on the basis of the following paragraph.

The aging housing inventory presents a broad spectrum of conditions, from good upkeep to unbelievable deterioration. Buildings, even relatively good buildings, are likely to have numerous minor violations rather than the gross and evident sanitary violations of an earlier age. Except for the serious violations in a relatively small number of slum buildings, the task is to deal with masses of minor violations that, though insignificant in themselves, amount in the aggregate to major deprivations of health and comfort to tenants. Caused by wear and tear, by the abrasions of time, and aggravated by neglect, these conditions do not readily yield to the dramatic *vacate and restore* measures of earlier times. Moreover, the lines between *good* and *bad* housing have become blurred in many parts of our cities; we find a range of *shades of gray* blending into each other. Different kinds of code enforcement efforts may be required to deal with different degrees of deterioration.

1. The above passage suggests that code enforcement efforts may have to be 1.____

   A. developed to cope with varying levels of housing dilapidation
   B. aimed primarily at the serious violations in slum buildings
   C. modeled on the *vacate and restore* measures of earlier times
   D. modified to reduce unrealistic penalties for petty violations

2. According to the above passage, during former times some buildings had sanitary violations which were 2.____

   A. irreparable and minor
   B. blurred and gray
   C. flagrant and obvious
   D. insignificant and numerous

3. According to the above passage, the aging housing stock presents a 3.____

   A. great number of rent-controlled buildings
   B. serious problem of tenant-caused deterioration
   C. significant increase in buildings without intentional violations
   D. wide range of physical conditions

Questions 4-5.

DIRECTIONS: Questions 4 and 5 are to be answered SOLELY on the basis of the following passage.

In general, housing code provisions relating to the safe and sanitary maintenance of dwelling units prescribe the maintenance required for foundations, walls, ceilings, floors, windows, doors, stairways, and also the facilities and equipment required in other sections. The more recent codes have, in addition, extensive provisions designed to ensure that the unit be maintained in a rat-free and rat-proof condition. Also, as an example of new approaches in code provisions, one proposed Federal model housing code prohibits the landlord from terminating vital services and utilities except during temporary emergencies or when actual repairs or maintenance are in process. This provision may be used to prevent a landlord from turning off utility services as a technique of self-help eviction or as a weapon against rent strikes.

4. According to the above passage, the more recent housing codes have extensive provisions designed to 4.___

   A. maintain a reasonably fire-proof living unit
   B. prohibit tenants from participating in rent strikes
   C. maintain the unit free from rats
   D. prohibit tenants from using lead-based paints

5. According to the above passage, one housing code would permit landlords to terminate vital services during 5.___

   A. a rent strike
   B. an actual eviction
   C. a temporary emergency
   D. the planning of repairs and maintenance

Questions 6-8.

DIRECTIONS: Questions 6 through 8 are to be answered SOLELY on the basis of the following passage.

City governments have long had building codes which set minimum standards for building and for human occupancy. The code (or series of codes) makes provisions for standards of lighting and ventilation, sanitation, fire prevention, and protection. As a result of demands from manufacturers, builders, real estate people, tenement owners, and building-trades unions, these codes often have established minimum standards well below those that the contemporary society would accept as a rock-bottom minimum. Codes often become outdated so that meager standards in one era become seriously inadequate a few decades later as society"s concept of a minimum standard of living changes. Out-of-date codes, when still in use, have sometimes prevented the introduction of new devices and modern building techniques. Thus, it is extremely important that building codes keep pace with changes in the accepted concept of a minimum standard of living.

6. According to the above passage, all of the following considerations in building planning would probably be covered in a building code EXCEPT 6.____

   A. closet space as a percentage of total floor area
   B. size and number of windows required for rooms of differing sizes
   C. placement of fire escapes in each line of apartments
   D. type of garbage disposal units to be installed

7. According to the above passage, if an ideal building code were to be created, how would the established minimum standards in it compare to the ones that are presently set by city governments? 7.____
   They would

   A. be lower than they are at present
   B. be higher than they are at present
   C. be comparable to the present minimum standards
   D. vary according to the economic group that sets them

8. On the basis of the above passage, what is the reason for difficulties in introducing new building techniques? 8.____

   A. Builders prefer techniques which represent the rock-bottom minimum desired by society.
   B. Certain manufacturers have obtained patents on various building methods to the exclusion of new techniques.
   C. The government does not want to invest money in techniques that will soon be outdated.
   D. New techniques are not provided for in building codes which are not up-to-date.

Questions 9-11.

DIRECTIONS: Questions 9 through 11 are to be answered SOLELY on the basis of the following paragraph.

When constructed within a multiple dwelling, such storage space shall be equipped with a sprinkler system and also with a system of mechanical ventilation in no way connected with any other ventilating system. Such storage space shall have no opening into any other part of the dwelling except through a fireproof vestibule. Any such vestibule shall have a minimum superficial floor area of fifty square feet, and its maximum area shall not exceed seventy-five square feet. It shall be enclosed with incombustible partitions having a fire-resistive rating of three hours. The floor and ceiling of such vestibule shall also be of incombustible material having a fire-resistive rating of at least three hours. There shall be two doors to provide access from the dwelling,to the car storage space. Each such door shall have a fire-resistive rating of one and one-half hours and shall be provided with a device to prevent the opening of one door until the other door is entirely closed.

9. According to the above paragraph, the one of the following that is REQUIRED in order for cars to be permitted to be stored in a multiple dwelling is a(n) 9.____

   A. fireproof vestibule
   B. elevator from the garage
   C. approved heating system
   D. sprinkler system

10. According to the above paragraph, the one of the following materials that would NOT be acceptable for the walls of a vestibule connecting a garage to the dwelling portion of a building is 10.____

A. 3" solid gypsum blocks
B. 4" brick
C. 4" hollow gypsum blocks, plastered both sides
D. 6" solid cinder concrete blocks

11. According to the above paragraph, the one of the following that would be ACCEPTABLE for the width and length of a vestibule connecting a garage that is within a multiple dwelling to the dwelling portion of the building is 11.____

A. 3'8" x 13'0"
B. 4'6" x 18'6"
C. 4'9" x 14'6"
D. 4'3" x 19'3"

Questions 12-13.

DIRECTIONS: Questions 12 and 13 are to be answered SOLELY on the basis of the following paragraph.

It shall be unlawful to place, use, or maintain in a condition intended, arranged, or designed for use, any gas-fired cooking appliance, laundry stove, heating stove, range or water heater or combination of such appliances in any room or space used for living or sleeping in any new or existing multiple dwelling unless such room or space has a window opening to the outer air or such gas appliance is vented to the outer air. All automatically operated gas appliances shall be equipped with a device which shall shut off automatically the gas supply to the main burners when the pilot light in such appliance is extinguished. A gas range or the cooking portion of a gas appliance incorporating a room heater shall not be deemed an automatically operated gas appliance. However, burners in gas ovens and broilers which can be turned on and off or ignited by non-manual means shall be equipped with a device which shall shut off automatically the gas supply to those burners when the operation of such non-manual means fails.

12. According to the above paragraph, an automatic shut-off device is NOT required on a gas 12.____

A. hot water heater
B. laundry dryer
C. space heater
D. range

13. According to the above paragraph, a gas-fired water heater is permitted 13.____

A. only in kitchens
B. only in bathrooms
C. only in living rooms
D. in any type of room

Questions 14-18.

DIRECTIONS: Questions 14 through 18 are to be answered SOLELY on the basis of the information contained in the statement below.

No multiple dwelling shall be erected to a height in excess of one and one-half times the width of the widest street on which it faces, except that above the level of such height, for each one foot that the front wall of such dwelling sets back from the street line, three feet shall be added to the height limit of such dwelling, but such dwelling shall not exceed in maximum height three feet plus one and three-quarter times the width of the widest street on which it faces.

Any such dwelling facing a street more than one hundred feet in width shall be subject to the same height limitations as though such dwelling faced a street one hundred feet in width.

14. The MAXIMUM height of a multiple dwelling set back five feet from the street line and facing a 60 foot wide street is feet. 14.____

A. 60 B. 90 C. 105 D. 165

15. The MAXIMUM height of a multiple dwelling set back six feet from the street line and facing a 120 foot wide street is ______ feet. 15.____

A. 198 B. 168 C. 120 D. 105

16. The MAXIMUM height of a multiple dwelling is 16.____

A. 100 ft. B. 150 ft. C. 178 ft. D. unlimited

17. The MAXIMUM height of a multiple dwelling set back 10 feet from the street line and facing a 110 foot wide street is feet. 17.____

A. 178 B. 180 C. 195 D. 205

18. The MAXIMUM height of a multiple dwelling set back eight feet from the street line and facing a 90 foot wide street is feet. 18.____

A. 135 B. 147 C. 178 D. 159

Questions 19-23.

DIRECTIONS: Questions 19 through 23 are to be answered SOLELY on the basis of the following statement.

The number of persons accommodated on any story in a lodging house shall not be greater than the sum of the following components,

a. 22 persons for each full multiple of 22 inches in the smallest clear width for each means of egress approved by the department, other than fire escapes
b. 20 persons for each lawful fire escape accessible from such story.

19. The MAXIMUM number of persons that may be accommodated on a story in a lodging house depends on the 19.____

A. number of lawful fire escapes *only*
B. number of approved means of egress *only*
C. smallest clear width in each approved means of egress *only*
D. number of lawful fire escapes and sum total of smallest clear widths in each approved means of egress

20. The MAXIMUM number of persons that may be accommodated on a story of a lodging house having one lawful fire escape and a sum total of 44 inches in the smallest clear widths of the two approved means of egress is 20.____

A. 20 B. 22 C. 42 D. 64

21. The MAXIMUM number of persons that may be accommodated on a story of a lodging house having two lawful fire escapes and a sum total of 60 inches in the smallest clear width of the approved means of egress is 21.___

A. 64 B. 84 C. 100 D. 106

22. The MAXIMUM number of persons that may be accommodated on a story of a lodging house having one lawful fire escape and a sum total of 33 inches in the smallest clear width of the approved means of egress is 22.___

A. 42 B. 53 C. 64 D. 73

23. The MAXIMUM number of persons that may be accommodated on a story of a lodging house having two lawful fire escapes and two approved means of egress, with 40 inches and 44 inches in the smallest clear widths, respectively, is 23.___

A. 84 B. 104 C. 106 D. 108

Questions 24-25.

DIRECTIONS: Questions 24 and 25 are to be answered SOLELY on the basis of the following paragraph.

Though the recent trend toward apartment construction may appear to be the Region's response to large-lot zoning and centralized industry, it really is not. It is mainly a function of the age of the population. Most of the apartments are occupied by one- and two-person families young people out of school but without a family of their own and older people whose children have grown. Both groups have been increasing in number; and, in this Region, they characteristically live in apartments. It is this increased demand for apartments and the simultaneous decrease in demand for one-family houses that dramatically raised the percentage of building permits issued for multi-family housing units from 36 percent in 1977 to 67 percent in 1981. The fact that three-fourths of the apartments were built in the Core between 1977 and 1981 at the same time as the Core was losing population underscores the failure of the apartment boom to slow the outward spread of the population.

24. According to the above paragraph, one of the reasons for the increase in the number of building permits issued for multi-family construction in the City Metropolitan Region is 24.___

A. that workers in industry want to live close to their jobs
B. an increase in the number of elderly people living in the Region
C. the inability of many families to afford the large lots necessary to build private homes
D. the new zoning ordinance made it easier to build apartments

25. According to the above paragraph, the apartment construction boom 25.___

A. increased the population density in the Core
B. spurred a population shift to the suburbs
C. did not halt the outward flow of the population from the Core
D. was most significant in the outer areas of the Region

KEY (CORRECT ANSWERS)

1. A
2. C
3. D
4. C
5. C

6. A
7. B
8. D
9. D
10. B

11. C
12. D
13. D
14. C
15. B

16. C
17. A
18. D
19. D
20. D

21. B
22. A
23. C
24. B
25. C

TEST 2

DIRECTIONS: Each question or incomplete statement is followed by several suggested answers or completions. Select the one that BEST answers the question or completes the statement. *PRINT THE LETTER OF THE CORRECT ANSWER IN THE SPACE AT THE RIGHT.*

Questions 1-4.

DIRECTIONS: Questions 1 through 4 are to be answered SOLELY on the basis of the following paragraph.

Although the suburbs have provided housing and employment for millions of additional families since 1950, many suburban communities have maintained controls over the kinds of families who can live in them. Suburban attitudes have been formed by reaction against a perception of crowded, harassed city life and threatening alien city people. As population, taxable income, and jobs have left the cities for the suburbs, the *urban crisis* of substandard housing, declining levels of education and public services, and decreasing employment opportunities has been created. The crisis, however, is not urban at all, but national, and in part a result of the suburban policy that discourages outward movement by the urban poor.

1. According to the above paragraph, the quality of urban life 1.____

   A. is determined by public opinion in the cities
   B. has worsened in recent years
   C. is similar to rural life
   D. can be changed by political means

2. According to the above paragraph, suburban communities have 2.____

   A. tried to show that the urban crisis is really a national crisis
   B. avoided taking a position on the urban crisis
   C. been involved in causing the urban crisis
   D. been the innocent victims of the urban crisis

3. According to the above paragraph, the poor have 3.____

   A. become increasingly sophisticated in their attempts to move to the suburbs
   B. generally been excluded from the suburbs
   C. lost incentive for betterment of their living conditions
   D. sought improvement of the central cities

4. As used in the above paragraph, the word perception means MOST NEARLY 4.____

   A. development B. impression
   C. opposition D. uncertainty

Questions 5-8.

DIRECTIONS: Questions 5 through 8 are to be answered SOLELY on the basis of the following paragraph.

The concentration of publicly assisted housing in central cities -- because the suburbs do not want them and effectively bar them -- is usually rationalized by a solicitous regard for keeping intact the city neighborhoods cherished by low-income groups. If one accepted this as valid, the devotion of minorities to blighted city neighborhoods in preference to suburban employment and housing would be an historic first. Certainly no such devotion was visible among the millions who have deserted their city neighborhoods in the last 25 years even if it meant an arduous daily trip from the suburbs to their jobs in the cities.

5. The writer implies that MOST poor people 5.____

A. prefer isolation
B. fear change
C. are angry
D. seek betterment

6. The general tone of the paragraph is BEST characterized as 6.____

A. uncertain B. skeptical C. evasive D. indifferent

7. As used in the above paragraph, the word rationalize means MOST NEARLY 7.____

A. dispute B. justify C. deny D. locate

8. According to the above paragraph, publicly assisted housing is concentrated in the central cities PRIMARILY because 8.____

A. city dwellers are unable to find satisfactory housing
B. deterioration of older housing has increased in recent years
C. suburbanites have opposed the movement of the poor to the suburbs
D. employment opportunities have decreased in the suburbs

Questions 9-11.

DIRECTIONS: Questions 9 through 11 are to be answered SOLELY on the basis of the following paragraph.

In recent years, new and important emphasis has been placed upon the maximum use of conservation and rehabilitation techniques in carrying out programs of urban renewal and revitalization. In urban renewal projects where existing structures are hopelessly deteriorated or land uses are incompatible with the community's overall plans, the entire area may be acquired, cleared, and sold for redevelopment. However, where existing structures are basically sound but have deteriorated to the point where they are a blighting influence on the neighborhood, they may be salvaged through a program of rehabilitation and reconditioning.

9. According to the above paragraph, the one of the following which is MOST likely to cause area-wide razing of the buildings in urban renewal programs is 9.____

A. a program of rehabilitation and reconditioning
B. concerted insistence by landlords and tenants that certain buildings be bulldozed
C. an inability of community groups to agree on priorities for staged clearance
D. land use contrary to the community's general plan

10. According to the above paragraph, rehabilitation of structures may take place if 10.____

A. new conservation and rehabilitation techniques are used
B. salvaging all the buildings in the entire area is hopeless
C. the community wishes to preserve historic structures
D. the existing buildings are structurally sound

11. As used in the above paragraph, the word blighting means MOST NEARLY 11.___

A. ruining B. infrequent C. recurrent D. traditional

Questions 12-13.

DIRECTIONS: Questions 12 and 13 are to be answered SOLELY on the basis of the following paragraphs.

We must also find better ways to handle the relocation of people uprooted by projects. In the past, many renewal plans have foundered on this problem, and it is still the most difficult part of the community development. Large-scale replacement of low-income residents -- many ineligible for public housing -- has contributed to deterioration of surrounding communities. However, thanks to changes in housing authority procedures, relocation has been accomplished in a far more satisfactory fashion. The step-by-step community development projects we advocate in this plan should bring further improvement.

But additional measures will be necessary. There are going to be more people to be moved; and, with the current shortage of apartments, large ones especially, it is going to be tougher to find places to move them to. The city should have more freedom to buy or lease housing that comes on the market because of normal turnover and make it available to relocatees.

12. According to the above paragraphs, one of the reasons a neighborhood may deteriorate is that 12.___

A. there is a scarcity of large apartments
B. step-by-step community development projects have failed
C. people in the given neighborhood are uprooted from their homes
D. a nearby renewal project has an inadequate relocation plan

13. From the above paragraphs, one might conclude that the relocation phase of community renewal has been improved. 13.___

A. by changes in housing authority procedures
B. by development of step-by-step community development projects
C. through expanded city powers to buy housing for relocation
D. by the addition of huge sums of money

Questions 14-15.

DIRECTIONS: Questions 14 and 15 are to be answered SOLELY on the basis of the following paragraphs.

Provision of decent housing for the lower half of the population (by income) was thus taken on as a public responsibility. Public housing was to assist the poorest quarter of urban families while the 221(d)(3) Housing Program would assist the next quarter. But limited funds meant that the supply of subsidized housing could not stretch nearly far enough to help this half of the population. Who were to be left out in the rationing process which was accomplished by the sifting of applicants for housing on the part of public and private authorities?

Discrimination on the grounds of race or color is not allowed under Federal law. In all sections of the country, encouragingly, housing programs are found which follow this law to the letter. Yet, housing programs in some cities still suffer from the residue of racial segregation policies and attitudes that for years were condoned or even encouraged.

Some sifting in the 221(d)(3) Housing Program follows the practice of many public housing authorities, the imposition of requirements with respect to character. This is a delicate matter. To fill a project overwhelmingly with broken families, alcoholics, criminals, delinquents, and other problem tenants would hardly make it a wholesome environment. Yet the total exclusion of such families is hardly an acceptable alternative. To the extent this exclusion is practiced, the very people whose lives are described in order to persuade lawmakers and the public to instigate new programs find the door shut in their faces when such programs come into being. The proper balance is difficult to achieve, but society's neediest families surely should not be totally denied the opportunities for rejuvenation in subsidized housing.

14. From the above paragraphs, it can be assumed that the 221(d)(3) Housing Program 14.____

A. served a population earning more than the median income
B. served a less affluent population than is served by public housing
C. excludes all problem families from its projects
D. is a subsidized housing program

15. According to this text, the provision of housing for the poor 15.____

A. has not been completely accomplished with public monies
B. is never influenced by segregationist policies
C. is limited to providing housing for only the neediest families
D. is primarily the responsibility of the Federal government

16. Five hundred persons attended a public hearing at which a proposed public housing project was being considered. Less than half favored the project while the majority opposed the project. 16.____
According to the above statement, it is REASONABLE to conclude that

A. the proposal stimulated considerable community interest
B. the public housing project was disapproved by the city because a majority opposed it
C. those who opposed the project lacked sympathy for needy persons
D. the supporters of the project were led by militants

17. A vacant lot close to a polluted creek is for sale. Two buyers compete. One owns an adjacent factory which provides 300 high paying unskilled jobs. He needs to expand or move from the city. If he expands, he will provide 300 additional jobs. The other is a community group in a changing residential area close by. They hope to stabilize the neighborhood by bringing in new housing. They would build an apartment building with 100 dwelling units on the lot. 17.____
According to the above paragraph, it is REASONABLE to conclude that

A. jobs are more important than housing
B. there is conflict between the factory owners and the neighborhood group
C. the neighborhood group will not succeed in stabilizing the area by constructing new housing
D. the polluted creek should be cleaned up

18. The housing authority faces every problem of the private developer, and it must also assume responsibilities of which private building is free. The authority must account to the community; it must conform to federal regulations; it must provide durable buildings of good standard at low cost; it must overcome the prejudices against public operations, of contractors, bankers, and prospective tenants. These authorities are being watched by anti-housing enthusiasts for the first error of judgment or the first evidence of high costs, to be torn to bits before a Congressional committee. 18.___
On the basis of this statement, it would be MOST correct to state that

A. private builders do not have the opposition of contractors, bankers, and prospective tenants
B. Congressional committees impede the progress of public housing by petty investigations
C. a housing authority must deal with all the difficulties encountered by the private builder
D. housing authorities are no more immune from errors in judgment than private developers

19. Another factor that has considerably added to the city's housing crisis has been the great influx of low-income workers and their families seeking better employment opportunities during wartime and defense boom periods. The circumstances of these families have forced them to crowd into the worst kind of housing and have produced on a renewed scale the conditions from which slums flourish and grow. 19.___
On the basis of this statement, one would be justified in stating that

A. the influx of low-income workers has aggravated the slum problem
B. the city has better employment opportunities than other sections of the country
C. the high wages paid by our defense industries have made many families ineligible for tenancy in public housing projects
D. the families who settled in the city during wartime and the defense build-up brought with them language and social customs conducive to the growth of slums

20. Much of the city felt the effects of the general postwar increase of vandalism and street crime, and the greatly expanded public housing program was no exception. Projects built in congested slum areas with a high incidence of delinquency and crime were particularly subjected to the depredations of neighborhood gangs. The civil service watchmen who patrolled the projects, unarmed and neither trained nor expected to perform police duties, were unable to cope with the situation. 20.___
On the basis of this statement, the MOST accurate of the following statements is:

A. Neighborhood gangs were particularly responsible for the high incidence of delinquency and crime in congested slum areas having public housing programs
B. Civil service watchmen who patrolled housing projects failed to carry out their assigned police duties
C. Housing projects were not spared the effects of the general postwar increase of vandalism and street crime
D. Delinquency and crime affected housing projects in slum areas to a greater extent than other dwellings in the same area

21. Another peculiar characteristic of real estate is the absence of liquidity. Each parcel is a discrete unit as to size, location, rental, physical condition, and financing arrangements. Each property requires investigation, comparison of rents with other properties, and individualized haggling on price and terms. 21.____
On the basis of this statement, the LEAST accurate of the following statements is:

A. Although the size, location, and rent of parcels vary, comparison with rents of other properties affords an indication of the value of a particular parcel
B. Bargaining skill is the essential factor in determining the value of a parcel of real estate
C. Each parcel of real estate has individual peculiarities distinguishing it from any other parcel
D. Real estate is not easily converted to other types of assets

22. In part, at least, the charges of sameness, monotony, and institutionalism directed at public housing projects result from the degree in which they differ from the city's normal housing pattern. They seem alike because their very difference from the usual makes them stand apart. 22.____
In many respects, there is considerably more variety between public housing projects than there is between different streets of apartment houses or tenements throughout the city.
On the basis of this statement, it would be LEAST accurate to state that:

A. There is considerably more variety between public housing projects than there is between different streets of tenements throughout the city
B. Public housing projects differ from the city's normal housing pattern to the degree that sameness, monotony, and institutionalism are characteristic of public buildings
C. Public housing projects seem alike because their deviation from the usual dwellings draws attention to them
D. The variety in structure between public housing projects and other public buildings is related to the period in which they were built

23. The amount of debt that can be charged against the city for public housing is limited by law. Part of the city's restricted housing means goes for cash subsidies it may be required to contribute to state-aided projects. Under the provisions of the state law, the city must match the state's contributions in subsidies; and while the value of the partial tax exemption granted by the city is counted for this purpose, it is not always sufficient. 23.____
On the basis of this statement, it would be MOST accurate to state that:

A. The amount of money the city may spend for public housing is limited by annual tax revenues
B. The value of tax exemptions granted by the city to educational, religious, and charitable institutions may be added to its subsidy contributions to public housing projects
C. The subsidy contributions for state-aided public housing projects are shared equally by the state and the city under the provisions of the state law
D. The tax revenues of the city, unless supplemented by state aid, are insufficient to finance public housing projects

24. Maintenance costs can be minimized and the useful life of houses can be extended by building with the best and most permanent materials available. The best and most permanent materials in many cases are, however, much more expensive than materials which require more maintenance. The most economical procedure in home building has been to compromise between the capital costs of high quality and enduring materials and the maintenance costs of less desirable materials. 24.____
On the basis of this statement, one would be justified in stating that:

A. Savings in maintenance costs make the use of less durable and less expensive building materials preferable to high quality materials that would prolong the useful life of houses constructed from them
B. Financial advantage can be secured by the home builder if he judiciously combines costly but enduring building materials with less desirable materials which, however, require more maintenance
C. A compromise between the capital costs of high quality materials and the maintenance costs of less desirable materials makes it easier for a home builder to estimate construction expenditures
D. The most economical procedure in home building is to balance the capital costs of the most permanent materials against the costs of less expensive materials that are cheaper to maintain

25. Personnel selection has been a critical problem for local housing authorities. The pool of qualified workers trained in housing procedures is small, and the colleges and universities have failed to grasp the opportunity for enlarging it. While real estate experience makes a good background for management of a housing project, many real estate men are deplorably lacking in understanding of social and governmental problems. Social workers, on the other hand, are likely to be deficient in business judgment. 25.____
On the basis of this statement, it would be MOST accurate to state that:

A. Colleges and universities have failed to train qualified workers for proficiency in housing procedures
B. Social workers are deficient in business judgment as related to the management of a housing project
C. Real estate experience makes a person a good manager of a housing project
D. Local housing authorities have been critical of present methods of personnel selection

KEY (CORRECT ANSWERS)

1. B
2. C
3. B
4. B
5. D
6. B
7. B
8. D
9. D
10. D
11. A
12. D
13. A
14. D
15. A
16. A
17. B
18. C
19. A
20. C
21. B
22. B
23. C
24. B
25. A

PREPARING WRITTEN MATERIAL

PARAGRAPH REARRANGEMENT COMMENTARY

The sentences which follow are in scrambled order. You are to rearrange them in proper order and indicate the letter choice containing the correct answer at the space at the right.

Each group of sentences in this section is actually a paragraph presented in scrambled order. Each sentence in the group has a place in that paragraph; no sentence is to be left out. You are to read each group of sentences and decide upon the best order in which to put the sentences so as to form as well-organized paragraph.

The questions in this section measure the ability to solve a problem when all the facts relevant to its solution are not given.

More specifically, certain positions of responsibility and authority require the employee to discover connections between events sometimes, apparently, unrelated. In order to do this, the employee will find it necessary to correctly infer that unspecified events have probably occurred or are likely to occur. This ability becomes especially important when action must be taken on incomplete information.

Accordingly, these questions require competitors to choose among several suggested alternatives, each of which presents a different sequential arrangement of the events. Competitors must choose the MOST logical of the suggested sequences.

In order to do so, they may be required to draw on general knowledge to infer missing concepts or events that are essential to sequencing the given events. Competitors should be careful to infer only what is essential to the sequence. The plausibility of the wrong alternatives will always require the inclusion of unlikely events or of additional chains of events which are NOT essential to sequencing the given events.

It's very important to remember that you are looking for the best of the four possible choices, and that the best choice of all may not even be one of the answers you're given to choose from.

There is no one right way to solve these problems. Many people have found it helpful to first write out the order of the sentences, as they would have arranged them, on their scrap paper before looking at the possible answers. If their optimum answer is there, this can save them some time. If it isn't, this method can still give insight into solving the problem. Others find it most helpful to just go through each of the possible choices, contrasting each as they go along. You should use whatever method feels comfortable, and works, for you.

While most of these types of questions are not that difficult, we've added a higher percentage of the difficult type, just to give you more practice. Usually there are only one or two questions on this section that contain such subtle distinctions that you're unable to answer confidently, and you then may find yourself stuck deciding between two possible choices, neither of which you're sure about.

EXAMINATION SECTION
TEST 1

DIRECTIONS: The sentences that follow are in scrambled order. You are to rearrange them in proper order and indicate the letter choice containing the correct answer. *PRINT THE LETTER OF THE CORRECT ANSWER IN THE SPACE AT THE RIGHT.*

1. Below are four statements labeled W., X., Y., and Z. 1.____
   - W. He was a strict and fanatic drillmaster.
   - X. The word is always used in a derogatory sense and generally shows resentment and anger on the part of the user.
   - Y. It is from the name of this Frenchman that we derive our English word, martinet.
   - Z. Jean Martinet was the Inspector-General of Infantry during the reign of King Louis XIV.

   The *PROPER* order in which these sentences should be placed in a paragraph is:

   A. X, Z, W, Y B. X, Z, Y, W C. Z, W, Y, X D. Z, Y, W, X

2. In the following paragraph, the sentences which are numbered, have been jumbled. 2.____
   1. Since then it has undergone changes.
   2. It was incorporated in 1955 under the laws of the State of New York.
   3. Its primary purpose, a cleaner city, has, however, remained the same.
   4. The Citizens Committee works in cooperation with the Mayor's Inter-departmental Committee for a Clean City.

   The order in which these sentences should be arranged to form a well-organized paragraph is:

   A. 2, 4, 1, 3 B. 3, 4, 1, 2 C. 4, 2, 1, 3 D. 4, 3, 2, 1

Questions 3-5.

DIRECTIONS: The sentences listed below are part of a meaningful paragraph but they are not given in their proper order. You are to decide what would be the *best order* in which to put the sentences so as to form a well-organized paragraph. Each sentence has a place in the paragraph; there are no extra sentences. You are then to answer questions 3 to 5 inclusive on the basis of your rearrangements of these secrambled sentences into a properly organized paragraph.

In 1887 some insurance companies organized an Inspection Department to advise their clients on all phases of fire prevention and protection. Probably this has been due to the smaller annual fire losses in Great Britain than in the United States. It tests various fire prevention devices and appliances and determines manufacturing hazards and their safeguards. Fire research began earlier in the United States and is more advanced than in Great Britain. Later they established a laboratory specializing in electrical, mechanical, hydraulic, and chemical fields.

3. When the five sentences are arranged in proper order, the paragraph starts with the sentence which begins 3.____

A. "In 1887..."
B. "Probably this ..."
C. "It tests ..."
D. "Fire research ..."
E. "Later they ..."

4. In the last sentence listed above, "they" refers to 4.____

A. insurance companies
B. the United States and Great Britain
C. the Inspection Department
D. clients
E. technicians

5. When the above paragraph is properly arranged, it ends with the words 5.____

A. "... and protection."
B. "... the United States."
C. "... their safeguards."
D. "... in Great Britain."
E. "... chemical fields."

KEY (CORRECT ANSWERS)

1. C
2. C
3. D
4. A
5. C

TEST 2

DIRECTIONS: In each of the questions numbered 1 through 5, several sentences are given. For each question, choose as your answer the group of numbers that represents the *most logical* order of these sentences if they were arranged in paragraph form. *PRINT THE LETTER OF THE CORRECT ANSWER IN THE SPACE AT THE RIGHT.*

1. 1. It is established when one shows that the landlord has prevented the tenant's enjoyment of his interest in the property leased. 1.____
   2. Constructive eviction is the result of a breach of the covenant of quiet enjoyment implied in all leases.
   3. In some parts of the United States, it is not complete until the tenant vacates within a reasonable time.
   4. Generally, the acts must be of such serious and permanent character as to deny the tenant the enjoyment of his possessing rights.
   5. In this event, upon abandonment of the premises, the tenant's liability for that ceases.

   The CORRECT answer is:

   A. 2, 1, 4, 3, 5   B. 5, 2, 3, 1, 4   C. 4, 3, 1, 2, 5
   D. 1, 3, 5, 4, 2

2. 1. The powerlessness before private and public authorities that is the typical experience of the slum tenant is reminiscent of the situation of blue-collar workers all through the nineteenth century. 2.____
   2. Similarly, in recent years, this chapter of history has been reopened by anti-poverty groups which have attempted to organize slum tenants to enable them to bargain collectively with their landlords about the conditions of their tenancies.
   3. It is familiar history that many of the workers remedied their condition by joining together and presenting their demands collectively.
   4. Like the workers, tenants are forced by the conditions of modern life into substantial dependence on these who possess great political arid economic power.
   5. What's more, the very fact of dependence coupled with an absence of education and self-confidence makes them hesitant and unable to stand up for what they need from those in power.

   The CORRECT answer is:

   A. 5, 4, 1, 2, 3   B. 2, 3, 1, 5, 4   C. 3, 1, 5, 4, 2
   D. 1, 4, 5, 3, 2

3. 1. A railroad, for example, when not acting as a common carrier may contract; away responsibility for its own negligence. 3.____
   2. As to a landlord, however, no decision has been found relating to the legal effect of a clause shifting the statutory duty of repair to the tenant.
   3. The courts have not passed on the validity of clauses relieving the landlord of this duty and liability.
   4. They have, however, upheld the validity of exculpatory clauses in other types of contracts.
   5. Housing regulations impose a duty upon the landlord to maintain leased premises in safe condition.

6. As another example, a bailee may limit his liability except for gross negligence, willful acts, or fraud.

The CORRECT answer is:

A. 2, 1, 6, 4, 3, 5 B. 1, 3, 4, 5, 6, 2 C. 3, 5, 1, 4, 2, 6
D. 5, 3, 4, 1, 6, 2

4. 1. Since there are only samples in the building, retail or consumer sales are generally eschewed by mart occupants, and,in some instances, rigid controls are maintained to limit entrance to the mart only to those persons engaged in retailing. 4.____
2. Since World War I, in many larger cities, there has developed a new type of property, called the mart building.
3. It can, therefore, be used by wholesalers and jobbers for the display of sample merchandise.
4. This type of building is most frequently a multi-storied, finished interior property which is a cross between a retail arcade and a loft building.
5. This limitation enables the mart occupants to ship the orders from another location after the retailer or dealer makes his selection from the samples.

The CORRECT answer is:

A. 2, 4, 3, 1, 5 B. 4, 3, 5, 1, 2 C. 1, 3, 2, 4, 5
D. 1, 4, 2, 3, 5

5. 1. In general, staff-line friction reduces the distinctive contribution of staff personnel. 5.____
2. The conflicts, however, introduce an uncontrolled element into the managerial system.
3. On the other hand, the natural resistance of the line to staff innovations probably usefully restrains over-eager efforts to apply untested procedures on a large scale.
4. Under such conditions, it is difficult to know when valuable ideas are being sacrificed.
5. The relatively weak position of staff, requiring accommodation to the line, tends to restrict their ability to engage .in free, experimental innovation.

The CORRECT answer is:

A. 4, 2, 3, 1, 3 B. 1, 5, 3, 2, 4 C. 5, 3, 1, 2, 4
D. 2, 1, 4, 5, 3

KEY (CORRECT ANSWERS)

1. A
2. D
3. D
4. A
5. B

TEST 3

DIRECTIONS: Questions 1 through 4 consist of six sentences which can be arranged in a logical sequence. For each question, select the choice which places the numbered sentences in the *most logical* sequence. *PRINT THE LETTER OF THE CORRECT ANSWER IN THE SPACE AT THE RIGHT.*

1. 1.____
   1. The burden of proof as to each issue is determined before trial and remains upon the same party throughout the trial.
   2. The jury is at liberty to believe one witness' testimony as against a number of contradictory witnesses.
   3. In a civil case, the party bearing the burden of proof is required to prove his contention by a fair preponderance of the evidence.
   4. However, it must be noted that a fair preponderance of evidence does not necessarily mean a greater number of witnesses.
   5. The burden of proof is the burden which rests upon one of the parties to an action to persuade the trier of the facts, generally the jury, that a proposition he asserts is true.
   6. If the evidence is equally balanced, or if it leaves the jury in such doubt as to be unable to decide the controversy either way, judgment must be given against the party upon whom the burden of proof rests.

   The CORRECT answer is:

   A. 3, 2, 5, 4, 1, 6
   B. 1, 2, 6, 5, 3, 4
   C. 3, 4, 5, 1, 2, 6
   D. 5, 1, 3, 6, 4, 2

2. 2.____
   1. If a parent is without assets and is unemployed, he cannot be convicted of the crime of non-support of a child.
   2. The term "sufficient ability" has been held to mean sufficient financial ability.
   3. It does not matter if his unemployment is by choice or unavoidable circumstances.
   4. If he fails to take any steps at all, he may be liable to prosecution for endangering the welfare of a child.
   5. Under the penal law, a parent is responsible for the support of his minor child only if the parent is "of sufficient ability."
   6. An indigent parent may meet his obligation by borrowing money or by seeking aid under the provisions of the Social Welfare Law.

   The CORRECT answer is:

   A. 6, 1, 5, 3, 2, 4
   B. 1, 3, 5, 2, 4, 6
   C. 5, 2, 1, 3, 6, 4
   D. 1, 6, 4, 5, 2, 3

3. 1. Consider, for example, the case of a rabble rouser who urges a group of twenty people to go out and break the windows of a nearby factory. 3.____
2. Therefore, the law fills the indicated gap with the crime of inciting to riot."
3. A person is considered guilty of inciting to riot when he urges ten or more persons to engage in tumultuous and violent conduct of a kind likely to create public alarm.
4. However, if he has not obtained the cooperation of at least four people, he cannot be charged with unlawful assembly.
5. The charge of inciting to riot was added to the law to cover types of conduct which cannot be classified as either the crime of "riot" or the crime of "unlawful assembly."
6. If he acquires the acquiescence of at least four of them, he is guilty of unlawful assembly even if the project does not materialize.

The CORRECT answer is:

A. 3, 5, 1, 6, 4, 2 B. 5, 1, 4, 6, 2, 3 C. 3, 4, 1, 5, 2, 6
D. 5, 1, 4, 6, 3, 2

4. 1. If, however, the rebuttal evidence presents an issue of credibility, it is for the jury to determine whether the presumption has, in fact, been destroyed. 4.____
2. Once sufficient evidence to the contrary is introduced, the presumption disappears from the trial.
3. The effect of a presumption is to place the burden upon the adversary to come forward with evidence to rebut the presumption.
4. When a presumption is overcome and ceases to exist in the case, the fact or facts which gave rise to the presumption still remain.
5. Whether a presumption has been overcome is ordinarily a question for the court.
6. Such information may furnish a basis for a logical inference.

The CORRECT answer is:

A. 4, 6, 2, 5, 1, 3 B. 3, 2, 5, 1, 4, 6 C. 5, 3, 6, 4, 2, 1
D. 5, 4, 1, 2, 6, 3

KEY (CORRECT ANSWERS)

1. D
2. C
3. A
4. B

PREPARING WRITTEN MATERIAL

EXAMINATION SECTION
TEST 1

DIRECTIONS: Each of Questions 1 through 5 consists of a sentence which may or may not be an example of good formal English usage.

Examine each sentence, considering grammar, punctuation, spelling, capitalization, and awkwardness. Then choose the correct statement about it from the four options below it.

If the English usage in the sentence given is better than any of the changes suggested in options B, C, or D, pick option A. (Do not pick an option that will change the meaning of the sentence.

1. I don't know who could possibly of broken it. 1.____

    A. This is an example of good formal English usage.
    B. The word "who" should be replaced by the word "whom."
    C. The word "of" should be replaced by the word "have."
    D. The word "broken" should be replaced by the word "broke."

2. Telephoning is easier than to write. 2.____

    A. This is an example of good formal English usage.
    B. The word "telephoning" should be spelled "telephoneing."
    C. The word "than" should be replaced by the word "then."
    D. The words "to write" should be replaced by the word "writing."

3. The two operators who have been assigned to these consoles are on vacation. 3.____

    A. This is an example of good formal English usage.
    B. A comma should be placed after the word "operators."
    C. The word "who" should be replaced by the word "whom."
    D. The word "are" should be replaced by the word "is."

4. You were suppose to teach me how to operate a plugboard. 4.____

    A. This is an example of good formal English usage.
    B. The word "were" should be replaced by the word "was."
    C. The word "suppose" should be replaced by the word "supposed."
    D. The word "teach" should be replaced by the word "learn."

5. If you had taken my advice; you would have spoken with him. 5.____

    A. This is an example of good formal English usage.
    B. The word "advice" should be spelled "advise."
    C. The words "had taken" should be replaced by the word "take."
    D. The semicolon should be changed to a comma.

KEY (CORRECT ANSWERS)

1. C
2. D
3. A
4. C
5. D

TEST 2

DIRECTIONS: Select the correct answer.

1. The *one* of the following sentences which is *MOST* acceptable from the viewpoint of correct grammatical usage is: 1.____

   A. I do not know which action will have worser results.
   B. tie should of known better.
   C. Both the officer on the scene, and his immediate supervisor, is charged with the responsibility.
   D. An officer must have initiative because his supervisor will not always be available to answer questions.

2. The *one* of the following sentences which is *MOST* acceptable from the viewpoint of correct grammatical usage is: 2.____

   A. Of all the officers available, the better one for the job will be picked.
   B. Strict orders were given to all the officers, except he.
   C. Study of the law will enable you to perform your duties more efficiently.
   D. It seems to me that you was wrong in failing to search the two men.

3. The *one* of the following sentences which does *NOT* contain a misspelled word is: 3.____

   A. The duties you will perform are similiar to the duties of a patrolman.
   B. Officers must be constantly alert to sieze the initiative.
   C. Officers in this organization are not entitled to special privileges.
   D. Any changes in procedure will be announced publically.

4. The *one* of the following sentences which does *NOT* contain a misspelled word is: 4.____

   A. It will be to your advantage to keep your firearm in good working condition.
   B. There are approximately fourty men on sick leave.
   C. Your first duty will be to pursuade the person to obey the law.
   D. Fires often begin in flameable material kept in lockers.

5. The *one* of the following sentences which does *NOT* contain a misspelled word is: 5.____

   A. Officers are not required to perform technical maintainance.
   B. He violated the regulations on two occasions.
   C. Every employee will be held responable for errors.
   D. This was his nineth absence in a year.

KEY (CORRECT ANSWERS)

1. D
2. C
3. C
4. A
5. B

TEST 3

DIRECTIONS: Select the correct answer.

1. You are answering a letter that was written on the letterhead of the ABC Company jind signed by James H. Wood, Treasurer. What is usually considered to be the correct salutation to use in your reply? 1.____

   A. Dear ABC Company:
   B. Dear Sirs:
   C. Dear Mr. Wood:
   D. Dear Mr. Treasurer:

2. Assume that one of your duties is to handle routine letters of inquiry from the public. The one of the following which is usually considered to be *MOST* desirable in replying to such a letter is a 2.____

   A. detailed answer handwritten on the original letter of inquiry
   B. phone call, since you can cover details more easily over the phone than in a letter
   C. *short letter giving the specific information requested*
   D. long letter discussing all possible aspects of the question raised

3. The *CHIEF* reason for dividing a letter into paragraphs is to 3.____

   A. make the message clear to the reader by starting a new paragraph for each new topic
   B. make a short letter occupy as much of the page as possible
   C. keep the reader's attention by providing a pause from time to time
   D. make the letter look neat and businesslike

4. Your superior has asked you to send an e-mail from your agency to a government agency in another city. He has written out the message and has indicated the name of the government agency.
   When you dictate the message to your secretary, which of the following items that your superior has *NOT* mentioned must you be sure to *include*? 4.____

   A. Today's date
   B. The full address of the government agency
   C. A polite opening such as "Dear Sirs"
   D. A final sentence such as "We would appreciate hearing from your agency in reply as soon as is convenient for you"

5. The one of the following sentence which is grammatically preferable to the others is: 5.____

   A. Our engineers will go over your blueprints so that you may have no problems in construction.
   B. For a long time he had been arguing that we, not he, are to blame for the confusion.
   C. I worked on this automobile for two hours and still cannot find out what is wrong with it.
   D. Accustomed to all kinds of hardships, fatigue seldom bothers veteran policemen.

KEY (CORRECT ANSWERS)

1. C
2. C
3. A
4. B
5. A

TEST 4

DIRECTIONS: Select the correct answer.

1. Suppose that an applicant for a job as snow laborer presents a letter from a former employer stating: "John Smith has a pleasing manner and never got into an argument with his fellow employees. He was never late or absent." This letter 1.____

   A. indicates that with some training Smith will make a good snow gang boss
   B. presents no definite evidence of Smith's ability to do snow work
   C. proves definitely that Smith has never done any snow work before
   D. proves definitely that Smith will do better than average work as a snow laborer

2. Suppose you must write a letter to a local organization in your section refusing a request in connection with collection of their refuse. 2.____
   You should *start* the letter by

   A. explaining in detail the consideration you gave the request
   B. praising the organization for its service to the community
   C. quoting the regulation which forbids granting the request
   D. stating your regret that the request cannot be granted

3. Suppose a citizen writes in for information as to whether or not he may sweep refuse into the gutter. A Sanitation officer answers as follows: 3.____
   Dear Sir:
   No person is permitted to litter, sweep, throw or cast, or direct, suffer or permit any person under his control to litter, sweep, throw or cast any ashes, garbage, paper, dust, or other rubbish or refuse into any public street or place, vacant lot, air shaft, areaway, backyard or court.

   Very truly yours,
   John Doe

   This letter is *poorly* written *CHIEFLY* because

   A. the opening is not indented
   B. the thought is not clear
   C. the tone is too formal and cold
   D. there are too many commas used

4. A section of a disciplinary report written by a Sanitation officer states: "It is requested that subject Sanitation man be advised that his future activities be directed towards reducing his recurrent tardiness else disciplinary action will be initiated which may result in summary discharge." This section of the report is *poorly* written *MAINLY* because 4.____

   A. at least one word is misspelled
   B. it is not simply expressed
   C. more than one idea is expressed
   D. the purpose is not stated

5. A section of a disciplinary report written by an officer states: “He comes in late. He takes too much time for lunch. He is lazy. I recommend his services be dispensed with.” This section of the report is *poorly* written *MAINLY* because 5.____

A. it ends with a preposition
B. it is not well organized
C. no supporting facts are stated
D. the sentences are too simple

KEY (CORRECT ANSWERS)

1. B
2. D
3. C
4. B
5. C

REPORT WRITING
EXAMINATION SECTION
TEST 1

DIRECTIONS: Each question or incomplete statement is followed by several suggested answers or completions. Select the one that BEST answers the question or completes the statement. *PRINT THE LETTER OF THE CORRECT ANSWER IN THE SPACE AT THE RIGHT.*

Questions 1-4.

DIRECTIONS: Answer Questions 1 through 4 on the basis of the following report which was prepared by a supervisor for inclusion in his agency's annual report.

On Oct. 13, I was assigned to study the salaries paid to clerical employees in various titles by the city and by private industry in the area.

In order to get the data I needed, I called Mr. Johnson at the Bureau of the Budget and the payroll officers at X Corp.–a brokerage house, Y Co.–an insurance company, and Z Inc.–a publishing firm. None of them was available and I had to call all of them again the next day.

When I finally got the information I needed, I drew up a chart, which is attached. Note that not all of the companies I contacted employed people at all the different levels used in the city service.

The conclusions I draw from analyzing this information is as follows: The city's entry-level salary is about average for the region; middle-level salaries are generally higher in the city government than in private industry; but salaries at the highest levels in private industry are better than city employees' pay.

1. Which of the following criticisms about the style in which this report is written is *most valid*? 1.____

   A. It is too informal.
   B. It is too concise.
   C. It is too choppy.
   D. The syntax is too complex.

2. Judging from the statements made in the report, the method followed by this employee in performing his research was 2.____

   A. *good;* he contacted a representative sample of businesses in the area
   B. *poor;* he should have drawn more definite conclusions
   C. *good;* he was persistent in collecting information
   D. *poor;* he did not make a thorough study

3. One sentence in this report contains a grammatical error. This sentence *begins* on line number 3.____

A. 4 B. 7 C. 10 D. 13

4. The type of information given in this report which should be presented in footnotes or in an appendix, is the 4.____

A. purpose of the study
B. specifics about the businesses contacted
C. reference to the chart
D. conclusions drawn by the author

5. The use of a graph to show statistical data in a report is *superior* to a table because it 5.____

A. features approximations
B. emphasizes facts and relationships more dramatically
C. C. presents data more accurately
D. is easily understood by the average reader

6. Of the following, the degree of formality required of a written report in tone is *most likely* to depend on the 6.____

A. subject matter of the report
B. frequency of its occurrence
C. amount of time available for its preparation
D. audience for whom the report is intended

7. Of the following, a distinguishing characteristic of a written report intended for the head of your agency as compared to a report prepared for a lower-echelon staff member, is that the report for the agency head should *usually* include 7.____

A. considerably more detail, especially statistical data
B. the essential details in an abbreviated form
C. all available source material
D. an annotated bibliography

8. Assume that you are asked to write a lengthy report for use by the administrator of your agency, the subject of which is "The Impact of Proposed New Data Processing Operations on Line Personnel" in your agency. You decide that the *most appropriate* type of report for you to prepare is an analytical report, including recommendations.
The MAIN reason for your decision is that 8.____

A. the subject of the report is extremely complex
B. large sums of money are involved
C. the report is being prepared for the administrator
D. you intend to include charts and graphs

9. Assume that you are preparing a report based on a survey dealing with the attitudes of employees in Division X regarding proposed new changes in compensating employees for working overtime. Three per cent of the respondents to the survey voluntarily offer an unfavorable opinion on the method of assigning overtime work, a question not specifically asked of the employees. 9.____
On the basis of this information, the *most appropriate* and *significant* of the following comments for you to make in the report with regard to employees' attitudes on assigning overtime work, is that

A. an insignificant percentage of employees dislike the method of assigning overtime work
B. three per cent of the employees in Division X dislike the method of assigning overtime work
C. three per cent of the sample selected for the survey voiced an unfavorable opinion on the method of assigning overtime work
D. some employees voluntarily voiced negative feelings about the method of assigning overtime work, making it impossible to determine the extent of this attitude

10. A supervisor should be able to prepare a report that is well-written and unambiguous. Of the following sentences that might appear in a report, select the one which communicates *most clearly* the intent of its author. 10.____

A. When your subordinates speak to a group of people, they should be well-informed.
B. When he asked him to leave, SanMan King told him that he would refuse the request.
C. Because he is a good worker, Foreman Jefferson assigned Assistant Foreman D'Agostino to replace him.
D. Each of us is responsible for the actions of our subordinates.

11. In some reports, especially longer ones, a list of the resources (books, papers, magazines, etc.) used to prepare it is included. This list is called the 11.____

A. accreditation
B. bibliography
C. summary
D. glossary

12. Reports are usually divided into several sections, some of which are more necessary than others. 12.____
Of the following, the section which is ABSOLUTELY necessary to include in a report is

A. a table of contents
B. the body
C. an index
D. a bibliography

13. Suppose you are writing a report on an interview you have just completed with a particularly hostile applicant. Which of the following BEST describes what you should include in this report? 13.____

A. What you think caused the applicant's hostile attitude during the interview
B. Specific examples of the applicant's hostile remarks and behavior
C. The relevant information uncovered during the interview
D. A recommendation that the applicant's request be denied because of his hostility

14. When including recommendations in a report to your supervisor, which of the following is MOST important for you to do? 14._

A. Provide several alternative courses of action for each recommendation
B. First present the supporting evidence, then the recommendations
C. First present the recommendations, then the supporting evidence
D. Make sure the recommendations arise logically out of the information in the report

15. It is often necessary that the writer of a report present facts and sufficient arguments to gain acceptance of the points, conclusions, or recommendations set forth in the report. 15._
Of the following, the LEAST advisable step to take in organizing a report, when such argumentation is the important factor, is a(n)

A. elaborate expression of personal belief
B. businesslike discussion of the problem as a whole
C. orderly arrangement of convincing data
D. reasonable explanation of the primary issues

16. In some types of reports, visual aids add interest, meaning, and support. They also provide an essential means of effectively communicating the message of the report. 16._
Of the following, the selection of the suitable visual aids to use with a report is LEAST dependent on the

A. nature and scope of the report
B. way in which the aid is to be used
C. aids used in other reports
D. prospective readers of the report

17. Visual aids used in a report may be placed either in the text material or in the appendix. 17._
Deciding where to put a chart, table, or any such aid *should* depend on the

A. title of the report
B. purpose of the visual aid
C. title of the visual aid
D. length of the report

18. A report is often revised several times before final preparation and distribution in an effort to make certain the report meets the needs of the situation for which it is designed. 18._
Which of the following is the BEST way for the author to be sure that a report covers the areas he intended?

A. Obtain a co-worker's opinion
B. Compare it with a content checklist
C. Test it on a subordinate
D. Check his bibliography

19. In which of the following situations is an oral report preferable to a written report? When a(n) 19._

A. recommendation is being made for a future plan of action
B. department head requests immediate information
C. long standing policy change is made
D. analysis of complicated statistical data is involved

20. When an applicant is approved, the supervisor must fill in standard forms with certain information. 20.____
The GREATEST advantage of using standard forms in this situation rather than having the supervisor write the report as he sees fit, is that

A. the report can be acted on quickly
B. the report can be written without directions from a supervisor
C. needed information is less likely to be left out of the report
D. information that is written up this way is more likely to be verified

21. Assume that it is part of your job to prepare a monthly report for your unit head that eventually goes to the director. The report contains information on the number of applicants you have interviewed that have been approved and the number of applicants you have interviewed that have been turned down. 21.____
Errors on such reports are serious because

A. you are expected to be able to prove how many applicants you have interviewed each month
B. accurate statistics are needed for effective management of the department
C. they may not be discovered before the report is transmitted to the director
D. they may result in loss to the applicants left out of the report

22. The frequency with which job reports are submitted should depend MAINLY on 22.____

A. how comprehensive the report has to be
B. the amount of information in the report
C. the availability of an experienced man to write the report
D. the importance of changes in the information included in the report

23. The CHIEF purpose in preparing an outline for a report is *usually* to insure that 23.____

A. the report will be grammatically correct
B. every point will be given equal emphasis
C. principal and secondary points will be properly integrated
D. the language of the report will be of the same level and include the same technical terms

24. The MAIN reason for requiring written job reports is to 24.____

A. avoid the necessity of oral orders
B. develop better methods of doing the work
C. provide a permanent record of what was done
D. increase the amount of work that can be done

25. Assume you are recommending in a report to your supervisor that a radical change in a standard maintenance procedure should be adopted. 25.____
Of the following, the MOST important information to be included in this report is

A. a list of the reasons for making this change
B. the names of others who favor the change
C. a complete description of the present procedure
D. amount of training time needed for the new procedure

KEY (CORRECT ANSWERS)

1. A
2. D
3. D
4. B
5. B

6. D
7. B
8. A
9. D
10. D

11. B
12. B
13. C
14. D
15. A

16. C
17. B
18. B
19. B
20. C

21. B
22. D
23. C
24. C
25. A

TEST 2

DIRECTIONS: Each question or incomplete statement is followed by several suggested answers or completions. Select the one that BEST answers the question or completes the statement. *PRINT THE LETTER OF THE CORRECT ANSWER IN THE SPACE AT THE RIGHT.*

1. It is often necessary that the writer of a report present facts and sufficient arguments to gain acceptance of the points, conclusions, or recommendations set forth in the report. Of the following, the LEAST advisable step to take in organizing a report, when such argumentation is the important factor, is a(n) 1.____

   A. elaborate expression of personal belief
   B. businesslike discussion of the problem as a whole
   C. orderly arrangement of convincing data
   D. reasonable explanation of the primary issues

2. Of the following, the factor which is generally considered to be LEAST characteristic of a good control report is that it 2.____

   A. stresses performance that adheres to standard rather than emphasizing the exception
   B. supplies information intended to serve as the basis for corrective action
   C. provides feedback for the planning process
   D. includes data that reflect trends as well as current status

3. An administrative assistant has been asked by his superior to write a concise, factual report with objective conclusions and recommendations based on facts assembled by other researchers.
   Of the following factors, the administrative assistant should give LEAST consideratio to 3.____

   A. the educational level of the person or persons for whom the report is being prepared
   B. the use to be made of the report
   C. the complexity of the problem
   D. his own feelings about the importance of the problem

4. When making a written report, it is often recommended that the findings or conclusions be presented near the beginning of the report.
   Of the following, the MOST important reason for doing this is that it 4.____

   A. facilitates organizing the material clearly
   B. assures that all the topics will be covered
   C. avoids unnecessary repetition of ideas
   D. prepares the reader for the facts that will follow

5. You have been asked to write a report on methods of hiring and training new employees. Your report is going to be about ten pages long.
   For the convenience of your readers, a brief summary of your findings *should* 5.____

   A. appear at the beginning of your report
   B. be appended to the report as a postscript
   C. be circulated in a separate memo
   D. be inserted in tabular form in the middle of your report

6. In preparing a report, the MAIN reason for writing an outline is *usually* to 6.___

   A. help organize thoughts in a logical sequence
   B. provide a guide for the typing of the report
   C. allow the ultimate user to review the report in advance
   D. ensure that the report is being prepared on schedule

7. The one of the following which is *most appropriate* as a reason for including footnotes in a report is to 7.___

   A. correct capitalization
   B. delete passages
   C. improve punctuation
   D. cite references

8. A completed formal report may contain all of the following EXCEPT 8.___

   A. a synopsis
   B. a preface
   C. marginal notes
   D. bibliographical references

9. Of the following, the MAIN use of proofreaders' marks is to 9.___

   A. explain corrections to be made
   B. indicate that a manuscript has been read and approved
   C. let the reader know who proofread the report
   D. indicate the format of the report

10. Informative, readable and concise reports have been found to observe the following rules: 10.___

    Rule I. Keep the report short and easy to understand.
    Rule II. Vary the length of sentences.
    Rule III. Vary the style of sentences so that, for example, they are not all just sub ject-verb, subject-verb.

    Consider this hospital laboratory report: The experiment was started in January. The apparatus was put together in six weeks. At that time the synthesizing process was begun. The synthetic chemicals were separated. Then they were used in tests on patients.

    Which one of the following choices MOST accurately classifies the above rules into those which are *violated* by this report and those which are *not*?

    A. II is violated, but I and III are not.
    B. III is violated, but I and II are not.
    C. II and III are violated, but I is not.
    D. I, II, and III are violated.

Questions 11-13.

DIRECTIONS: Questions 11 through 13 are based on the following example of a report. The report consists of eight numbered sentences, some of which are not consistent with the principles of good report writing.

(1) I interviewed Mrs. Loretta Crawford in Room 424 of County Hospital. (2) She had collapsed on the street and been brought into emergency. (3) She is an attractive woman with many friends judging by the cards she had received. (4) She did not know what her husband's last job had been, or what their present income was. (5) The first thing that Mrs. Crawford said was that she had never worked and that her husband was presently unemployed. (6) She did not know if they had any medical coverage or if they could pay the bill. (7) She said that her husband could not be reached by telephone but that he would be in to see her that afternoon. (8) I left word at the nursing station to be called when he arrived.

11. A good report should be arranged in logical order. Which of the following sentences from the report does NOT appear in its proper sequence in the report? Sentence 11._____

A. 1 B. 4 C. 7 D. 8

12. Only material that is relevant to the main thought of a report should be included. Which of the following sentences from the report contains material which is LEAST relevant to this report? Sentence 12._____

A. 3 B. 4 C. 6 D. 8

13. Reports should include all essential information. Of the following, the MOST important fact that is *missing* from this report is: 13._____

A. Who was involved in the interview
B. What was discovered at the interview
C. When the interview took place
D. Where the interview took place

Questions 14-15.

DIRECTIONS: Each of Questions 14 and 15 consists of four numbered sentences which constitute a paragraph in a report. They are not in the right order. Choose the numbered arrangement appearing after letter A, B, C, or D which is MOST logical and which BEST expresses the thought of the paragraph.

14. 14._____
I. Congress made the commitment explicit in the Housing Act of 1949, establishing as a national goal the realization of a decent home and suitable environment for every American family.
II. The result has been that the goal of decent home and suitable environment is still as far distant as ever for the disadvantaged urban family.
III. In spite of this action by Congress, federal housing programs have continued to be fragmented and grossly under-funded.
IV. The passage of the National Housing Act signaled a new federal commitment to provide housing for the nation's citizens.

A. I, IV, III, II
B. IV, I, III, II
C. IV, I, II, III
D. II, IV, I, III

15. I. The greater expense does not necessarily involve "exploitation," but it is often perceived as exploitative and unfair by those who are aware of the price differences involved, but unaware of operating costs. 15.____
II. Ghetto residents believe they are "exploited" by local merchants, and evidence substantiates some of these beliefs.
III. However, stores in low-income areas were more likely to be small independents, which could not achieve the economies available to supermarket chains and were, therefore, more likely to charge higher prices, and the customers were more likely to buy smaller-sized packages which are more expensive per unit of measure.
IV. A study conducted in one city showed that distinctly higher prices were charged for goods sold in ghetto stores than in other areas.

A. IV, II, I, III
B. IV, I, III, II
C. II, IV, III, I
D. II, III, IV, I

16. In organizing data to be presented in a formal report, the FIRST of the following steps should be 16.____

A. determining the conclusions to be drawn
B. establishing the time sequence of the data
C. sorting and arranging like data into groups
D. evaluating how consistently the data support the recommendations

17. All reports should be prepared with *at least* one copy so that 17.____

A. there is one copy for your file
B. there is a copy for your supervisor
C. the report can be sent to more than one person
D. the person getting the report can forward a copy to someone else

18. Before turning in a report of an investigation he has made, a supervisor discovers some additional information he did not include in this report. 18.____
Whether he rewrites this report to include this additional information should PRIMARILY depend on the

A. importance of the report itself
B. number of people who will eventually review this report
C. established policy covering the subject matter of the report
D. bearing this new information has on the conclusions of the report

KEY (CORRECT ANSWERS)

1.	A	11.	B
2.	A	12.	A
3.	D	13.	C
4.	D	14.	B
5.	A	15.	C
6.	A	16.	C
7.	D	17.	A
8.	C	18.	D
9.	A		
10.	C		

TRENDS IN HOUSING

CONTENTS

TRENDS IN HOUSING

Members of countless communities throughout America are raising critical questions about the adequacy and effectiveness of local housing code enforcement programs. These critics feel deep concern over the fact that 1966 found "some four million urban families living in homes of such disrepair as to violate decent housing standards." For this reason, they insist everything possible be done to guarantee that present and future inspection efforts lead to rapid and adequate upgrading of the substandard but salvageable housing in each community and that the neighborhoods be made more desirable places in which to live.

In order to meet these demands effectively, inspectors of housing and their supervisors should first acquaint themselves with the origin of public concern about housing problems; the past, present, and new approaches to housing code administration; the expanded role of the inspection function in the neighborhood improvement effort; and the general nature of their role and responsibilities

I. The History of Housing

The first public policies on housing in this country were established during the Colonial period. Many of the early settlers built houses with wooden chimneys and thatched roofs which were the causes of frequent fires. Consequently, several of the colonies passed regulations prohibiting these. One of the first was the Plymouth Colony, which in 1626 passed a law stipulating that new houses should not be thatched but roofed with either board or pale and the like. In 1648 wooden or plastered chimneys were prohibited on new houses in New Amsterdam, and chimneys on existing houses were decreed to be inspected regularly. In Charlestown in 1740, following a disastrous fire, the general assembly passed an act that declared that all buildings should be of brick or stone, that all "tall" wooded houses must be pulled down by 1745, and that the use of wood was to be confined to window frames, shutters, and to exterior work. This law was obviously unenforceable because, as we learn from other publications during that period, more Charlestown houses were made of timber than of brick.

Social control over housing was exerted in other ways. Early settlers in Pennsylvania frequently dug caves out of the banks of the Delaware River and used these as primitive-type dwellings. Some of these shelters were still in use as late as 1687 when the Provincial Council ordered inhabitants to provide for themselves other habitations, in order to have the said caves or houses destroyed. In some New England communities, around the turn of the 18th century, standards were raised considerably higher by local ordinances. In East Greenwich, it had been the custom to build houses 14 feet square with posts 9 feet high; in 1727 the town voted that houses shall be built 18 feet square with-posts 15 feet high with chimneys of stone or brick as before.

During the early days of this country, basic sanitation was very poor, primarily because outdoor privies served as the general means of sewage disposal. The principal problems created by the use of these privies involved their nearness to the streets and their easy accessibility to hogs and goats. In 1652, Boston prohibited the building of privies within 12 feet of the street. The Dutch of New Amsterdam in 1657 prohibited the throwing of rubbish and filth into the streets or canal and required the householders to keep the streets clean and orderly.

After the early Colonial period we pass into an era of very rapid metropolitan growth along the eastern seashore. This growth was due largely to the immigration of people from Europe. Frequently these immigrants arrived without money or jobs and were forced to move in with friends or relatives. This led to severe overcrowding. Most of the information available pertains to New York City, because the situation there was worse than that in any other city in the country. It received the majority of the immigrants, many of whom were unable to move beyond the city. The most serious housing problems began in New York about 1840 when the first tenements were built. These provided such substandard housing and such unhealthy, crowded living conditions that a social reform movement was imminent in New York.

During the early part of the 19th century, the only housing control authority was that vested in the fire wardens, whose objective was to prevent fires, and the health wardens, who were charged with the enforcement of general sanitation. In 1867, with the passing of the Tenement Housing Act, New York City began to face the problem of substandard housing. This law represented the first comprehensive legislation of its kind in this country. The principal features of the act are summarized as follows: for every room occupied for sleeping in a tenement or lodging house, if it does not communicate directly with the external air, a ventilating or transom window to the neighboring room or hall; a proper fire escape on every tenement or lodging house; the roof to be kept in repair and the stairs to have bannisters; water closets or privies – at least one to every twenty occupants for all such houses; after July 1, 1867, permits for occupancy of every cellar not previously occupied as a dwelling; cleansing of every lodging house to the satisfaction of the Board of Health, which is to have access at any time; reporting of all cases of infectious disease to the Board by the owner or his agent; inspection and, if necessary, disinfection of such houses; and vacation of buildings found to be out of repair. There were also regulations governing distances between buildings, heights of rooms, and dimensions of windows. The terms "tenement house," "lodging house," and "cellar" were defined.

Although this act had some beneficial influences on overcrowding, sewage disposal, lighting, and ventilation, it did not correct the evils of crowding on lots and did not provide for adequate ventilation for inner rooms. In 1879, a second tenement act, amending the first, was passed adding restrictions on the amount of lot coverage and providing for a window opening of at least 12 square feet in every room. Several attempts in 1882, 1884, and 1895 were made to amend this original act and provide for occupancy standards, but they were relatively unenforceable. While these numerous acts remedied only slightly the serious problems of the tenements, they did show the city's acknowledgment of the problems. This public acknowledgment, however, was seldom shared by the owners of the tenements, or, in some cases, by the courts. The most famous case, in 1892, involved Trinity Church, at that time one of the largest owners of tenements in New York City. In the case, the City of New York accused Trinity Church of violating provisions of the Act of 1882 by failing to provide running water on every floor of its buildings. A district court levied a fine of $200 against the Church, which in turn appealed to the Court of Common Pleas to have the law set aside as unconstitutional. Incredibly, the court agreed unanimously to uphold the landlord's position, stating there is no evidence nor can the court judicially know that the presence and distribution of water on the several floors will conduce to the health of the occupants ... there is no necessity for legislative compulsion on a landlord to distribute water through the stories of his building; since if tenants require it, self-interest and the rivalry of competition are sufficient to secure it ... now, if it be competent for the legislature to impose an expense upon a landlord in order that tenants be furnished with water in their rooms instead of in the yard or basement, at what point must this police power pause? ... a conclusion contrary to the present decision would involve the essential principle of that species of socialism under the regime of which the individual disappears and is absorbed by a collective being called the 'state', a principle utterly repugnant to the spirit of our political system and necessarily fatal to our form of liberty. Fortunately, 3 years later, the city health department was granted an appeal from the court order, and eventually the constitutionality of the law was upheld.

Jacob A. Riis, Lawrence Veiller, and others did much during this period to champion the cause of better living conditions. Their efforts resulted in the Tenement House Act of 1901, a milestone in housing and an extremely comprehensive document for its time. It began with concise definitions of certain terms that were to become important in court actions. It contained provisions for protection from fire, requiring that every tenement erected thereafter, and exceeding 60 feet in height, should be fireproof. In addition, there were specific provisions regarding fire escapes on both new and existing houses. More light and ventilation were required; coverage was restricted to not more than 70 percent on interior lots and 90 percent on corner lots. There were special provisions governing rear yards, inner courts, and buildings on the same lot with the tenement house. At least one window of specified dimensions was required for every room, including the bathroom. Minimum size of rooms was specified as were certain characteristics for public halls. Significantly included were provisions concerning planning for the individual apartments in order to assure privacy. One of the most important provisions of the Tenement Act was the requirement for running water and water closets in each apartment in new tenement houses. Special attention was given to basements and cellars, the law requiring not only that they be damp-proof but also that permits be obtained before they were occupied. One novel section of this act prohibited the use of any part of the building as a house of prostitution.

The basic principles and methodology established in the Tenement Act of 1901 still underlie much of the housing efforts in New York City today. Philadelphia, a city that can be compared with New York from the standpoint of age, was fortunate to have farsighted leaders in its early stage of development. Since 1909, with the establishment of the Philadelphia Housing Association, the city has had almost continual inspection and improvement.

Although Chicago is approximately two centuries younger than New York, it enacted housing legislation as early as 1889 and health legislation as early as 1881. Regulations on ventilation, light, drainage, and plumbing of dwellings were put into effect in 1896. Many of the structures, however, were built of wood, were dilapidated, and constituted serious fire hazards.

Before 1892, all government involvement in housing was at a local level. In 1892, however, the Federal Government passed a resolution authorizing investigation of slum conditions in cities containing 200,000 or more inhabitants. At that time these included the cities of Baltimore, Boston, Brooklyn, Buffalo, Chicago, Cincinnati, Cleveland, Detroit, Milwaukee, New Orleans, New York, Philadelphia, Pittsburgh, St. Louis, San Francisco, and Washington. Much controversy surrounded the involvement of the Federal Government in housing. The Commissioner of Labor was forced to write an extensive legal opinion concerning the constitutionality of expenditures by the Federal Government in this area. The result was that Congress appropriated only $20,000 to cover the expenses of this project. The lack of funds limited actual investigations to Baltimore, Chicago, New York, and Philadelphia and did not cover housing conditions in toto within these cities. Facts obtained from the investigation were very broad, covering items such as the number of saloons per number of inhabitants, number of arrests, distribution of males and females, proportion of foreign-born inhabitants, degree of illiteracy, kinds of occupations of the residents, conditions of their health, their earnings, and the number of voters.

The 20th century started off rather poorly in the area of housing. No significant housing legislation was passed until 1929 when the New York State legislature passed its Multiple Dwelling Law. This law continued the Tenement Act of New York City but replaced many provisions of the 1901 law with less strict requirements. Other cities and states followed New York State's example and permitted less strict requirements in their codes. This decreased what little emphasis there was in enforcement of building laws so that during the 1920's the cities had worked themselves into a very poor state of housing. Conditions in America declined to such a state by the 30's that President Franklin D. Roosevelt's shocking report to the people was "that one-third of the nation is ill-fed, ill-housed, and ill-clothed." With this the Federal Government launched itself extensively into the field of housing. The first Federal housing law was passed in

1934. One of the purposes of this act was to create a sounder mortgage system through the provision of a permanent system of government insurance for residential mortgages. The Federal Housing Administration was created to carry out the objectives of this act. Many other Federal laws followed: the Veterans Administration becoming involved in guaranteeing of loans, the Home Loan Bank Board, Federal National Mortgage Association, Communities Facilities Administration, Public Housing Administration, and the Public Works Administration. With the U.S. Housing Act of 1937, the Federal Government entered the area of slum clearance and urban renewal, requiring one slum dwelling to be eliminated for every new unit built under the Housing Administration program. It was not until the passage of the Housing Act of 1949 that the Federal Government entered into slum clearance on a comprehensive basis.

The many responsibilities in housing administered by various agencies within the Federal Government proved to be unwieldy. Hence, in 1966 the Department of Housing and Urban Development was created to have prime responsibilities for the Federal Government's involvement in the field of housing.

II. Trends in Housing Inspection

Historically, local provisions for the inspection of housing have been completely inadequate. Usually the function has been split among two or more agencies, and the pertinent code sections have been spread among several local ordinances.

Following the work of C.E.A. Winslow, minimum code standards were made available and resulted in the passing of housing codes. This consolidation of housing requirements resulted in the field of housing inspection. Originally much of the work was devoted to complaint and referral inspections

A Complaint and Referral Inspections

In most communities the housing inspectors are expected to center their efforts primarily on complaint and referral inspections. This approach satisfies the persons making the complaints and referrals and helps improve some of the municipality's substandard housing. However, it does little to bring about general improvements in any section of the community and actually constitutes an inefficient way of using the available inspection manpower because the men have to spend so much time traveling from one area to another. Many supervisors and inspectors realize this unsystematic method not only wastes time but also is an ineffective way of upgrading housing and curbing blight. First, on complaint inspections the inspectors are usually instructed to confine their investigations to the dwelling unit specifically involved unless the general conditions are so bad that an inspection of the entire building is deemed necessary. This means most complaint inspections are piecemeal and do not ordinarily bring entire dwellings up to code standards. Second, even though numerous complaints are unwarranted, inspectors are often given so many to check each day that they do not have time to inspect other obviously substandard houses in the vicinity of those complained about. Consequently, these "rotten apples" are left to spoil the block, while the house that has been improved stands alone.

Too often inspection agencies have found they did not have enough facts on hand about the extent and distribution of the substandard housing in their communities. Thus, they were unable to convince their superiors and the public about the inadequacy of complaint inspections as the major method of uncovering violations and checking residential blight in neighborhoods. It is the consensus of housing officials that area inspections are the most effective way of doing both. Fortunately, in the 1960's, as one city after another began developing the comprehensive community renewal plans provided for in the Housing Act of 1959, this information finally started to become available. It verified the need for systematic inspections on a neighborhood basis. Congress further emphasized the importance of this new approach by including Section 301 in the Housing Act of 1964. This required all cities engaged in urban renewal to have comprehensive area inspection programs in operation by March 1967, and thereafter, in order to remain eligible for national renewal funds.

B Neighborhood Inspection Technique

The area or neighborhood inspection technique is a more recent type of inspection and one which begins to face up to the problems of saving neighborhoods from urban blight. While this is a step forward, it is merely one of several steps required if urban blight and its associated human suffering are to be minimized or controlled.

Throughout this manual the terms "area" or "neighborhood" are used interchangeably and refer to a readily identifiable portion of a community.

Whether this consists of so many blocks, an entire neighborhood, or a section thereof, it should be of such size as to permit the local code enforcement team to inspect and systematically effect minimum housing standards within a manageable time.

This means that area inspection programs involve systematic cellar-to-roof, house-to-house, block-to-block inspections of all properties within the specific area and include all the follow-up work required to bring the substandard housing up to code standards within a reasonable period. By putting major emphasis on this type of effort instead of on the complaint-oriented approach, blight is checked and an overall upgrading of residential sections is achieved in one portion of a community after another. Thus, systematic area inspection is both a longer lasting and a much more effective method of improving housing and stabilizing property values than the traditional complaint method.

Usually a municipality combines its area work with some complaint and referral inspections. This is not objectionable so long as major emphasis is given to the area programs, and the inspectors move through the various sections of town systematically. Only in this way can a community's housing inspection program contribute adequately to the municipal efforts to upgrade all substandard housing and stem the deterioration of individual homes and neighborhoods. A percentage of the inspection force should, however, be primarily assigned to complaint and referral work so that prompt action can be taken on all cases in which the problems are too severe to await action in connection with the area inspections.

While the area-wide or neighborhood inspections will correct violations of the housing code, this is all they will accomplish. Once these neighborhoods are brought up to standard, inspectors will move on to other neighborhoods but be forced to return at a later time and repeat the process.

If a neighborhood has declined to the extent that there is a large number of housing violations, then it is obvious that something or someone or both have caused the neighborhood to deteriorate. Any effort that does not also eliminate the cause for deterioration can only be a token effort and frequently a *wasted effort*. Unless a housing program evaluates the total neighborhood for both housing violations and for environmental stresses within the neighborhood that may have caused the deterioration of housing, then the inspectional effort has not been complete.

What then are these "environmental stresses"? Environmental stresses are the elements within a neighborhood that influence the physical, mental, and emotional well-being of the occupants. They include items such as noise, glare, excessive land covering, nonresidential land uses, and extensive traffic problems. If a housing program is to be complete, these stresses must be identified and assessed. Then efforts must be made in conjunction with other departments within the city to program capital improvement budgets to alleviate or minimize these stresses.

These two types of inspection are the field involvement of the housing inspector. He must inspect not only the houses for violations but also the neighborhoods for environmental stresses. This will provide him with knowledge of physical conditions within the neighborhood. As mentioned previously, however, this is not the whole problem in most neighborhoods. Generally, the very difficult problem of the human element is involved. Many buildings and neighborhoods deteriorate because of apathy on the part of the neighborhood inhabitants. Efforts must be made to motivate the slum dweller to work towards a better living environment. Experience by the Public Health Service (PHS) in motivational training has shown it to be very effective in raising the living standards of neighborhood populations.

In summary then, a housing inspection effort should be made up of three parts: First, a neighborhood or area-wide housing inspection procedure; second, a neighborhood analysis procedure to identify, assess, and eventually control environmental stresses; and third, a program of motivational training for slum dwellers to raise the living standards of the neighborhood.

III. Role of Health Agencies in Housing

Up until the end of World War II, most local housing hygiene programs were carried on by the health departments. After World War II, health agencies began to drift away from the field of housing hygiene. This gap was filled by a variety of other city agencies including building departments, police departments, fire departments, and more recently created departments of licenses and inspections. Regardless which department administers the housing code, the health department, if it is to live up to its responsibilities of protecting the public health, must have an involvement in housing. A general statement of PHS policy is that the basic responsibility of health agencies with regard to housing is to see to it that local and state governments take action to ensure that all occupied housing meets minimum public health standards. This basic responsibility falls upon federal, state, and local health agencies alike.

Several kinds of governmental action are required. These include: (1) adoption of minimum health standards in housing, (2) conduct of a program to achieve and maintain these standards, (3) periodic evaluation of the standards to ensure their current adequacy, and (4) monitoring of the standards enforcement effort to guarantee that public health values are provided. Health agencies, in order to meet their responsibilities, must accept the role of either stimulating or carrying out these four required kinds of governmental action.

In communities that have neither standards nor program, the health agency has the responsibility of initiating both by stimulating the required governmental action. Stimulation may be direct, through elected or appointed officials, or indirect, by generating public support that will trigger official action.

IV. Summary

Several basic thoughts are contained in this chapter.

1. Housing is an old, well-established but often overlooked topic within this country. Indications are, however, that the broad field of housing will receive much more attention from the policymakers throughout the country within the coming years.

2. No single agency can eliminate urban blight. A concentrated effort of all city departments, private concerns, and political bodies must be focused on small sections (neighborhoods) to minimize or control urban blight and its associated human sufferings.

3. A housing effort cannot be successful if it is merely an inspection of houses for code compliance. There must also be a united effort to eliminate environmental stresses within the neighborhood and instill motivation in slum dwellers to desire and work towards improving their environment.

GLOSSARY OF HOUSING, BUILDING CONSTRUCTION, CARPENTRY, AND WOOD TERMS

CONTENTS

GLOSSARY OF HOUSING, BUILDING CONSTRUCTION, CARPENTRY, AND WOOD TERMS

A

AIR-DRIED LUMBER - Lumber that has been piled in yards or sheds for any length of time. For the United States as a whole the minimum moisture content of thoroughly air-dried lumber is 12 to 15 percent and the average is somewhat higher.
AIRWAY - A space between roof insulation and roof boards for movement of air.
ALLIGATORING - Coarse checking pattern characterized by a slipping of the new coating over the old coating to the extent that the old coating can be seen through the fissures.
ANCHOR - Irons of special form used to fasten together timbers or masonry.
ANCHOR BOLTS - (1) Bolts which fasten columns, girders, or other members to concrete or masonry.
(2) Bolts to secure a wooden sill to concrete or masonry floor or wall.
ANNUAL GROWTH RING - The growth layer put on in a single growth year, including springwood and summerwood.
APRON - The flat member of the inside trim of a window placed against the wall immediately beneath the stool.
AREAWAY - An open subsurface space adjacent to a building used to admit light or air or as a means of access to a basement or cellar.
ASPHALT - Most native asphalt is a residue from evaporated petroleum. It is insoluble in water but soluble in gasoline and melts when heated. Used widely in building for such items as waterproof roof coverings of many types, exterior wall coverings, and flooring tile.
ASTRAGAL - A molding, attached to one of a pair of swinging doors, against which the other door strikes.
ATTIC VENTILATORS - In houses, screened openings provided to ventilate an attic space. They are located in the soffit area as inlet ventilators and in the gable end or along the ridge as outlet ventilators. They can also consist of powerdriven fans used as an exhaust system. (See also LOUVER)

B

BACKBAND - Molding used on the side of a door or window casing for ornamentation or to increase the width of the trim.
BACKING - The bevel on the top edge of a hip rafter that allows the roofing board to fit the top of the rafter without leaving a triangular space between it and the lower side of the roof covering.
BACK-FILL - The replacement of excavated earth into a trench or pier excavation around and against a basement foundation.
BALLOON FRAME - The lightest and most economical form of construction, in which the studding and corner posts are set up in continuous lengths from first-floor line or sill to the roof plate.
BALUSTER - A small pillar or column used to support a rail.
BALUSTERS - Usually small vertical members in a railing used between a top rail and the stair treads or a bottom rail.

BALUSTRADE - A series of balusters connected by a rail, generally used for porches, balconies, and the like.
BAND - A low, flat molding.
BARK - Outer layer of a tree, comprising the inner bark, or thin, inner living part (phloem) and the outer bark, or corky layer, composed of dry, dead tissue.
BASE - The bottom of a column; the finish of a room at the junction of the walls and floor.
BASE OR BASEBOARD - A board placed around a room against the wall next to the floor to finish properly between floor and plaster or dry wall.
BASE MOLDING - Molding used to trim the upper edge of interior baseboard.
BASE SHOE - Molding used next to the floor on interior baseboard. Sometimes called a carpet strip.
BATTEN - Narrow strips of wood used to cover joints or as decorative vertical members over plywood or wide boards.
BATTEN (CLEAT) - A narrow strip of board used to fasten several pieces together.
BATTER BOARD - One of a pair of horizontal boards nailed to posts set at the corners of an excavation, used to indicate the desired level, also as a fastening for stretched strings to indicate outlines of foundation walls.
BAY WINDOW - Any window space projecting outward from the walls of a building, either square or polygonal in plan.
BEAM - (1) An inclusive term for joists, girders, rafters, and purlins.
(2) A large structural member transversely supporting a load.
One example is a beam under the floor of a house.
BEARING PARTITION - A partition that supports any vertical load in addition to its own weight.
BEARING WALL - A wall that supports any vertical load in addition to its own weight.
BED MOLDING - A molding in an angle, as between the overhanging cornice, or eaves, of a building and the sidewalls.
BEDDING - A filling of mortar, putty, or other substance in order to secure a firm bearing.
BELT COURSE - A horizontal board across or around a building, usually made of a flat member and a molding.
BENDING, STEAM - The process of forming curved wood members by steaming or boiling the wood and bending it to a form.
BEVEL - One side of a solid body is said to be on a bevel with respect to another when the angle between the two sides is greater or less than a right angle.
BEVEL BOARD (PITCH BOARD) - A board used in framing a roof or stairway to lay out bevels.
BEVEL SIDING (LAP SIDING) - Used as the finish siding on the exterior of a house or other structure. It is usually manufactured by "resaw-ing dry, square surfaced boards diagonally to produce two wedge-shaped pieces. These pieces commonly run from three-sixteenths inch thick on the thin edge to one-half to three-fourths inch thick on the other edge, depending on the width of the siding.
BIRD'S-EYE - Small localized areas in wood with the fibers indented and otherwise contorted to form few to many small circular or elliptical figures remotely resembling birds' eyes on the tangential surface. Common in sugar maple and used for decorative purposes; rare in other hardwood species.
BLIND-NAILING - Nailing in such a way that the nailheads are not visible on the face of the work. Usually at the tongue of matched boards.
BLIND STOP - A rectangular molding, usually 3/4 by 1 3/8 inches or more in width, used in the assembly of a window frame. Serves as a stop for storm and screen or combination windows and to resist air infiltration.

BLINDS (SHUTTERS) - Light wood sections in the form of doors to close over windows to shut out light, give protection, or add temporary insulation. Commonly used now for ornamental purposes, in which case they are fastened rigidly to the building.
BLUE STAIN - A bluish or grayish discoloration of the sapwood caused by the growth of certain moldlike fungi on the surface and in the interior of the piece, made possible by the same conditions that favor the growth of other fungi. BOARD - Lumber less than 2 inches thick.
BOARD FOOT - The equivalent of a board 1 foot square and 1 inch thick.
BOARDING IN - The process of nailing boards on the outside studding of a house.
BODIED LINSEED OIL - Linseed oil that has been thickened in viscosity by suitable processing with heat or chemicals. Bodied oils are obtainable in a great range of viscosity from a little greater than that of raw oil to just short of a jellied condition.
BOILED LINSEED OIL - Linseed oil in which enough lead, manganese, or cobalt salts have been incorporated to make the oil harden more rapidly when spread in thin coatings.
BOLSTER - A short horizontal timber resting on the top of a column for the support of beams or girders.
BOLTS, ANCHOR - Bolts to secure a wooden sill plate to concrete or masonry floor or wall or pier.
BOSTON RIDGE - A method of applying asphalt or wood shingles at the ridge or at the hips of a roof as a finish.
BOW - The distortion in a board that deviates from flatness lengthwise but not across its faces.
BRACE - An inclined piece of framing lumber used to complete a triangle and applied to wall or floor to stiffen the structure. Often used on walls as temporary bracing until framing has been completed.
BRACES - Pieces fitted and firmly fastened to two others at any angle in order to strengthen the angle thus threated.
BRACKET - A projecting support for a shelf or other structure.
BREAK JOINTS - To arrange joints so that they do not come directly under or over the joints of adjoining pieces, as in shingling, siding, etc.
BRICK VENEER - A facing of brick laid against frame or tile wall construction .
BRIDGING - (1) Pieces fitted in pairs from the bottom of one floor joist to the top of adjacent joists, and crossed to distribute the floor load; sometimes pieces of width equal to the joists and fitted neatly between them.
(2) Small wood or metal members that are inserted in a diagonal position between the floor joists to act both as tension and compression members for the purpose of bracing the joists and spreading the action of loads.
BROAD-LEAVED TREES - (See HARDWOODS)
BUCK - Often used in reference to rough frame opening members. Door bucks used in reference to metal door frame.
BUILDING CODE - A collection of legal requirements the purpose of which is to protect the safety, health, morals, and general welfare of those in and about buildings.
BUILDING PAPER - Cheap, thick paper, used to insulate a building before the siding or roofing is put on; sometimes placed between double floors.
BUILT-UP ROOF - A roofing composed of three to five layers of asphalt felt laminated with coal tar, pitch, or asphalt. The top is finished with crushed slag or gravel. Generally used on flat or low-pitched roofs.
BUILT-UP TIMBER - A timber made of several pieces fastened together, and forming one of larger dimension.

BUTT JOINT - The junction where the ends of two timbers or other members meet in a square-cut joint.

C

CABINET - A shop-or-job-built unit for kitchens or other rooms. Often includes combinations of drawers, doors, and the like.
CAMBIUM - The one-cell-thick layer of tissue between the bark and wood that repeatedly subdivides to form new wood and bark cells.
CANT STRIP - A wedge or triangular-shaped piece of lumber used at gable ends under shingles or at the junction of the house and a flat deck under the roofing.
CAP - The upper member of a column, pilaster, door cornice, molding, and the like.
CARRIAGES - The supports or the steps and risers of a flight of stairs.
CASEMENT - A window in which the sash opens upon hinges.
CASEMENT FRAMES AND SASH - Frames of wood or metal enclosing part or all of the sash, which may be opened by means of hinges affixed to the vertical edges.
CASING - (1) Molding of various widths and thicknesses used to trim door and window openings at the jambs.
(2) The trimming around a door or window opening, either outside or inside, or the finished lumber around a post or beam, etc.
CEILING - Narrow, matched boards; sheathing of the surfaces that inclose the upper side of a room.
CELL - A general term for the minute units of wood structure, including wood fibers, vessels, members, and other elements of diverse structure and function.
CEMENT, KEENE'S - The whitest finish plaster obtainable that produces a wall of extreme durability. Because of its density it excels for a wainscoting plaster for bathrooms and kitchens and is also used extensively for the finish coat in auditoriums, public buildings, and other places where walls will be subjected to unusually hard wear or abuse.
CENTER-HUNG SASH - A sash hung on its centers so that it swings on a horizontal axis.
CHAMFER - A beveled surface cut upon the corner of a piece of wood.
CHECK - A lengthwise separation of the wood, usually extending across the rings of annual growth and commonly resulting from stresses set up in the wood during seasoning.
CHECKING - Fissures that appear with age in many exterior paint coatings, at first superficial, but which in time may penetrate entirely through the coating.
CHECKRAILS - Meeting rails sufficiently thicker than a window to fill the opening between the top and bottom sash made by the parting stop in the frame. They are usually beveled.
CHECKS - Splits or cracks in a board, ordinarily caused by seasoning.
CLAMP - A mechanical device used to hold two or more pieces together.
CLAPBOARDS - A special form of outside covering of a house; siding.
COLLAPSE - The flattening of groups of cells in heartwood during the drying or pressure treatment of wood, characterized by a caved-in or corrugated appearance.
COLLAR BEAM - (1) Nominal 1- or 2-inch-thick members connecting opposite roof rafters. They serve to stiffen the roof structure.
(2) A tie beam connecting the rafters considerably above the wall plate. It is also called a rafter tie.
(3) A beam connecting pairs of opposite roof rafters above the attic floor.

COLUMN - In architecture: A perpendicular supporting member, circular or rectangular in section, usually consisting of a base, shaft, and capital. In engineering: A structural compression member, usually vertical, supporting loads acting on or near and in the direction of its longitudinal axis.
COLUMNS - A support, square, rectangular, or cylindrical in section, for roofs, ceilings, etc., composed of base, shaft, and capital.
COMBINATION DOORS - Combination doors have an inside removable section so that the same frame serves for both summer and winter protective devices. A screen is inserted in warm weather to make a screen door, and a glazed or a glazed-and-wood paneled section in winter to make a storm door. The inconvenience of handling a different door in each season is eliminated.
COMBINATION DOORS OR WINDOWS - Combination doors or windows used over regular openings. They provide winter insulation and summer protection. They often have self-storing or removable glass and screen inserts. This eliminates the need for handling a different unit each season.
COMBINATION FRAME - A combination of the principal features of the full and balloon frames.
CONCRETE - An artificial building material made by mixing cement and sand with gravel, broken stone, or other aggregate, and sufficient water to cause the cement to set and bind the entire mass.
CONCRETE, PLAIN - Concrete without reinforcement, or reinforced only for shrinkage or temperature changes.
CONDENSATION - Beads or drops of water, and frequently frost in extremely cold weather, that accumulate on the inside of the exterior covering of a building when warm, moisture-laden air from the interior reaches a point where the temperature no longer permits the air to sustain the moisture it holds. Use of louvers or attic ventilators will reduce moisture condensation in attics. A vapor barrier under the gypsum lath or dry wall on exposed walls will reduce condensation in walls.
CONDUCTORS - Pipes for conducting water from a roof to the ground or to a receptacle or drain; downspout.
CONDUIT, ELECTRICAL - A pipe, usually metal, in which wire is installed.
CONSTRUCTION, DRY-WALL - A type of construction in which the interior wall finish is applied in a dry condition, generally in the form of sheet materials or wood paneling, as contrasted to plaster.
CONSTRUCTION, FRAME - A type of construction in which the structural parts are of wood or depend upon a wood frame for support. In building codes, if masonry veneer is applied to the exterior walls, the classification of this type of construction is usually unchanged.
COPED JOINT - Fitting woodwork to an irregular surface. In moldings, cutting the end of one piece to fit the molded face of the other at an interior angle to replace a miter joint.
CORBEL OUT - To build out one or more courses of brick or stone from the face of a wall, to form a support for timbers.
CORNER BEAD - A strip of formed galvanized iron, sometimes combined with a strip of metal lath, placed on corners before plastering to reinforce them. Also, a strip of wood finish three-quarters-round or angular placed over a plastered corner for protection.
CORNER BOARDS - Used as trim for the external corners of a house or other frame structures against which the ends of the siding are finished.
CORNER BRACES - Diagonal braces at the corners of frame structure to stiffen and strengthen the wall.

CORNERITE - Metal-mesh lath cut into strips and bent to a right angle. Used in interior corners of walls and ceilings on lath to prevent cracks in plastering.
CORNICE - (1) Overhang of a pitched roof at the eave line, usually consisting of a facia board, a soffit for a closed cornice, and appropriate moldings.
(2) The molded projection which finishes the top of the wall of a building.
(3) A decorative element made up of molded members usually placed at or near the top of an exterior or interior wall.
CORNICE RETURN - That portion of the cornice that returns on the gable end of a house.
COUNTERFLASHING - A flashing usually used on chimneys at the roofline to cover shingle flashing and to prevent moisture entry.
COUNTERFLASHINGS - Strips of metal used to prevent water from entering the top edge of the vertical side of a roof flashing; they also allow expansion and contraction without danger of breaking the flashing.
COVE MOLDING - (1) A molding with a concave face used as trim or to finish interior corners.
(2) A three-sided molding with concave face used wherever small angles are to be covered.
CRAWL SPACE - A shallow space below the living quarters of a house. It is generally not excavated or paved and is often enclosed for appearance by a skirting or facing material.
CRICKET - A small drainage diverting roof structure of single or double slope placed at the junction of larger surfaces that meet at an angle.
CROOK - The distortion in a board that deviates edgewise from a straight line from end to end of the board.
CROWN MOLDING - A molding used on cornice or wherever a large angle is to be covered.
CUP - The distortion in a board that deviates flatwise from a straight line across the width of the board.

D

d - (See PENNY)
DADO - A rectangular groove across the width of a board or plank. In interior decoration, a special type of wall treatment.
DEADENING - Construction intended to prevent the passage of sound.
DECAY - The decomposition of wood substance by fungi.
DECAY, ADVANCED (OR TYPICAL) - The older stage of decay in which the destruction is readily recognized because the wood has become punky, soft and spongy, stringy, ringshaked, pitted, or crumbly. Decided discoloration or bleaching of the rotted wood is often apparent.
DECAY, INCIPIENT - The early stage of decay that has not proceeded far enough to soften or otherwise perceptibly impair the hardness of the wood. It is usually accompanied by a slight discoloration or bleaching of the wood.
DECK PAINT - An enamel with a high degree of resistance to mechanical wear, designed for use on such surfaces as porch floors.
DENSITY - (1) The mass of substance in a unit volume. When expressed in the metric system (in g. per cc), it is numerically equal to the specific gravity of the same substance.

(2) The weight of a body per unit volume. When expressed in the c. g. s. (centimeter-gram-second) system, it is numerically equal to the specific gravity of the same substance.

DIFFUSE-POROUS WOOD - Certain hardwoods in which the pores tend to be uniform in size and distribution throughout each annual ring or to decrease in size slightly and gradually toward the outer border of the ring.

DIMENSION - (See LUMBER)

DIMENSION STOCK - A term largely superseded by the term hardwood dimension lumber. It is hardwood stock processed to a point where the maximum waste is left at a dimension mill, and the maximum utility is delivered to the user. It is stock of specified thickness, width, and length, in multiples thereof. According to specification, it may be solid or glued; rough or surfaced; semifabricated or completely fabricated.

DIMENSIONAL STABILIZATION - Reduction through special treatment in swelling and shrinking of wood, caused by changes in its moisture content with changes in relative humidity.

DIRECT NAILING - To nail perpendicular to the initial surface, or to the junction of the pieces joined. Also termed face nailing.

DOORJAMB, INTERIOR - The surrounding case into which and out of which a door closes and opens. It consists of two upright pieces, called jambs, and a head, fitted together and rabbeted.

DORMER - (1) A projection in a sloping roof, the framing of which forms a vertical wall suitable for windows or other openings.

(2) An internal recess, the framing of which projects a sloping roof.

DOWNSPOUT - A pipe, usually of metal, for carrying rainwater from roof gutters.

DRESSED AND MATCHED (TONGUED AND GROOVED) - Boards or planks machined in such a manner that there is a groove on one edge and a corresponding tongue on the other.

DRIER, PAINT - Usually oil-soluble soaps of such metals as lead, manganese, or cobalt, which, in small proportions, hasten the oxidation and hardening (drying) of the drying oils in paints. DRIP - (1) The projection of a window sill or water table to allow the water to drain clear of the side of the house below it.

(2) A member of a cornice or other horizontal exterior-finish course that has a projection beyond the other parts for throwing off water.

(3) A groove in the underside of a sill to cause water to drop off on the outer edge, instead of drawing back and running down the face of the building.

DRIP CAP - A molding placed on the exterior top side of a door or window frame to cause water to drip beyond the outside of the frame.

DROP SIDING - Usually 3/4 inch thick and 6 inches wide, machined into various patterns. Drop siding has tongue and groove or shiplap joints, is heavier, and has more structural strength than bevel siding.

DRY KILN - (See KILN)

DRY ROT - A term loosely applied to any dry, crumbly rot but especially to that which, when in an advanced stage, permits the wood to be crushed easily to a dry powder. The term is actually a misnomer, since all wood-rotting fungi require considerable moisture for growth.

DRY-WALL - (See CONSTRUCTION, DRY WALL)

DUCTS - In a house, usually round or rectangular metal pipes for distributing warm air from the heating plant to rooms, or air from a conditioning device, or as cold air returns. Ducts are also made of asbestos and composition materials.

E

EARLY WOOD - (See SPRINGWOOD)
EAVES - (1) The overhang of a roof projecting over the walls.
(2) The margin or lower part of a roof projecting over the wall.
EDGE-GRAINED - (See GRAIN)
EXPANSION JOINT - A bituminous fiber strip used to separate blocks or units of concrete to prevent cracking due to expansion as a result of temperature changes.
EXTRACTIVES - Substances in wood, not an integral part of the cellular structure, that can be removed by solution in hot or cold water, ether, benzene, or other solvents that do not react chemically with wood components.

F

FACE NAILING - To nail perpendicular to the initial surface or to the junction of the pieces joined.
FACIA OR FASCIA - (1) A flat board, band, or face, used sometimes by itself but usually in combination with moldings, often located at the outer face of the cornice.
(2) A flat member of a cornice or other finish, generally the board of the cornice to which the gutter is fastened.
FIBER, WOOD - A comparatively long (one twenty-fifth or less to one-third inch), narrow, tapering wood cell closed at both ends.
FIGURE - The pattern produced in a wood surface by annual growth rings, rays, knots, deviations from regular grain such as interlocked and wavy grain, and irregular coloration.
FILLER (WOOD) - A heavily pigmented preparation used for filling and leveling off the pores in open-pored woods.
FINISH - Wood products to be used in the joiner work, such as doors and stairs, and other fine work required to complete a building, especially the interior.
FIRE-RESISTIVE - In the absence of a specific ruling by the authority having jurisdiction, applies to materials for construction not combustible in the temperatures of ordinary fires and that will withstand such fires without serious impairment of their usefulness for at least 1 hour.
FIRE-RETARDANT CHEMICAL - A chemical or preparation of chemicals used to reduce flammability or to retard spread of flame.
FIRE STOP - A solid, tight closure of a concealed space, placed to prevent the spread of fire and smoke through such a space.
FLAGSTONE (FLAGGING OR FLAGS) - Flat stones, from 1 to 4 inches thick, used for rustic walks, steps, floors, and the like. Usually sold by the ton.
FLAKES - (See RAYS, WOOD)
FLASHING - (1) The material used and the process of making watertight the roof intersections and other exposed places on the outside of the house.
(2) Sheet metal or other material used in roof and wall construction to protect a building from seepage of water.
FLAT-GRAINED - (See GRAIN)
FLAT PAINT - An interior paint that contains a high proportin of pigment, and dries to a flat or lusterless finish.

FLUE - The space or passage in a chimney through which smoke, gas, or fumes ascend. Each passage is called a flue, which, together with any others and the surrounding masonry, make up the chimney.
FLUE LINING - Fire clay or terracotta pipe, round or square, usually made in all of the ordinary flue sizes and in 2-foot lengths, used for the inner lining of chimneys with a brick or masonry work around the outside. Flue lining in chimneys runs from about a foot below the flue connection to the top of the chimney.
FLUSH - Adjacent surfaces even, or in some plane (with reference to two structural pieces).
FLY RAFTER - End rafters of the gable overhang supported by roof sheathing and look-outs.
FOOTING - (1) A masonry section, usually concrete, in a rectangular form, wider than the bottom of the foundation wall or pier it supports.
(2) The spreading course or courses at the base or bottom of a foundation wall, pier, or column.
(3) An enlargement at the lower end of a wall, pier or column, to distribute the load.
FOOTING FORM - A wooden or steel structure, placed around the footing that will hold the concrete to the deserved shape and size.
FOUNDATION - (1) The supporting portion of a structure below the first floor construction, or below grade, including the footings.
(2) That part of a building or wall which supports the super-structure.
FRAME - The surrounding or inclosing woodwork of windows, doors, etc., and the timber skeleton of a building.
FRAMING - (1) The rough timber structure of a building, including interior and exterior walls, floor, roof, and ceiling.
(2) Lumber used for the structural members of a building, such as studs and joists.
FRAMING SYSTEMS:
BALLOON FRAMING - A system of framing a building in which all vertical structural elements of the exterior walls, particularly the studs, consist of single pieces extending from the foundation sill to the roof plate, and support intermediate floor and ceiling joists.
BRACED FRAMING - A system of framing a building in which all vertical structural elements of the bearing walls and partitions except corner posts, extend for one story only, starting at the foundation sill for the first-story framing and at the top plate of the story below for all stories above the first. Corner posts extend from foundation sill to roof plate and are braced by diagonal members usually extending the full height of each story and crossing several of the studs in each outer wall.
PLATFORM FRAMING - A system of framing a building on which floor joists of each story rest on the top plates of the story below (or on the foundation sill for the first story) and the bearing walls and partitions rest on the subfloor of each story.
FRIEZE - (1) In house construction, a horizontal member connecting the top of the siding with the soffit of the cornice or roof sheathing.
(2) Any sculptured or ornamental band in a building. Also the horizontal member of a cornice set vertically against the wall.
FROSTLINE - The depth of frost penetration in soil. This depth varies in different parts of the country. Footings should be placed below this depth to prevent movement.
FULL FRAME - The old fashioned mortised-and-tenoned frame, in which every joint was mortised and tenoned. Rarely used at the present time.

FUNGI, WOOD - Microscopic plants that live in damp wood and cause mold, stain, and decay.
FUNGICIDE - A chemical that is poisonous to fungi.
FURRING - (1) Narrow strips of board nailed upon the walls and ceilings to form a straight surface upon which to lay the laths or other finish.
(2) Strips of wood or metal applied to a wall or other surface to even it and usually to serve as a fastening base for finish material.

G

GABLE - (1) The vertical triangular end of a building from the eaves to the apex of the roof.
(2) That portion of a wall contained between the slopes of a double-sloped roof, on a single-sloped roof, that portion contained between the slope of and a line projected horizontally through the lowest elevation of the roof construction.
GABLE END - An end wall having a gable.
GAGE - A tool used by carpenters; to strike a line parallel to the edge of a board.
GAMBREL - A symmetrical roof with two different pitches or slopes on each side.
GIRDER - (1) A timber used to support wall beams or joists.
(2) A large or principal beam of wood or steel used to support concentrated loads at isolated points along its length.
GIRT (RIBBAND) - The horizontal member of the walls of a full or combination frame house which supports the floor joists or is flush with the top of the joists.
GLOSS ENAMEL - A finishing material made of varnish and sufficient pigments to provide opacity and color, but little or no pigment of low opacity. Such an enamel forms a hard coating with maximum smoothness of surface and a high degree of gloss.
GLOSS (PAINT OR ENAMEL) - A paint or enamel that contains a relatively low proportion of pigment and dries to a sheen or luster.
GRADE - The designation of quality of a manufactured piece of wood or of logs.
GRAIN - The direction, size, arrangement, appearance, or quality of the elements in wood or lumber. To have a specific meaning the term must be qualified.
CLOSE-GRAINED WOOD - Wood with narrow, inconspicuous annual rings. The term is sometimes used to designate wood having small and closely spaced pores, but in this sense the term "fine textured" is more often used.
COARSE-GRAINED WOOD - Wood with wide conspicuous annual rings in which there is considerable difference between springwood and summer-wood. The term is sometimes used to designate wood with large pores, such as oak, ash, chestnut, and walnut, but in this sense the term "coarse textured" is more often used.
CROSS-GRAINED WOOD - Wood in which the fibers deviate from a line parallel to the sides of the piece. Cross grain may be either diagonal or spiral grain, or a combination of the two.
CURLY-GRAINED WOOD - Wood in which the fibers are distorted so that they have a curled appearance, as in "bird's-eye" wood. The areas showing curly grain may vary up to several inches in diameter.
DIAGONAL-GRAINED WOOD - Wood in which the annual rings are at an angle with the axis of a piece as a result of sawing at an angle with the bark of the tree or log. A form of cross grain.
EDGE-GRAINED LUMBER - Lumber that has been sawed so that the wide surfaces extend approximately at right angles to the annual growth rings. Lumber is considered

edge grained when the rings form an angle of 45° to 90° with the wide surface of the piece.
FINE-GRAINED WOOD - (See GRAIN, CLOSE-GRAINED WOOD)
FLAT-GRAINED LUMBER - Lumber that has been sawed so the wide surfaces extend approximately parallel to the annual growth rings. Lumber is considered flat grained when the annual growth rings make an angle of less than 45° with the surface of the piece.
INTERLOCKED-GRAINED WOOD - Wood in which the fibers are inclined in one direction in a number of rings of annual growth, then gradually reverse and are inclined in an opposite direction in succeeding growth rings, then reverse again.
OPEN-GRAINED WOOD - Common classification by painters for woods with large pores, such as oak, ash, chestnut, and walnut. Also known as "coarse textured."
PLAINSAWED LUMBER - Another term for flat-grained lumber.
QUARTERSAWED LUMBER - Another term for edge-grained lumber.
SPIRAL-GRAINED WOOD - Wood in which the fibers take a spiral course around the trunk of a tree instead of the normal vertical course. The spiral may extend in a right-handed or left-handed direction around the tree trunk. Spiral grain is a form of cross grain.
STRAIGHT-GRAINED WOOD - Wood in which the fibers run parallel to the axis of a piece.
VERTICAL-GRAINED LUMBER - Another form for edge-grained lumber.
WAVY-GRAINED WOOD - Wood in which the fibers collectively take the form of waves or undulations.
GREEN - Freshly sawed lumber, or lumber that has received no intentional drying; unseasoned. The term does not apply to lumber that may have become completely wet through waterlogging.
GROOVE - A long hollow channel cut by a tool, into which a piece fits or in which it works. Two special types of grooves are the
DADO, a rectangular groove cut across the full width of a piece, and the
HOUSING, a groove cut at any angle with the grain and part way across a piece. Dados are used in sliding doors, window frames, etc.; housings are used for framing stair risers and threads in a string.
GROUND - A strip of wood assisting the plasterer in making a straight wall and in giving a place to which the finish of the room may be nailed.
GROUNDS - Strips of wood, of same thickness as lath and plaster, that are attached to walls before the plastering is done. Used around windows, doors, and other openings as a plaster stop and in other places for attaching baseboards or other trim.
GROUT - (1) Mortar made of such consistency by the addition of water that it will just flow into the joints and cavities of the masonry work and fill them solid.
(2) Mortar made so thin by the addition of water that it will all run into the joints and cavities of the masonwork and fill them up solid.
GUSSET - A flat wood, plywood, or similar type member used to provide a connection at the intersection of wood members. Most commonly used at joints of wood trusses. They are fastened by nails, screws, bolts, or adhesives.
GUTTER OR EAVE TROUGH - A shallow channel or conduit of metal or wood set below and along the eaves of a house to catch and carry off rainwater from the roof.
GYPSUM PLASTER - Gypsum formulated to be used with the addition of sand and water for base-coat plaster.

H

HARDWOODS - Generally, the botanical group of trees that have broad leaves, in contrast to the conifers or softwoods. The term has no reference to the actual hardness of the wood.

HEADER - (1) A beam placed perpendicular to joists and to which joists are nailed in framing for a chimney, stairway, or other opening. More generally, a piece or member that makes a T-joint with other members; often a short piece extending between other members and at right angles to them; frequently used instead of lintel.

(2) A short joist supporting tail beams and framed between trimmer joists; the piece of stud or finish over an opening; a lintel.

HEADROOM - The clear space between floor line and ceiling, as in a stairway.

HEARTH - The floor of a fireplace, usually made of brick, tile, or stone.

HEARTWOOD - The wood extending from the pith to the sapwood, the cells of which no longer participate in the life processes of the tree. Heartwood may be infiltrated with gums, resins, and other materials that usually make it darker and more decay resistant than sapwood.

HEEL OF A RAFTER - The end or foot that rests on the wall plate. HIP - The external angle formed by the meeting of two sloping sides of a roof.

HIP ROOF - (1) A roof that rises by inclined planes from all four sides of a building.

(2) A roof which slopes up toward the center from all sides, necessitating a hip rafter at each corner.

HONEYCOMBING - Checks, often not visible at the surface, that occur in the interior of a piece of wood, usually along the wood rays.

HUMIDIFIER - A device designed to discharge water vapor into a confined space for the purpose of increasing or maintaining the relative humidity in an enclosure.

I

I-BEAM - A steel beam with a cross"section resembling the letter "I." INSULATING BOARD OR FIBERBOARD - A low-density board made of wood, sugarcane, cornstalks, or similar materials, usually formed by a felting process, dried and usually pressed to thicknesses 1/2 and 25/32 inch.

INSULATION BOARD, RIGID - A structural building board made of wood or cane fiber in 1/2" and 25/32" thicknesses. It can be obtained in various size sheets, in various densities, and with several treatments.

INSULATION, BUILDING - Any material high in resistance to heat transmission that, when placed in the walls, ceilings, or floors of a structure, will reduce the rate of heat flow.

INSULATION, THERMAL - Any material high in resistance to heat transmission that, when placed in the walls, ceilings, or floors of a structure, will reduce the rate of heat flow.

J

JACK RAFTER - (1) A rafter that spans the distance from the wallplate to a hip, or from a valley to a ridge.

(2) A short rafter framing between the wall plate; a hip rafter.

JAMB - (1) The side piece or post of an opening; sometimes applied to the door frame.

(2) The side and head lining of a doorway, window, or other opening.

JOINT - (1) The space between the adjacent surfaces of two members or components joined and held together by nails, glue, cement, mortar, or other means.

(2) The junction of two pieces of wood or veneer.

JOINT-BUTT - Squared ends or ends and edges adjoining each other.

DOVETAIL - Joint made by cutting pins the shape of dovetails which fit between dovetails upon another piece.

DRAWBOARD - A mortise-and-tenon joint with holes so bored that when a pin is driven through, the joint becomes tighter.

FISHED - An end butt splice strengthened by pieces nailed on the sides.

HALVED - A joint made by cutting half the wood away from each piece so as to bring the sides flush.

HOUSED - A joint in which a piece is grooved to receive the piece which is to form the other part of the joint.

GLUE - A joint held together with glue.

LAP - A joint of two pieces lapping over each other.

MORTISED - A joint made by cutting a hole or mortise, in one piece, and a tenon, or piece to fit the hole, upon the other.

RUB - A flue joint made by carefully fitting the edges together, spreading glue between them, and rubbing the pieces back and forth until the pieces are well rubbed together.

SCARFED - A timber spliced by cutting various shapes of shoulders, or jogs, which fit each other.

JOINT CEMENT - A powder that is usually mixed with water and used for joint treatment in gypsum - wallboard finish. Often called "spackle."

JOIST - One of a series of parallel beams, usually 2 inches thick, used to support floor and ceiling loads, and supported in turn by larger beams, girders, or bearing walls.

JOISTS - Timbers supporting the floor boards.

K

KERF - The cut made by a saw.

KILN - A heated chamber for drying lumber, veneer, and other wood products.

KNEE BRACE - A corner brace, fastened at an angle from wall stud to rafter, stiffening a wood or steel frame to prevent angular movement.

KNOT - (1) That portion of a branch or limb which has been surrounded by subsequent growth of the wood of the trunk or other portion of the tree. As a knot appears on the sawed surface, it is merely a section of the entire knot, its shape depending upon the direction of the cut.

(2) In lumber, the portion of a branch or limb of a tree that appears on the edge or face of the piece.

L

LANDING - A platform between flights of stairs or at the termination of a flight of stairs.

LATH - A building material of wood, metal, gypsum, or insulating board that is fastened to the frame of a building to act as a plaster base.

LATHS - Narrow strips to support plastering.

LATTICE - (1) Crossed wood, iron plate, or bars.

(2) An assemblage of wood or metal strips, rods, or bars made by crossing them to form a network.

LEADER - (See DOWNSPOUT)

LEDGER STRIP - A strip of lumber nailed along the bottom of the side of a girder on which joists rest.

LEDGERBOARD - The support for the second-floor joists of a balloon-frame house, or for similar uses; ribband.
LEVEL - A term describing the position of a line or plane when parallel to the surface of still water; an instrument or tool used in testing for horizontal and vertical surfaces, and in determining differences of elevation.
LIGHT - Space in a window sash for a single pane of glass. Also, a pane of glass.
LINTEL - A horizontal structural member that supports the load over an opening such as a door or window.
LINTEL (HEADER) - The piece of construction or finish, stone, wood, or metal, which is over an opening; a header.
LONGITUDINAL - Generally, the direction along the length of the grain of wood.
LOOKOUT - (1) The end of a rafter, or the construction which projects beyond the sides of a house to support the eaves; also the projecting timbers at the gables which support the verge boards.
(2) A short wood bracket or cantilever to support an overhanging portion of a roof or the like, usually concealed from view.
LOUVER - (1) An opening with a series of horizontal slats so arranged as to permit ventilation but to exclude rain, sunlight, or vision. See also ATTIC VENTILATORS.
(2) A kind of window, generally in peaks of gables and the tops of towers, provided with horizontal slots which exclude rain and snow and allow ventilation.
LUMBER - (1) Lumber is the product of the sawmill and planing mill not further manufactured other than by sawing, resawing, and passing lengthwise through a standard planing machine, cross cutting to length, and matching.
(2) Sawed parts of a log such as boards, planks, scantling, and timber.
LUMBER, BOARDS - Yard lumber less than 2 inches thick and 2 or more inches wide.
LUMBER, DIMENSION - Yard lumber from 2 inches to, but not including, 5 inches thick, and 2 or more inches wide. Includes joists, rafters, studs, plank, and small timbers. The actual size dimension of such lumber after shrinking from green dimension and after machining to size or pattern is called the dress size.
LUMBER, DRESSED SIZE - The dimensions of lumber after shrinking from the green dimension and after planing, usually 3/8 inch less than the nominal or rough size. For example, a 2 by 4 stud actually measures 1 5/8 by 3 5/8 inches.
LUMBER, MATCHED - Lumber that is edge-dressed and shaped to make a close tongue-and-groove joint at the edges or ends when laid edge to edge or end to end.
LUMBER, NOMINAL SIZE - As applied to timber or lumber, the rough-sawed commercial size by which it is known and sold in the market.
LUMBER, SHIPLAP - Lumber that is edge-dressed to make a close rabbeted or lapped joint.
STRUCTURAL LUMBER - Lumber that is 2 or more inches thick and 4 or more inches wide, intended for use where working stresses are required. The grading of structural lumber is based on the strength of the piece and the use of the entire piece.
LUMBER, TIMBERS - Yard lumber 5 or more inches in least dimension. Includes beams, stringers, posts, caps, sills, girders, and purlins.
LUMBER, YARD - Lumber of those grades, sizes, and patterns which are generally intended for ordinary construction, such as framework and rough coverage of houses.

M

MANTEL - The shelf above a fireplace. Originally referred to the beam or lintel supporting the arch above the fireplace opening. Used also in referring to the entire finish around a fireplace, covering the chimney breast in front and sometimes on the sides.
MASONRY - Stone, brick, concrete, hollow-tile, concrete-block, gypsum-block, or other similar building units or materials or a combination of the same, bonded together with mortar to form a wall, pier, buttress , or similar mass.
MATCHING, OR TONGUING AND GROOVING - The method used in cutting the edges of a board to make a tongue on one edge and a groove on the other.
MEDULLARY RAYS - (See RAYS, WOOD)
MEETING RAIL - The bottom rail of the upper sash of a double-hung window. Sometimes called the check rail.
MEETING RAILS - Rails sufficiently thicker than a window to fill the opening between the top and bottom sash made by the parting stop in the frame of double-hung windows. They are usually beveled.
MEMBER - A single piece in structure, complete in itself.
METAL LATH - Sheets of metal that are slit and drawn out to form openings on which plaster is spread.
MILLWORK - Generally all building materials made of finished wood and manufactured in millwork plants and planing mills are included under the term "millwork." It includes such items as inside and outside doors, window and doorframes, blinds, porchwork, mantels, panel-work, stairways, moldings, and interior trim. It normally does not include flooring, ceiling, or siding.
MITER - (1) The joining of two pieces at an angle that bisects the angle of junction.
(2) The joint formed by two abutting pieces meeting at an angle.
MITER JOINT - The joint of two pieces at an angle that bisects the joining angle. For example, the miter joint at the side and head casing at a door opening is made at a 45° angle.
MOISTURE CONTENT OF WOOD - Weight of the water contained in the wood, usually expressed as a percentage of the weight of the oven-dry wood.
MOLDING - (1) A wood strip having a curved or projecting surface used for decorative purposes.
(2) Material, usually patterned strips, used to provide ornamental variation of outline or contour, whether projections or cavities, such as cornices, bases, window and doorjambs, and heads.
MOLDING BASE - The molding on the top of a base board.
BED - A molding used to cover the joint between the plancier and frieze; also used as a base molding upon heavy work, and sometimes as a member of a cornice.
LIP - A molding with a lip which overlaps the piece against which the back of the molding rests.
RAKE - The cornice upon the gable edge of a pitch roof, the members of which are made to fit those of the molding of the horizontal eaves.
PICTURE - A molding shaped to form a support for picture hooks, often placed at some distance from the ceiling upon the wall to form the lower edge of the frieze.
MORTISE - The hole which is to receive a tenon, or any hole cut into or through a piece by a chisel; generally of rectangular shape.
MULLION - The construction between the openings of a window frame to accommodate two or more windows.

MUNTIN - The vertical member between two panels of the same piece of panel work. The vertical sash-bars separating the different panels of glass.

N

NATURAL FINISH - (1) A transparent^inish which does not seriously alter the original color or grain of the natural wood. Natural finishes are usually provided by sealers, oils, varnishes, water-repellent, preservatives, and other similar materials.

(2) A transparent finish, usually a drying oil, sealer, or varnish, applied on wood for the purpose of protection against soiling or weathering. Such a finish may not seriously alter the original color of the wood or obscure its grain pattern.

NAVAL STORES - A term applied to the oils, resins, tars, and pitches derived from oleoresin contained in, exuded by, or extracted from trees chiefly of the pine species (genus *Pinus)* or from the wood of such trees.

NEWEL - (1) The principal post of the foot of a staircase; also the central support of a winding flight of stairs.

(2) A post to which the end of a stair railing or balustrade is fastened. Also, any post to which a railing or balustrade is fastened.

NONBEARING WALL - A wall supporting no load other than its own weight.

NONLOADBEARING WALL - A wall supporting no load other than its own weight.

NOSING - (1) The part of a stair tread which projects over the riser, or any similar projection; a term applied to the rounded edge of a board.

(2) The projecting edge of a molding or drip. Usually applied to the projecting molding on the edge of a stair tread.

NOTCH - A crosswise rabbet at the end of a board.

O

O.C. ON CENTER - The measurement of spacing for studs, rafters, joists, and the like in a building from center of one member to the center of the next.

O.G. OR OGEE - A molding with a profile in the form of a letter S; having the outline of a reversed curve.

OLD GROWTH - Timber growing in or harvested from a mature, naturally established forest. When the trees have grown most or all of their individual lives in active competition with their companions for sunlight and moisture, this timber is usually straight and relatively free of knots.

OVENDRY WOOD - Wood dried to constant weight in an oven at temperatures above that of boiling water (usually 101° to 105°C. or 214° to 221°F.).

P

PAINT — (1) A combination of pigments with suitable thinners or oils to provide decorative and protective coatings.

(2) L, pure white lead (basic-carbonate) paint; TLZ, titanium-lead-zinc paint; TZ, titanium-zinc paint.

PANEL - (1) A large, thin board or sheet of lumber, plywood, or other material. A thin board with all its edges inserted in a groove of a surrounding frame of thick material. A portion of a flat surface recessed or sunk below the surrounding area, distinctly set off by molding or some other decorative device. Also, a section of floor, wall, ceiling, or roof, usually prefabricated and of large size, handled as a single unit in the operations of assembly and erection.

(2) In house construction, a thin flat piece of wood, plywood, or similar material, framed by stiles and rails as in a door or fitted into grooves of thicker material with molded edges for decorative wall treatment.

PAPER, BUILDING - A general term for papers, felts, and similar sheet materials used in buildings without reference to their properties or uses.

PAPER, SHEATHING - A building material, generally paper or felt, used in wall and roof construction as a protection against the passage of air and sometimes moisture.

PARTING STOP OR STRIP - A small wood piece used in the side and head jambs of double-hung windows to separate upper and lower sash.

PARTITION A wall that subdivides spaces within any story of a building.

PARTITION TYPES:

BEARING PARTITION - A partition which supports any vertical load in addition to its own weight.

NONBEARING PARTITION - A partition extending from floor to ceiling but which supports no load other than its own weight.

PECK - Pockets or areas of disintegrated wood caused by advanced stages of localized decay in the living tree. It is usually associated with cypress and incense-cedar. There is no further development of peck once the lumber is seasoned.

PENNY - As applied to nails, it originally indicated the price per hundred. The term now serves as a measure of nail length and is abbreviated by the letter d.

PERM - A measure of water vapor movement through a material (grains per square foot per hour per inch of mercury difference in vapor pressure).

PIER - A column of masonry, usually rectangular in horizontal cross-section, used to support other structural members.

PIGMENT - A powdered solid in suitable degree of subdivision for use in paint or enamel.

PILASTER - A portion of a square column usually set within or against a wall.

PILES - Long posts driven into the soil in swampy locations or whenever it is difficult to secure a firm foundation, upon which the footing course of masonry or other timbers are laid.

PITCH - (1) The incline or rise of a roof. Pitch is expressed in inches or rise per foot of run, or by the ratio of the rise to the span.

(2) The incline slope of a roof, or the ratio of the total rise to the total width of a house; i.e., an 8-foot rise and a 24-foot width are a 1/3 pitch roof.

ROOF SLOPE is expressed in inches of rise per 12 inches of run.

(3) Inclination or slope, as for roofs or stairs, or the rise divided by the span.

PITCH BOARD - A board sawed to the exact shape formed by the stair tread, riser, and slope of the stairs and used to lay out the carriage and stringers.

PITCH POCKET - An opening that extends parallel to the annual growth rings and that contains, or has contained, either solid or liquid pitch.

PITCH STREAK - A well-defined accumulation of pitch in a more or less regular streak in the wood of certain softwoods.

PITH - The small, soft core occurring in the structural center of a tree trunk, branch, twig, or log.

PLAINSAWED - (See GRAIN)

PLAN - A horizontal geometrical section of a building, showing the walls, doors, windows, stairs, chimneys, columns, etc.

PLANING-MILL PRODUCTS - Products worked to pattern, such as flooring, ceiling, and siding.

PLANKS OR LUMBER - Material 2 or 3 inches thick and more than 4 inches wide, such as joists, flooring, etc.
PLASTER - A mixture of lime, hair, and sand, or of lime, cement, and sand, used to cover outside and inside wall surfaces.
PLATE - (1) The top horizontal piece of the walls of a frame building upon which the roof rests.
(2) A. A horizontal structural member placed on a wall or supported on posts, studs, or corbels to carry the trusses of a roof or to carry the rafters directly.
B. A shoe or base member, as of a partition or other frame.
C. A small, relatively thin member placed on or in a wall to support girders, rafters, etc.
(3) Sill plate - A horizontal member anchored to a masonry wall.
Sole plate - Bottom horizontal member of a frame wall.
Top plate - Top horizontal member of a frame wall supporting ceiling joists, rafters, or other members.
PLATE CUT - The cut in a rafter which rests upon the plate; sometimes called the seat cut.
PLOUGH - To cut a groove, as in a plank.
PLUMB - Exactly perpendicular; vertical.
PLUMB CUT - Any cut made in a vertical plane; the vertical cut at the top end of a rafter.
PLY - (1) A term used to denote a layer or thickness of building or roofing paper as two-ply, three-ply, etc.
(2) A term to denote the number of thicknesses or layers of roofing felt, veneer in plywood, or layers in built-up materials, in any finished piece of such material.
PLYWOOD - (1) A piece of wood made of three or more layers of veneer joined with glue and usually laid with the grain of adjoining plies at right angles. Almost always an odd number of plies are used to provide balanced construction.
(2) An assembly made of layers (plies) of veneer, or of veneer in combination with a lumber core, joined with an adhesive. The grain of adjoining plies is usually laid at right angles, and almost always an odd number of plies are used to obtain balanced construction.
PORCH - (1) An ornamental entrance way.
(2) A floor extending beyond the exterior walls of a building. It may be enclosed or unenclosed, roofed or uncovered.
(3) A roofed area extending beyond the main house. May be open or enclosed and with concrete or wood frame floor system.
PORE - (See VESSELS)
PORES - Wood cells of comparatively large diameter that have open ends and are set one above the other to form continuous tubes. The openings of the vessels on the surface of a piece of wood are referred to as pores.
POROUS WOODS - Another name for hardwoods, which frequently have vessels or pores large enough to be seen readily without magnification.
POST - A timber set on end to support a wall, girder, or other member of the structure.
PLOW - To cut a groove running in the same direction as the grain of the wood.
PRESERVATIVE - Any substance that, for a reasonable length of time, will prevent the action of wood-destroying fungi, borers of various kinds, and similar destructive life when the wood has been properly coated or impregnated with it.
PRIMER - The first coat of paint in a paint job that consists of two or more coats; also the paint used for such a first coat.

PULLEY STILE - The member of a window frame which contains the pulleys and between which the edges of the sash slide.
PURLIN - A timber supporting several rafters at one or more points, or the roof sheeting directly.
PUTTY - A type of cement usually made of whiting and boiled linseed oil, beaten or kneaded to the consistency of dough, and used in sealing glass in sash, filling small holes and crevices in wood, and for similar purposes.

Q

QUARTER ROUND - A small molding that has the cross-section of a quarter circle.

R

RABBET or REBATE - (1) A corner cut out of an edge of a piece of wood.
(2) A rectangular longitudinal groove cut in the corner of a board or other piece of material.
RADIAL - Coincident with a radius from the axis of the tree or log to the circumference. A radial section is a lengthwise section in a plane that extends from pith to bark.
RADIANT HEATING - A method of heating, usually consisting of coils or pipes placed in the floor, wall, or ceiling.
RAFTER - One of a series of structural members of a roof designed to support roof loads. The rafters of a flat roof are sometimes called roof joists.
RAFTERS, COMMON - Those which run square with the plate and extend to the ridge.
CRIPPLE - Those which cut between valley and hip rafters.
HIP - Those extending from the outside angle of the plates toward the apex of the roof.
JACKS - Those square with the plate and intersecting the hip rafter.
VALLEY - Those extending from an inside angle of the plates toward the ridge or center line of the house.
RAIL - (1) The horizontal members of a balustrade or panel work.
(2) Cross members of panel doors or of a sash. Also the upper and lower members of a balustrade or staircase extending from one vertical support, such as a post, to another.
(3) A horizontal bar or timber of wood or metal extending from one post or support to another as a guard or barrier in a fence, balustrade, staircase, etc. Also, the cross or horizontal members
of the framework of a sash, door, blind, or any paneled assembly.
RAKE - (1) The trim of a building extending in an oblique line, as rake dado or molding.
(2) The trim members that run parallel to the roof slope and from the finish between wall and roof.
(3) The inclined edge of a gable roof (the trim member is a rake molding).
RATE OF GROWTH - The rate at which a tree has laid on wood, measured radially in the trunk or in lumber cut from the trunk. The unit of measure in use is number of annual growth rings per inch.
RAW LINSEED OIL - The crude product expressed from flaxseed and usually without much subsequent treatment.
RAYS, WOOD - Strips of cells extending radially within a tree and varying in height from a few cells in some species to 4 or more inches in oak. The rays serve primarily to store food and transport it horizontally in the tree.

REFLECTIVE INSULATION - Sheet material with one or both surfaces of comparatively low heat emissivity that, when used in building construction so that the surfaces face air spaces, reduces the radiation across the air space.
REINFORCING - Steel rods or metal fabric placed in concrete slabs, beams, or columns to increase their strength.
RELATIVE HUMIDITY - The amount of water vapor expressed as a percentage of the maximum quantity that could be present in the atmosphere at a given temperature. (The actual amount of water vapor that can be held in space increases with the temperature.)
RESIN-EMULSION PAINT - Paint, the vehicle (liquid part) of which consists of resin or varnish dispersed in fine droplets in water, analogous to cream, which consists of butter-fat dispersed in water.
RESIN PASSAGE (OR DUCT) - Intercellular passages that contain and transmit resinous materials. On a cut surface, they are usually inconspicuous. They may extend vertically parallel to the axis of the tree or at right angles to the axis and parallel to the rays.
RETURN - The continuation of a molding or finish of any kind in a different direction.
RIBBAND - (See LEDGERBOARD)
RIBBON - A narrow board let into the studding to add support to joists.
RIDGE - The horizontal line at the junction of the top edges of two sloping roof surfaces. The rafters of both slopes are nailed to the ridge board. (See PLUMB CUT)
RIDGE BOARD - The board placed on edge at the ridge of the roof into which the upper ends of the rafters are fastened.
RING-POROUS WOODS - A group of hardwoods in which the pores are comparatively large at the beginning of each annual ring and decrease in size more or less abruptly toward the outer portion of the ring, thus forming a distinct inner zone of pores, known as the springwood, and an outer zone with smaller pores, known as the summerwood.
RISE - (1) The height a roof rising in horizontal distance (run) from the outside face of a wall supporting the rafters or trusses to the ridge of the roof. In stairs, the perpendicular height of a step or flight of steps.
(2) The vertical distance through which anything rises, as the rise of a roof or stair.
RISER - Each of the vertical boards closing the spaces between the treads of stairways.
ROLL ROOFING - Roofing material, composed of fiber and saturated with asphalt, that is supplied in rolls containing 108 square feet in 36-inch widths. It is generally furnished in weights of 55 to 90 pounds per roll.
ROOF - The entire construction used to close in the top of a building.
ROOF SHEATHING - The boards or sheet material fastened to the roof rafters on which the shingle or other roof covering is laid.
ROOFING - The material put on a roof to make it wind and waterproof.
ROUTED - (See MORTISED)
RUBBER-EMULSION PAINT - Paint, the vehicle of which consists of rubber or synthetic rubber dispersed in fine droplets in water.
RUBBLE - Roughly broken quarry stone.
RUBBLE MASONRY - Uncut stone, used for rough work, foundations, backing, and the like.
RUN - (1) The length of the horizontal projection of a piece such as a rafter when in position.
(2) In reference to roofs, the horizontal distance from the face of a wall to the ridge of the roof. Referring to stairways, the net width of a step; also the horizontal distance covered by a flight of steps.

S

SADDLE BOARD - The finish of the ridge of a pitch-roof house. Sometimes called comb board.
SAP - All the fluids in a tree except special secretions and excretions , such as oleoresin.
SAPWOOD - (1) The living wood of pale color near the outside of the log. Under most conditions the sapwood is more susceptible to decay than heartwood.
(2) The outer zone of wood, next to the bark. In the living tree it contains some living cells (the heartwood contains none), as well as dead and dying cells. In most species, it is lighter colored than the heartwood. In all species, it is lacking in decay resistance. SASH-(1) A single light frame containing one or more lights of glass.
(2) The framework which holds the glass in a window.
SASH BALANCE - A device, usually operated with a spring, designed to counterbalance window sash. Use of sash balances eliminates the need for sash weights, pulleys, and sash cord.
SATURATED FELT - A felt which is impregnated with tar or asphalt.
SAWING, PLAIN - Lumber sawed regardless of the grain, the log simply squared and sawed to the desired thickness; sometimes called slash or bastard sawed.
SCAB - (1) A short piece of lumber used to splice, or to prevent movement of two other pieces.
(2) A short piece of wood or plywood fastened to two abutting timbers to splice them together.
SCAFFOLD or STAGING - A temporary structure or platform enabling workmen to reach high places.
SCALE - A short measurement used as a proportionate part of a larger dimension. The scale of a drawing is expressed as 1/4 inch = 1 ft.
SCANTLING - Lumber with a cross-section ranging from 2 by 4 inches to 4 by 4 inches.
SCARFING - A joint between two pieces of wood which allows them to be spliced lengthwise.
SCOTIA - A hollow molding used as a part of a cornice, and often under the nosing of a stair tread.
SCRATCH COAT - The first coat of plaster, which is scratched to form a bond for the second coat.
SCRIBING - (1) The marking of a piece of work to provide for the fitting of one of its surfaces to the irregular surface of another.
(2) Fitting woodwork to an irregular surface.
SEALER - A finishing material, either clear or pigmented, that is usually applied directly over uncoated wood for the purpose of sealing the surface.
SEASONING - Removing moisture from green wood in order to improve its serviceability.
AIR-DRIED - Dried by exposure to air, usually in a yard, without artificial heat.
KILN-DRIED - Dried in a kiln with the use of artificial heat.
SEAT CUT or PLATE CUT - The cut at the bottom end of a rafter to allow it to fit upon the plate.
SEAT OF A RAFTER - The horizontal cut upon the bottom end of a rafter which rests upon the top of the plate.
SECOND GROWTH - Timber that has grown after removal by cutting, fire, wind, or other agency, of all or a large part of the previous stand.
SECTION - A drawing showing the kind, arrangement, and proportions of the various parts of a structure. It is assumed that the structure is cut by a plane, and the section is the view gained by looking in one direction.
SEMIGLOSS PAINT OR ENAMEL - A paint or enamel made with a slight insufficiency of nonvolatile vehicle so that its coating when dry, has some luster but is not very glossy.

SHAKE - A thick handsplit shingle, resawed to form two shakes, usually edge grained.
SHAKES - Imperfections in timber caused during the growth of the tree by high winds or imperfect conditions of growth.
SHEATHING - (1) The structural covering, usually wood boards or plywood, used over studs or rafters of a structure. Structural building board is normally used only as wall sheathing.
(2) Wall boards, roofing boards; generally applied to narrow boards laid with a space between them, according to the length of a shingle exposed to weather.
SHEATHING PAPER - (1) The paper used under siding or shingles to in-sulate in the house; building papers.
(2) A building material used in wall, floor, and roof construction to resist the passage of air.
SHELLAC - A transparent coating made by dissolving lac, a resinous secretion of the lac bug (a scale insect that thrives in tropical countries, especially India), in alcohol.
SHINGLES - Roof covering of asphalt, asbestos, wood, tile, slate, or other material cut to stock lengths, widths, and thicknesses.
SHINGLES, SIDING - Various kinds of shingles, such as wood shingles or shakes and non-wood shingles, that are used over sheathing for exterior sidewall covering of a structure.
SHIPLAP - (See LUMBER, SHIPLAP)
SIDING - The finish covering of the outside wall of a frame building, whether made of horizontal weatherboards, vertical boards with battens, shingles, or other material.
SIDING, BEVEL (LAP SIDING) - Used as the finish siding on the exterior of a house or other structure. It is usually manufactured by resawing dry square-surfaced boards diagonally to produce two wedge-shaped pieces. These pieces commonly run from 3/16 inch thick on the thin edge to 1/2 to 3/4 inch thick on the other edge, depending on the width of the siding.
SIDING, DROP - Usually 3/4 inch thick and 6 inches wide, machined into various patterns. Drop siding has tongue-and-groove joints, is heavier, has more structural strength, and is frequently used on buildings that require no sheathing, such as garages and barns.
SIDING, PANEL - Large sheets of plywood or hardboard which serve as both sheathing and siding.
SILL - The lowest member of the frame of a structure, resting on the foundation and supporting the floor joists or the uprights of the wall. The member forming the lower side of an opening, as a door sill, window sill, etc.
SILLS - The horizontal timbers of a house which either rest upon the masonry foundations or, in the absence of such, form the foundations.
SIZING - Working material to the desired size; a coating of glue, shellac, or other substance applied to a surface to prepare it for painting or other method of finish.
SLEEPER - A timber laid on the ground to support a floor joist.
SOFFIT - The underside of the members of a building, such as staircases, cornices, beams, and arches, relatively minor in area as compared with ceilings.
SOFTWOODS - Generally, the botanical group of trees that bear cones and in most cases have needlelike or scalelike leaves; also the wood produced by such trees. The term has no reference to the actual hardness of the wood.
SOIL COVER (GROUND COVER) - A light covering of plastic film, rool roofing, or similar material used over the soil in crawl spaces of buildings to minimize moisture permeation of the area.

SOIL STACK - A general term for the vertical main of a system of soil, waste, or vent piping.
SOLE OR SOLEPLATE - A member, usually a 2 by 4, on which wall and partition studs rest.
SPAN - The distance between structural supports such as walls, columns, piers, beams, girders, and trusses.
SPECIFIC GRAVITY - The ratio of the weight of a body to the weight of an equal volume of water at 4°C. or other specified temperature.
SPECIFICATIONS - The written or printed directions regarding the details of a building or other construction.
SPLASH BLOCK - A small masonry block laid with the top close to the ground surface to receive roof drainage and to carry it away from the building.
SPLICE - Joining of two similar members in a straight line.
SPRINGWOOD - The portion of the annual growth ring that is formed during the early part of the season's growth. In most softwoods and in ring-porous hardwoods, it is less dense and weaker mechanically than summerwood.
SQUARE - (1) A tool used by mechanics to obtain accuracy; a term applied to a surface including 100 square feet.
(2) A unit of measure - 100 square feet - usually applied to roofing material. Sidewall coverings are sometimes packed to cover 100 square feet and are sold on that basis.
STAIN - A discoloration in wood that may be caused by such diverse agencies as micro-organisms, metal, or chemicals. The term also applies to materials used to color wood.
STAIN, SHINGLE - A form of oil paint, very thin in consistency, intended for coloring wood with rough surfaces, like shingles, without forming a coating of significant thickness or gloss.
STAIR CARRIAGE - (1) Supporting member for stair treads. Usually a 2-inch plank notched to receive the treads; sometimes termed a "rough horse."
(2) A stringer for steps on stairs.
STAIR LANDING - A platform between flights of stairs or at the termination of a flight of stairs.
STAIR RISE - The vertical distance from the top of one stair tread to the top of the cne next above.
STAIRS, BOX - Those built between walls, and usually with no support except the wall strings.
STANDING FINISH - Term applied to the finish of the openings and the base, and all other finish work necessary for the inside.
STOOL - (1) The flat, narrow shelf forming the top member of the interior trim at the bottom of a window.
(2) A flat molding fitted over the window sill between jambs and contacting the bottom rail of the lower sash.
STORM SASH OR STORM WINDOW - An extra window usually placed on the outside of an existing window as additional protection against cold weather.
STORY - That part of a building between any floor and the floor or roof next above.
STRENGTH - The term in its broader sense includes all the properties of wood that enable it to resist different forces or loads. In its more restricted sense, strength may apply to any one of the mechanical properties, in which event the name of the property under consideration should be stated, thus: strength in compression parallel to grain, strength in bending, hardness, and so on.
STRESS - Force per unit of area.

STRING, STRINGER - A timber or other support for cross members in floors or ceilings. In stairs, the support on which the stair treads rest; also stringboard.
STRINGER - A long horizontal timber in a structure supporting a floor.
STUCCO - (1) Most commonly refers to an outside plaster made with Portland cement as its base.
(2) A fine plaster used for interior decoration and fine work; also for rough outside wall coverings.
STUD - (1) An upright beam in the framework of a building.
(2) One of a series of slender wood or metal vertical structural members placed as supporting elements in walls and partitions. (Plural: studs or studding.)
STUDDING - The framework of a partition or the wall of a house; usually referred to as 2 by 4's.
SUBFLOOR - (1) A wood floor which is laid over the floor joists and on which the finished floor is laid.
(2) Boards or plywood laid on joists over which a finish floor is to be laid.
SUMMERWOOD - The portion of the annual growth ring that is formed after the springwood formation has ceased. In most softwoods and in ring-porous hardwoods, it is denser and stronger mechanically than springwood.

T

TAIL BEAM - A relatively short beam or joist supported in a wall on one end and by a header at the other.
TANGENTIAL - Strictly, coincident with a tangent at the circumference of a tree or log, or parallel to such a tangent. In practice, however, it often means roughly coincident with a growth ring. A tangential section is a longitudinal section through a tree or limb and is perpendicular to a radius. Flat-grained and plainsawed lumber is sawed tangentially.
TERMITE SHIELD - A shield, usually of noncorrodible metal, placed in or on a foundation wall or other mass of masonry or around pipes to prevent passage of termites.
TERMITES - Insects that superficially resemble ants in size, general appearance, and habit of living in colonies; hence, frequently called "white ants." Subterranean termites do not establish themselves in buildings by being carried in with lumber, but by entering from ground nests after the building has been constructed. If unmolested they eat out the woodwork, leaving a shell of sound wood to conceal their activities, and damage may proceed so far so to cause collapse of parts of a structure before discovery. There are about 56 species of termites known in the United States; but the two main species, classified from the manner in which they attack wood, subterranean (ground-inhabiting) termites, the most common, and drywood termites, found almost exclusively along the extreme southern border and the Gulf of Mexico in the United States.
TEXTURE - A term often used interchangeably with grain. Sometimes used to combine the concepts of density and degree of contrast between springwood and summerwood. In this publication, texture refers to the finer structure of the wood (see GRAIN) rather than the annual rings.
THRESHOLD - (1) A strip of wood or metal with beveled edges used over the finished floor and the sill of exterior doors.
(2) The beveled piece over which the door swings; sometimes called a carpet strip.
TIE BEAM (COLLAR BEAM)- A beam so situated that it ties the principal rafters of a roof together and prevents them from thrusting the plate out of line.
TIMBER - Lumber with cross-section over 4 by 6 inches; such as posts, sills, and girders.
TIN SHINGLE - A small piece of tin used in flashing and repairing a shingle roof.

TO THE WEATHER - A term applied to the projecting of shingles or siding beyond the course above.
TOENAILING - To drive a nail at a slant with the initial surface in order to permit it to penetrate into a second member.
TREAD - The horizontal board in a stairway on which the foot is placed.
TRIM - (1) The finish materials in a building, such as moldings, applied around openings (window trims, door trim) or at the floor and ceiling of rooms (baseboard, cornice, picture molding).
(2) A term sometimes applied to outside or interior finished woodwork and the finish around openings.
TRIMMER - A beam or joist to which a header is nailed in framing for a chimney, stairway, or other opening.
TRIMMING - Putting the inside and outside finish and hardware upon a building.
TRUSS - (1) Structural framework of triangular units for supporting loads over long spans.
(2) A frame or jointed structure designed to act as a beam of long span, while each member is usually subjected to longitudinal stress only, either tension or compression.
TURPENTINE - A volatile oil used as a thinner in paints, and as a solvent in varnishes. Chemically, it is a mixture of terpenes.
TWIST - A distortion caused by the turning or winding of the edges of a board so that the four corners of any face are no longer in the same plane.
TYLOSES - Masses of cells appearing somewhat like froth in the pores of some hardwoods, notably white oak and black locust. In hardwoods, tyloses are formed when walls of living cells surrounding vessels extend into the vessels. They are sometimes formed in softwoods in a similar manner by the extension of cell walls into resin-passage cavities.

U

UNDERCOAT - A coating applied prioT to the finishing or top coats of a paint job. It may be the first of two or the second of three coats. In some usage of the word it may become synonymous with priming coat.

V

VALLEY - The internal angle formed by the junction of two sloping sides of a roof.
VAPOR BARRIER - Material used to retard the flow of vapor or moisture into walls and thus to prevent condensation within them. There are two types of vapor barriers, the membrane that comes in rolls and is applied as a unit in the wall or ceiling construction, and the paint type, which is applied with a brush. The vapor barrier must be a part of the warm side of the wall.
VARNISH - A thickened preparation of drying oil or drying oil and resin suitable for spreading on surfaces to form continuous, transparent coatings, or for mixing with pigments to make enamels.
VEHICLE - The liquid portion of a finishing material; it consists of the binder (nonvolatile) and volatile thinners.
VENEER - A thin layer or sheet of wood cut on a veneer machine.
ROTARY-CUT VENEER - Veneer cut in a lathe which rotates a log or bolt, chucked in the center, against a knife.
SAWED VENEER - Veneer produced by sawing.
SLICED VENEER - Veneer that is sliced off a log, bolt, or flitch with a knife.

VENT - A pipe installed to provide a flow of air to or from a drainage system or to provide a circulation of air within such system to protect trap seals from siphonage and back pressure.
VERGE BOARDS - The boards which serve as the eaves finish on the gable end of a building.
VERMICULITE - A mineral closely related to mica, with the faculty of expanding on heating to form lightweight material with insulation quality. Used as bulk insulation and also as aggregate in insulating and acoustical plaster and in insulating concrete floors.
VERTICAL GRAIN - (See GRAIN)
VESSELS - Wood cells of comparatively large diameter that have open ends and are set one above the other so as to form continuous tubes. The openings of the vessels on the surface of a piece of wood are usually referred to as *pores*.
VESTIBULE - An entrance to a house; usually inclosed.
VIRGIN GROWTH - The original growth of mature trees.
VOLATILE THINNER - A liquid that evporates readily and is used to thin or reduce the consistency of finishes without altering the relative volumes of pigments and nonvolatile vehicle.

W

WAINSOOTING - Matched boarding or panel work covering the lower portion of a wall.
WALE - A horizontal beam.
WALL, BEARING - A wall which supports any vertical load in addition to its own weight.
WALLBOARD - Wood pulp, gypsum, or similar materials made into large, rigid sheets that may be fastened to the frame of a building to provide a surface finish.
WANE - Bark or lack of wood from any cause on the edge or corner of a piece of lumber.
WARP - Any variation from a true or plane surface. Warp includes bow, crook, cup, and twist, or any combination thereof.
WASH - (1) The upper surface of a member or material when given a slope to shed water.
(2) The slant upon a sill, capping, etc., to allow the water to run off easily.
WATER REPELLENT - A liquid designed to penetrate into wood and to impart water repellency to the wood.
WATER-REPELLENT PRESERVATIVE - A liquid designed to penetrate into wood and impart water repellency and a moderate preservative protection. It is used for millwork, such as sash and frames, and is usually applied by dipping.
WATER TABLE - (1) A ledge or offset on or above a foundation wall, for the purpose of shedding water.
(2) The finish at the bottom of a house which carries the water away from the foundation.
WEATHERING - The mechanical or chemical disintegration and discoloration of the surface of wood that is caused by exposure to light, the action of dust and sand carried by winds, and the alternate shrinking and swelling of the surface fibers with the continual variation in moisture content brought by changes in the weather. Weathering does not include decay.
WEATHERSTRIP - (1) Narrow strips made of metal, or other material, so designed that when installed at doors or windows they will retard the passage of air, water, moisture, or dust around the door or window sash.
(2) Narrow or jamb-width sections of thin metal or other material to prevent infiltration of air and moisture around windows and doors.

WIND ("i" pronounced as in kind) - A term used to describe the surface of a board when twisted (winding) or when resting upon two diagonally opposite corners, if laid upon a perfectly flat surface.
WOODEN BRICK - Piece of seasoned wood, made the size of a brick, and laid where it is necessary to provide a nailing space in masonry walls.
WOOD RAYS - Strips of cells extending radially within a tree and varying in height from a few cells in some species to 4 inches or more in oak. The rays serve primarily to store food and to transport it horizontally in the tree.
WOOD SUBSTANCE - The solid material of which wood is composed. It usually refers to the extractive-free solid substance of which the cell walls are composed, but this is not always true. There is no wide variation in chemical composition or specific gravity between the wood substance of various species; the characteristic differences of species are largely due to differences in infiltrated materials and variations in relative amounts of cell walls and cell cavities.
WORKABILITY - The degree of ease and smoothness of cut obtainable with hand or machine tools.

HOUSING AND COMMUNITY DEVELOPMENT GLOSSARY

ACRONYMS AND ABBREVIATED REFERENCES

ACC .... Annual contributions contract.
AHOP .... Areawide housing opportunity plan.
AHS .... Annual housing survey.
AML .... Adjustable mortgage loan.
APA .... Administrative Procedure Act (5 U.S.C. 551 et seq.)
ARM .... Adjustable rate mortgage.
BMIR .... Below-market interest rate.
Budget Act .... Congressional Budget and Impoundment Control Act of 1974.
Budget Res. .... Concurrent resolution on the budget.
CBO .... Congressional Budget Office.
CD .... Community development.
CDBG .... Community development block grant.
CFR .... Code of Federal Regulations.
CIAP .... Comprehensive improvement assistance program.
Continuing Res .... Joint resolution continuing appropriations for the next fiscal year.
CPI .... Consumer Price Index.
DOE .... Department of Energy.
EDA .... Economic Development Administration.
EIS .... Environmental impact statement.
ERTA .... Economic Recovery Tax Act of 1981.
Fannie Mae .... Federal National Mortgage Association.
FDIC .... Federal Deposit Insurance Corporation.
FEMA .... Federal Emergency Management Agency.
FFB .... Federal Financing Bank.
FHA .... Federal Housing Administration.
FHLBB .... Federal Home Loan Bank Board.
FHLMC .... Federal Home Loan Mortgage Corporation (Freddie Mac).
FmHA .... Farmers Home Administration.
FMR .... Fair market rent.
FNMA .... Federal National Mortgage Association (Fannie Mae).
FR .... Federal Register.
Freddie Mac .... Federal Home Loan Mortgage Corporation.
FSLIC .... Federal Savings and Loan Insurance Corporation.
GAO .... Government Accounting Office.
Garn-St Germain .... Garn-St Germain Depository Institutions Act of 1982.
GEM .... Growing equity mortgage.
Ginnie Mae .... Government National Mortgage Association.
GNMA .... Government National Mortgage Association (Ginnie Mae).

GLOSSARY

GPM .... Graduated payment mortgage.
Gramm-Latta .... Omnibus Budget Reconciliation Act of 1981.
HAP .... Housing assistance plan.
HFA .... Housing finance agency.
HHS .... Department of Health and Human Services.
HoDAG .... Housing development grant.
HUD .... Department of Housing and Urban Development.
HURRA. .... Housing and Urban-Rural Recovery Act of 1983.
IG .... Inspector General.
IRS .... Internal Revenue Service.
MBS .... Mortgage-backed securities.
Mod Rehab .... Moderate rehabilitation.
MPS .... Minimum property standards.
MSA .... Metropolitan statistical area.
NHP .... National Housing Partnership.
NIBS .... National Institute of Building Sciences.
NOFA .... Notice of funding availability.
NSA .... Neighborhood strategy area.
OBRA .... Omnibus Budget Reconciliation Act of 1981.
OMB .... Office of Management and Budget.
PAM .... Pledged account mortgage.
PC .... Participation certificate.
PFS .... Performance funding system.
PHA .... Public housing agency.
PLAM .... Price-level adjusted mortgage.
PMI .... Private mortgage insurance.
PUD .... Planned unit development.
RAM .... Reverse annuity mortgage.
RAP .... Rental assistance payments.
REIT .... Real estate investment trust.
RESPA .... Real Estate Settlement Procedures Act of 1974.
SAM .... Shared appreciation mortgage.
Solar Bank .... Solar Energy and Energy Conservation Bank.
SRO .... Single room occupancy housing.
Sub Rehab .... Substantial rehabilitation.
TEFRA .... Tax Equity and Fiscal Responsibility Act of 1982.
TMAP .... Temporary mortgage assistance payments.
UDAG .... Urban development action grant.
U.S.C .... United States Code.
VA .... Veterans' Administration.

ABBREVIATED STATUTORY CITATIONS

Sec. 5 .... United States Housing Act of 1937 (funding for public housing and section 8 housing).
Sec. 7(o) .... Department of Housing and Urban Development Act (legislative review of HUD rules and regulations).

GLOSSARY

Sec. 8 .... United States Housing Act of 1937 (low-income rental housing assistance).
Sec. 9 .... United States Housing Act of 1937 (operating subsidies).
Sec. 14 .... United States Housing Act of 1937 (CLAP).
Sec. 17 .... United States Housing Act of 1937 (rental rehabilitation and development).
Sec. 101 .... Housing and Urban Development Act of 1965 (rent supplement).
Sec. 104 .... Housing and Community Development Act of 1974 (CDBG applications and review).
Sec. 105 .... Housing and Community Development Act of 1974 (CDBG eligible activities).
Sec. 106 .... Housing and Community Development Act of 1974 (CDBG allocation and distribution of funds).
Sec. 107 .... Housing and Community Development Act of 1974 (CD discretionary fund).
Sec. 108 .... Housing and Community Development Act of 1974 (CD loan guarantees).
Sec. 119 .... Housing and Community Development Act of 1974 (UDAG).
Sec. 201 .... Housing and Community Development Amendments of 1978 (troubled projects).
Sec. 202 .... Housing Act of 1959 (elderly and handicapped housing).
Sec. 203 .... Housing and Community Development Amendments of 1978 (management and preservation of HUD-owned projects). National Housing Act (single-family mortgage insurance).
Sec. 207 .... National Housing Act (multifamily mortgage insurance).
Sec. 213 .... Housing and Community Development Act of 1974 (allocation of funds for assisted housing). National Housing Act (cooperative housing mortgage insurance).
Sec. 221 .... National Housing Act (multifamily mortgage insurance).
Sec. 221(d)(3) .... National Housing Act (BMIR rental housing mortgage insurance).
Sec. 231 .... National Housing Act (mortgage insurance for elderly and handicapped rental housing).
Sec. 235 .... National Housing Act (home mortgage interest reduction payments).
Sec. 236 .... National Housing Act (rental and cooperative housing interest reduction payments).
Sec. 302(b)(2) .... Federal National Mortgage Association Charter Act (FNMA authority to deal in conventional mortgages).

GLOSSARY

Sec. 305(a)(2) .... Federal Home Loan Mortgage Corporation Act (FHLMC authority to deal in conventional mortgages).
Sec. 312 .... Housing Act of 1964 (rehabilitation loans).
Sec. 502 .... Housing Act of 1949 (rural housing loans and loan guarantees).
Sec. 513 .... Housing Act of 1949 (rural housing authorization amounts).
Sec. 515 .... Housing Act of 1949 (elderly and handicapped rural housing).
Sec. 521 .... Housing Act of 1949 (rural housing loan interest credits and RAP).
Sec. 533 .... Housing Act of 1949 (housing preservation grants).
Title I .... Housing and Community Development Act of 1974 (CDBG and UDAG). Housing Act of 1949 (urban renewal). National Housing Act (FHA property improvement loan insurance).
Title II .... National Housing Act (FHA mortgage insurance).
Title V .... Housing Act of 1949 (rural housing).

TERMS

Adjustable mortgage loan—See "adjustable rate mortgage".

Adjustable rate mortgage—A mortgage covering a loan the interest rate of which may vary periodically over the term of the loan, generally according to an established index. Also referred to as an adjustable mortgage loan.

Amortization—Gradual reduction of the principal of a loan, together with the payment of interest, according to a schedule of periodic payments so that the principal is fully paid by the end of the term of the loan.

Annual contributions contract—A contract under which HUD makes payments to a public housing agency equal to the amount of principal and interest owed by the PHA under obligations issued by it for the development, operation, or modernization of a public housing project.

Annual housing survey—An annual study by HUD and the Bureau of the Census regarding housing units, homeowners, and renters.

Appropriation—Constitutionally required legislation that grants Federal agencies the authority to make payments out of the Treasury for general or particular purposes. There are three general categories of appropriations legislation: general, supplemental, and continuing.

Areawide housing opportunity plan—A program to reduce the geographical concentration of lower income families by expanding housing opportunities throughout a wide area.

Assistance payments—Federal payments, made directly or through public housing agencies, to owners or prospective owners of rental housing to pay part of the rent of lower income tenants. See "interest-reduction payments".

Assumable mortgage—Mortgage in which the existing debt may be taken over by a third party without approval of the lender.

GLOSSARY

Authorization—Legislation granting authority for the congressional consideration of appropriations for general or particular purposes. Although unauthorized appropriations may be subject to points of order, they are legally valid if enacted.

Balloon mortgage—Mortgage under which the loan matures before the principal is fully repaid.

Below-market interest rate—HUD-insured mortgages financing homes for lower income families and displaced families bearing interest rates lower than the market rate, with the Federal Government bearing the cost of the difference in rates by purchase of the mortgages. See section 221(d)(3) of the National Housing Act.

Block grants—Grants by HUD on a noncategorical formula basis to assist community development and rehabilitation, including slum and blight elimination, conservation of housing, increased public services, improved use of land, and preservation of property. See title I of the Housing and Community Development Act of 1974.

Borrowing authority—Authority to incur indebtedness for which the Federal Government is liable, which authority is granted in advance of the provision of appropriations to repay such debts. Borrowing authority may take the form of authority to borrow from the Treasury or authority to borrow from the public by means of the sale of Federal agency obligations. Borrowing authority is not an appropriation since it provides a Federal agency only with the authority to incur a debt, and not the authority to make payments from the Treasury under the debt. Subsequent appropriations are required to liquidate the borrowing authority.

Budget authority—Legal authority to enter into obligations that will result in immediate or future outlays of Federal funds. Appropriations (unless liquidating borrowing authority or contract authority), contract authority, and borrowing authority are the three primary types of budget authority.

Coinsurance—HUD insurance of a mortgage, advance, or loan with the lender assuming a percentage of the loss on the insured obligation. See section 244 of the National Housing Act.

Commitment—An agreement to make or purchase a mortgage loan at a future date, or an agreement to insure a mortgage at a future date, if prescribed conditions are met by the mortgagee. Under HUD mortgage insurance, a traditional administration distinction exists between a special type of commitment known as a "conditional commitment" and other commitments known as "firm commitments". Under the former, a commitment is made to insure a mortgage (on a specific property for a definite loan amount) to be given by a future purchaser of the property involved if such a purchaser meets certain eligibility requirements. The term "standby commitment" is commonly used in the secondary market for residential mortgages to describe a commitment to purchase a mortgage loan or loans with specific terms, both parties understanding that the purchase is not likely to be completed unless particular circumstances make that advantageous to the seller of the mortgage. These commitments are typically used to enable the borrower to obtain construction financing at a lower cost on the assumption that permanent financing of the project will be available on more favorable terms than under the commitment when the project is completed and generating income.

Community development block grants—Block grants for community development made to States, urban counties, and metropolitan cities under section 106 of the Housing and Community Development Act of 1974.

GLOSSARY

Comprehensive improvement assistance—Assistance provided for the modernization of public housing projects under section 14 of the United States Housing Act of 1937.

Concurrent resolution on the budget—Concurrent resolution of the Congress establishing minimum revenues and maximum outlays for the congressional budget for the Federal Government.

Conditional commitment—See "commitment".

Condominiums—Multifamily housing projects with individual units owned by occupants, who also own an undivided interest in the common areas and facilities of the project.

Contract authority—Authority to enter into contracts obligating the Federal Government to make payments in the future, which authority is granted in advance of the provision of appropriations to make such payments. Contract authority is not an appropriation since it provides a Federal agency only with the authority to incur an obligation, and not the authority to make payments from the Treasury under the obligation. Subsequent appropriations are required to liquidate the contract authority.

Conventional mortgage—A mortgage covering a loan that is not insured by the HUD or guaranteed by the FmHA or VA.

Cooperatives—Multifamily housing projects owned by cooperative corporations with the stockholders of the corporations having the right to occupancy of the units.

Cost certification—A limitation, under HUD mortgage insurance for multifamily housing, on the amount of a mortgage eligible for insurance, which limitation is determined after completion of the project on the basis of the builder's certification as to the actual dollar amount of his costs for specific items of construction and prescribed related expenditures. Under this requirement, the insured mortgage is limited to a fixed percentage of that certified amount.

Deep subsidy program—Program of rental assistance payments under section 236(f)(2) of the National Housing Act.

Default—Failure to meet the terms of a mortgage or other loan agreement. Generally, a delinquency of more than 30 days under a mortgage is considered a default.

Delinquency—Failure to make any timely payment due under a mortgage or other loan agreement.

Direct endorsement—HUD program of delegated private mortgage processing of FHA loan applications under the single family mortgage insurance programs.

Discount point—An amount that may be payable to a lender by a borrower or seller in addition to principal and interest, equal to 1 percent of the principal amount of the loan.

Discretionary fund—Funds set aside for discretionary grants by HUD under section 107 of the Housing and Community Development Act of 1974.

Due-on-sale clause—A clause that may be included in a mortgage to authorize the mortgagee to require full repayment of the loan upon any transfer of the property.

Economic mix—Occupancy of rental housing by families of varying economic levels, including very low-income families, which is to be promoted by housing assistance payments. See section 8 of the United States Housing Act of 1937.

Elderly and handicapped housing—Generally refers to housing for elderly and handicapped persons developed by nonprofit sponsors with assistance provided by HUD under section 202 of the Housing Act of 1959.

GLOSSARY

Entitlement community—An urban county or metropolitan city eligible to receive a community development block grant directly from HUD.

Environmental impact statements—Statements required to be made under section 102(2)(C) of the National Environmental Policy Act of 1969 by Federal agencies in their recommendations or reports on proposals for legislation and other major Federal actions significantly affecting the quality of the human environment, as to the environmental impact of the proposed action; any adverse environmental effects that cannot be avoided should the proposal be implemented; relationship between local short-term use of man's environment and the maintenance and enhancement of long-term productivity; and any irreversible or irretrievable commitments of resources that would be involved in the proposed action should it be implemented. Applicants for block grants can assume responsibility for this statement under the community development program. See section 104(f) of the Housing and Community Development Act of 1974.

Estimated value—The basis of one of the limits on the amount of a mortgage that can be insured by HUD. For example, under certain programs the mortgage may not exceed 90 percent of the estimated value of the property when completed.

Fair market rent—An amount determined by HUD to be the cost of modest rental units in a particular market area.

Federal Home Loan Mortgage Corporation—A federally established and sponsored corporation, under the supervision of the Federal Home Loan Bank Board, that provides a secondary market primarily for conventional mortgages.

Federal Housing Administration—Part of HUD that has responsibility for carrying out the mortgage insurance programs of the National Housing Act.

Federal National Mortgage Association—A federally established and sponsored private corporation, under the general supervision of HUD, that provides a secondary market for mortgages.

Firm commitment—See "commitment".

Fiscal year—Annual accounting period of the Federal Government, beginning October 1 and ending September 30 of the subsequent calendar year. The fiscal year is designated by the calendar year in which it ends, so that fiscal year 2005 refers to the fiscal year beginning October 1, 2004 and ending September 30, 2005.

Flood insurance program—Program under which FEMA makes flood insurance available to participating communities under the National Flood Insurance Act of 1968.

Forebearance—The act of postponing or refraining from taking legal action against a mortgagor even though mortgage payments are in arrears.

Foreclosure—Legal procedure under which the property securing a loan is sold to pay the debt owed by a borrower who has defaulted.

Government National Mortgage Association—Federal corporation, and part of HUD, that provides a secondary market for federally guaranteed mortgages.

Graduated payment mortgage—A mortgage under which payments are comparatively low initially and then increase over a specified period before reaching a constant level.

Ground lease—Lease of land without improvements.

Growing equity mortgage—Mortgage under which payments increase over a specified period in order to accelerate the repayment of principal and thereby shorten the term of the loan.

Guaranteed loan—Loan in which a private lender is assured repayment by the Federal Government of part or all of the principal or interest, or both, in the event of a default by the borrower. Unlike an insured loan, no insurance fund exists and no insurance premiums are paid.

Hold-harmless provision—Statutory provision ensuring the continued eligibility of a specified class for certain assistance for a limited period of time. The most commonly cited examples are contained in paragraphs (4) and (6) of section 102(a) of the Housing and Community Development Act of 1974.

Home equity conversion mortgage—A form of mortgage in which the lender makes periodic payments to the borrower using the borrower's equity in the home as security.

Housing allowance payments—Payments made by HUD under section 504 of the Housing Act of 1970 to assist families in meeting rental or homeownership expenses.

Housing assistance planA part of the CDBG application describing local housing conditions and sets quantitative goals for providing housing to low- and moderate-income residents.

Housing development grant—Grant made by HUD under section 17(d) of the United States Housing Act of 1937 for the new construction or substantial rehabilitation of rental housing.

Housing finance agency—State agency responsible for financing housing and administering assisted housing programs.

Housing preservation grant—Grant made by FmHA under section 533 of the Housing Act of 1949 for the rehabilitation of single-family housing, rental housing, or cooperatives for low- and very low-income families and persons.

Industrial revenue bond—A debt instrument issued by a municipality or development corporation to finance the development of revenue-producing projects. Project revenues are then used to pay the debt service on the bonds. Section 103(b) of the Internal Revenue Code of 1954 establishes certain limitations.

Installment land contract—See "land contract".

Insured loan—Loan in which a private lender is assured repayment by the Federal Government of part or all of the principal or interest, or both, and for which the borrower pays insurance premiums.

Interest rate credits—Generally refers to the FmHA program of subsidized interest rate loans for single-family and multifamily housing for low or moderate income families under section 521(a)(1)(B) of the Housing Act of 1949. The subsidy may reduce the interest rate to as low as 1 percent.

Interest reduction payments—Periodic assistance payments by HUD to mortgagees to permit lower interest rate payments by lower income families (varying with fluctuations in incomes) on HUD insured mortgages financing homes, rental housing, or cooperative housing. See sections 235 and 236 of the National Housing Act.

Land contract—An agreement to transfer title to a property upon fulfillment of the contract conditions. Under an "installment land contract", the purchaser assumes possession immediately and makes periodic payments to the vendor (the owner of the property); title is transferred only when all payments have been made.

Leased housing—Low-rent housing provided by public housing agencies in housing leased from private owners.

Leveraging—The maximization of the effect of Federal assistance for a project by obtaining additional project funding from non-Federal sources. See section 119 of the Housing and Community Development Act of 1974.

Lien—Any legal claim on a property for payment of a debt. A mortgage is one example.

GLOSSARY

Loan-to-value ratio—The relationship between the amount of the mortgage loan and the appraised value of the property involved, expressed as a percentage of the appraised value. It is one of the traditional limitations on a mortgage eligible for mortgage insurance.

Lower income family—Generally, a family whose income does not exceed 80 percent of the median family income of the area involved.

Manufactured home—Housing, including a mobile home, that is factory-built or prefabricated.

Market rent—Rental that would be charged by the owner of a HUD-insured multifamily dwelling unit if the owner were paying interest on the loan at the HUD-approved market interest rate.

Metropolitan city—For purposes of the CDBG program, a city that is the central city of a metropolitan area or that has a population of not less than 50,000.

Metropolitan statistical area—Metropolitan area defined by the Office of Management and Budget. Previously referred to as standard metropolitan statistical area.

Minimum property standards—HUD regulations establishing minimum acceptable standards for properties to be purchased with HUD-insured mortgage loans.

Moderate income family—For purposes of the CDBG program, a family whose income exceeds 50 percent of the median family income of the area involved, but does not exceed 80 percent of the median family income of the area.

Moderate rehabilitation—Rehabilitation that is less comprehensive than substantial rehabilitation, such as repair or replacement of the heating or electrical system of a project.

Modernization—See “comprehensive improvement assistance”.

Mortgage—Conveyance of an interest in real property as security for repayment of a loan, including a loan made for the purchase or improvement of the real property.

Mortgage-backed securities—Obligations issued by an organization that has held and set aside mortgages as security for payment of the obligations. FNMA, GNMA, and FHLMC, as well as private organizations, issue such obligations.

Mortgage insurance programs—Generally refers to the insured loan programs carried out by HUD, through the FHA, under the National Housing Act.

Mortgage revenue bonds—Tax-exempt bonds issued by State and local governments and agencies to finance the sale or repair of single-family housing. The bonds are payable from revenues derived from repayments of interest on the mortgage loans financed from the proceeds of the bonds. Section 103A of the Internal Revenue Code of 1954 establishes certain limitations. Referred to as mortgage subsidy bonds in the Internal Revenue Code of 1954.

Mortgagee—A lender who is conveyed an interest in real property under a mortgage.

Mortgagor—A borrower who conveys an interest in real property under a mortgage.

Multifamily housingGenerally a project containing dwelling units for more than 4 families.

National Housing Partnership—A private limited partnership established under title IX of the Housing and Urban Development Act of 1969 for the purpose of carrying out the building, maintenance, or rehabilitation of housing and related facilities for lower or moderate income families. It can enter into partnerships or joint ventures, conduct research, provide technical assistance, and make loans or grants to accomplish its purpose.

GLOSSARY

National Institute of Building Sciences—A nonprofit nongovernmental organization established under section 809 of the Housing and Community Development Act of 1974 to make findings and to advise public and private sectors of the economy with respect to the use of building science and technology in achieving nationally acceptable standards for use in housing and building regulations.

Negative amortization—A loan prepayment schedule under which payments do not cover the full amount of interest due. The unpaid interest is added to the principal and, as a result, the outstanding principal balance increases rather than decreases.

Neighborhood development grant—A grant made by HUD to an eligible neighborhood nonprofit organization under section 123 of the Housing and Urban-Rural Recovery Act of 1983 to assist the organization in carrying out certain neighborhood development activities.

Neighborhood strategy area—Area in which concentrated housing rehabilitation and community development block grant activities are being undertaken.

Nonentitlement area—For purposes of the CDBG program, an area that is neither a metropolitan city nor urban county, and is therefore generally ineligible for direct grants from HUD.

Nonprofit sponsor—A group organized to undertake a housing project for reasons other than making a profit.

Notice of funding availability—A notice by HUD to inform potential project sponsors that contract authority is available.

Off-budget program—Federal program the transactions of which are not included in the Budget of the United States Government as a result of statutory requirement.

Operating subsidies—HUD payments to public housing agencies to assist the payment of operating expenses of public housing, or to the owners of certain multifamily projects for low income families. See section 9 of the United States Housing Act of 1937.

Participation loan—Loans made by the FmHA or others when another lender makes part of the loan.

Pass through—Principal and interest receipts on housing mortgages are “passed through” by GNMA, FNMA, FHLMC, or other organizations to the purchasers of their securities or obligations that have been sold and secured by the mortgages set aside as security for the obligations.

Planned unit development—Development and construction of a residential community as a unit in accordance with a plan for the entire development.

Pledged account mortgage—A graduated payment mortgage in which part of the buyer’s down payment is deposited in a savings account. Funds are drawn from the account to supplement the buyer’s monthly payments during the early years of the loan.

Pocket of poverty—For purposes of the UDAG program, a contiguous area of particularly severe poverty in a city or urban county. A city or urban county that fails to meet the general eligibility standards for UDAG assistance may be eligible if it contains such an area.

Prepayment penalty—A penalty that may be levied for repayment of a loan before it falls due.

Price-level adjusted mortgage—Mortgage under which the outstanding balance is adjusted according to an established price index, while the interest rate remains fixed.

Principal—The amount of debt, exclusive of accrued interest, remaining on a loan. Before any principal has been repaid, the total loaned amount is the principal.

GLOSSARY

Private mortgage insurance—Insurance by private companies of lenders against losses on mortgage loans.

Program reservation—HUD action reserving funds for a specific approved public housing project. This reservation is subject to PHA fulfillment of all HUD requirements.

Public housing—Lower income housing owned and operated by a public housing agency and assisted under the United States Housing Act of 1937 (other than under section 8 or 17).

Public housing agency—Public agency established by a State or local government to finance or operate low-income housing assisted under the United States Housing Act of 1937.

Real estate investment trust—A trust established by real estate investors primarily for the management and control of investments in mortgages and to sell obligations secured by mortgages and property held by the trust.

Recapture—Requiring repayment of assistance provided, either because the assistance has not been used within a certain period of time or a specified event (such as the sale of assisted property) occurs that permits repayment of all or a part of the assistance. See section 235(c)(2) of the National Housing Act.

Refinancing—Payment of a loan with amounts borrowed under a new loan.

Rehabilitation—The improvement or repair of property. Such term includes substantial and moderate rehabilitation, but excludes new construction.

Rehabilitation loans—Loans made by HUD under section 312 of the Housing Act of 1964 for the rehabilitation of property.

Reinsurance—Program under section 249 of the National Housing Act to demonstrate possible advantages of having private mortgage insurance companies enter into reinsurance contracts with HUD, under which such private insurers would assume a percentage of the risk on certain single-family mortgages insured by HUD.

Rent control—Limitation of annual rent increases by municipal ordinance, State, or Federal law.

Rent supplements—Annual Federal payments to owners of housing built with certain HUD mortgage insurance on behalf of prescribed types of lower income families.

Rental assistance payments—Generally refers to the FmHA program of rental assistance for low income families in rural areas under section 521(a)(2)(A) of the Housing Act of 1949.

Replacement cost—The basis of one of the limits placed on the amount of a mortgage that can be insured by HUD under certain programs, such as the mortgage may not exceed 90 percent of replacement cost of the housing when completed.

Reverse annuity mortgage—See "home equity conversion mortgage".

Rural area—A non-urban area meeting the requirements of section 520 of the Housing Act of 1949 and eligible assistance under the FmHA housing programs.

Second mortgage—A mortgage that grants rights subordinate to the rights granted by the initial mortgage. A second mortgage generally bears a higher rate of interest than the initial mortgage to reflect the greater risk of the lender.

Secondary mortgage market—Nationwide market for the purchase and sale of mortgages. FHLMC, FNMA, and GNMA are the 3 federally established entities that purchase mortgages in the secondary mortgage market, thereby increasing the availabilty of funds to financial institutions for additional residential loans.

Seed money—Advances, loans, or grants to cover preliminary expenses of constructing housing projects, such as the cost of planning and obtaining financing.

GLOSSARY

Shared appreciation mortgage—Mortgage under which the borrower receives financial assistance in purchasing a property and agrees in return to give the lender a portion of the future increase in the value of the property.

Shared housing—Generally refers to arrangements under which elderly and handicapped persons share the facilities of a dwelling with others in order to meet their housing needs and reduce the costs of housing. See section 8(p) of the United States Housing Act of 1937.

Single-family housing—Generally a structure containing dwelling units for 1 to 4 families.

Single room occupancy housing—Residential properties in which some or all dwelling units do not contain bathroom or kitchen facilities. See section 8(n) of the United States Housing Act of 1937.

Small city—A city that does not qualify as a metropolitan city for purposes of receiving a community development block grant under section 106 of the Housing and Community Development Act of 1974.

Standby commitment—See "commitment".

Substantial rehabilitationImprovements of a property from substandard to safe and sanitary conditions. It can vary from gutting and reconstruction to accumulated deferred maintenance. It may also involve conversion of nonresidential property to residential use.

Supplemental loans—HUD-insured loans under section 241 of the National Housing Act for improvements or additions to multifam-ily housing, nursing homes, group practice facilities, or hospitals.

Tandem plan purchases—The purchase by GNMA of certain housing mortgages at higher prices than would be paid by FNMA, FHLMC or other mortgage purchasers, with subsequent resale by GNMA at the best price obtainable, or as back-up of GNMA's mortgage-backed securities. The term derives from the original practice of FNMA purchasing from GNMA "in tandem" with the GNMA purchase.

Temporary mortgage assistance payments—Mortgage assistance payments authorized to be made under section 230(a) of the National Housing Act to a mortgagor of a single-family residence who defaults on the mortgage due to circumstances beyond the mortgagor's control. Constitutes an alternative to acquisition of the mortgage by HUD under section 230(b) of the National Housing Act.

Tenant contribution—The monthly amount of rent required to be paid by a tenant receiving rental assistance under a Federal housing program. Currently is 30 percent of monthly adjusted family income. See section 3(a) of the United States Housing Act of 1937.

Total development costs—The sum of all HUD-approved costs for planning, administration, site acquisition, relocation, demolition, construction and equipment, interest and carrying charges, on-site streets and utilities, nondwelling facilities, a contingency allowance, insurance premiums, off-site facilities, any initial operating deficit, and all other costs necessary to develop the project.

Troubled housing—Rental or cooperative housing project receiving assistance from HUD under section 201 of the Housing and Community Development Amendments of 1978 to restore financial soundness, improve management, and maintain the low and moderate income character of the project.

GLOSSARY

Turnkey housing—Housing initially financed and built by private sponsors and purchased upon completion by public housing agencies for use by lower income families under the public housing program.

Unit of general local government—A general purpose political subdivision of a State, such as a county, city, township, town, or village.

Urban county—For purposes of the CDBG and UDAG programs, generally refers to a county in a metropolitan area that has a combined population of not less than 200,000.

Urban development action grant—A grant made to an urban county, city, or unincorporated portion of an urban county under section 119 of the Housing and Community Development Act of 1974.

Urban homesteading—Program of HUD transfers of unoccupied residences under section 810 of the Housing and Community Development Act of 1974 to individuals or families without any substantial consideration where the individuals or families agree to occupy the residences not less than 5 years and to make repairs and improvements required to meet health and safety standards within certain time limits. Under a demonstration multifamily homestead-ing program, HUD transfers properties to local governments for conversion or rehabilitation to use primarily as housing for lower income families.

Urban renewal—Elimination and prevention of the development or spread of slums and blight, including slum clearance and redevelopment, or rehabilitation and conservation, assisted by HUD advances, loans, and grants under title I of the Housing Act of 1949. Program is being terminated under the provisions of title I of the Housing and Community Development Act of 1974.

Usury laws—Laws limiting the maximum rate of interest that may be charged on a loan.

Vacancy rate—In reference to dwelling units, the percentage of the total dwelling units in an area that are vacant and available for residence.

Variable interest rate—A means by which a lender is permitted to adjust the interest rate on a loan to reflect changes in the prime rateusually within a prescribed range and with advanced notice.

Very low-income family—Generally, a family whose income does not exceed 50 percent of the median family income of the area involved.

Voucher demonstration—Demonstration program of rental assistance under section 8(o) of the United States Housing Act of 1937. Assistance payments are provided for an eligible family based on the difference between the payment standard established by the Secretary for the area involved and 30 percent of the family's monthly adjusted income. The tenant contribution is the difference between the rent negotiated by the family and the amount of the monthly assistance payment.

ANSWER SHEET

TEST NO. ____________ PART ______ TITLE OF POSITION ____________________
(AS GIVEN IN EXAMINATION ANNOUNCEMENT - INCLUDE OPTION, IF ANY)

PLACE OF EXAMINATION ____________________ ____________ DATE ____________
(CITY OR TOWN) (STATE)

RATING

USE THE SPECIAL PENCIL. MAKE GLOSSY BLACK MARKS.

1 A B C D E	26 A B C D E	51 A B C D E	76 A B C D E	101 A B C D E
2 A B C D E	27 A B C D E	52 A B C D E	77 A B C D E	102 A B C D E
3 A B C D E	28 A B C D E	53 A B C D E	78 A B C D E	103 A B C D E
4 A B C D E	29 A B C D E	54 A B C D E	79 A B C D E	104 A B C D E
5 A B C D E	30 A B C D E	55 A B C D E	80 A B C D E	105 A B C D E
6 A B C D E	31 A B C D E	56 A B C D E	81 A B C D E	106 A B C D E
7 A B C D E	32 A B C D E	57 A B C D E	82 A B C D E	107 A B C D E
8 A B C D E	33 A B C D E	58 A B C D E	83 A B C D E	108 A B C D E
9 A B C D E	34 A B C D E	59 A B C D E	84 A B C D E	109 A B C D E
10 A B C D E	35 A B C D E	60 A B C D E	85 A B C D E	110 A B C D E

Make only ONE mark for each answer. Additional and stray marks may be counted as mistakes. In making corrections, erase errors COMPLETELY.

11 A B C D E	36 A B C D E	61 A B C D E	86 A B C D E	111 A B C D E
12 A B C D E	37 A B C D E	62 A B C D E	87 A B C D E	112 A B C D E
13 A B C D E	38 A B C D E	63 A B C D E	88 A B C D E	113 A B C D E
14 A B C D E	39 A B C D E	64 A B C D E	89 A B C D E	114 A B C D E
15 A B C D E	40 A B C D E	65 A B C D E	90 A B C D E	115 A B C D E
16 A B C D E	41 A B C D E	66 A B C D E	91 A B C D E	116 A B C D E
17 A B C D E	42 A B C D E	67 A B C D E	92 A B C D E	117 A B C D E
18 A B C D E	43 A B C D E	68 A B C D E	93 A B C D E	118 A B C D E
19 A B C D E	44 A B C D E	69 A B C D E	94 A B C D E	119 A B C D E
20 A B C D E	45 A B C D E	70 A B C D E	95 A B C D E	120 A B C D E
21 A B C D E	46 A B C D E	71 A B C D E	96 A B C D E	121 A B C D E
22 A B C D E	47 A B C D E	72 A B C D E	97 A B C D E	122 A B C D E
23 A B C D E	48 A B C D E	73 A B C D E	98 A B C D E	123 A B C D E
24 A B C D E	49 A B C D E	74 A B C D E	99 A B C D E	124 A B C D E
25 A B C D E	50 A B C D E	75 A B C D E	100 A B C D E	125 A B C D E

ANSWER SHEET

TEST NO. ______________ PART ______ TITLE OF POSITION ______________________________
(AS GIVEN IN EXAMINATION ANNOUNCEMENT - INCLUDE OPTION. IF ANY)

PLACE OF EXAMINATION ______________________________ (CITY OR TOWN) ______________ (STATE) DATE ______________

RATING

USE THE SPECIAL PENCIL. MAKE GLOSSY BLACK MARKS.

1 A B C D E	26 A B C D E	51 A B C D E	76 A B C D E	101 A B C D E
2 A B C D E	27 A B C D E	52 A B C D E	77 A B C D E	102 A B C D E
3 A B C D E	28 A B C D E	53 A B C D E	78 A B C D E	103 A B C D E
4 A B C D E	29 A B C D E	54 A B C D E	79 A B C D E	104 A B C D E
5 A B C D E	30 A B C D E	55 A B C D E	80 A B C D E	105 A B C D E
6 A B C D E	31 A B C D E	56 A B C D E	81 A B C D E	106 A B C D E
7 A B C D E	32 A B C D E	57 A B C D E	82 A B C D E	107 A B C D E
8 A B C D E	33 A B C D E	58 A B C D E	83 A B C D E	108 A B C D E
9 A B C D E	34 A B C D E	59 A B C D E	84 A B C D E	109 A B C D E
10 A B C D E	35 A B C D E	60 A B C D E	85 A B C D E	110 A B C D E

Make only ONE mark for each answer. Additional and stray marks may be counted as mistakes. In making corrections, erase errors COMPLETELY.

11 A B C D E	36 A B C D E	61 A B C D E	86 A B C D E	111 A B C D E
12 A B C D E	37 A B C D E	62 A B C D E	87 A B C D E	112 A B C D E
13 A B C D E	38 A B C D E	63 A B C D E	88 A B C D E	113 A B C D E
14 A B C D E	39 A B C D E	64 A B C D E	89 A B C D E	114 A B C D E
15 A B C D E	40 A B C D E	65 A B C D E	90 A B C D E	115 A B C D E
16 A B C D E	41 A B C D E	66 A B C D E	91 A B C D E	116 A B C D E
17 A B C D E	42 A B C D E	67 A B C D E	92 A B C D E	117 A B C D E
18 A B C D E	43 A B C D E	68 A B C D E	93 A B C D E	118 A B C D E
19 A B C D E	44 A B C D E	69 A B C D E	94 A B C D E	119 A B C D E
20 A B C D E	45 A B C D E	70 A B C D E	95 A B C D E	120 A B C D E
21 A B C D E	46 A B C D E	71 A B C D E	96 A B C D E	121 A B C D E
22 A B C D E	47 A B C D E	72 A B C D E	97 A B C D E	122 A B C D E
23 A B C D E	48 A B C D E	73 A B C D E	98 A B C D E	123 A B C D E
24 A B C D E	49 A B C D E	74 A B C D E	99 A B C D E	124 A B C D E
25 A B C D E	50 A B C D E	75 A B C D E	100 A B C D E	125 A B C D E